CELTIC BATTLE HEROES

CUCHULAINN · BOADICEA · FIONN MacCUMHAIL · MACBETH

JOHN MATTHEWS & BOB STEWART

Plates by JAMES FIELD

Firebird Books

First published in the UK 1988 by Firebird Books

Copyright © 1988 Firebird Books Ltd, P.O. Box 327, Poole, Dorset BH15 2RG
Text copyright © 1988 John Matthews *Boadicea* and *Fionn MacCumhail*
R.J. Stewart *Cuchulainn* and *Macbeth*

Distributed in the United States by
Sterling Publishing Co, Inc
2 Park Avenue, New York, NY 10016

Distributed in Australia by
Capricorn Link (Australia) Pty Ltd
PO Box 665, Lane Cove, NSW 2066

British Library Cataloguing in Publication Data
Matthews, John, *1948-*
   Celtic battle heroes: Cuchulainn: Boadicea: Fionn Mac Cumhaill: Macbeth.——
   (Heroes and warriors series).
   1. Legends, Celtic 2. War——Folklore
   I. Title II. Stewart, Bob III. Series
   398'. 392 GR137

ISBN 1 85314 100 3

Series editor Stuart Booth
Designed by Kathryn S.A. Booth
Typeset by Colset Private Limited, Singapore
Colour separations by Kingfisher Facsimile
Colour printed by Butler and Tanner, Frome and London
Printed and bound in Great Britain by Richard Clay Ltd, Chichester, Sussex.

Contents

CUCHULAINN

HOUND OF ULSTER

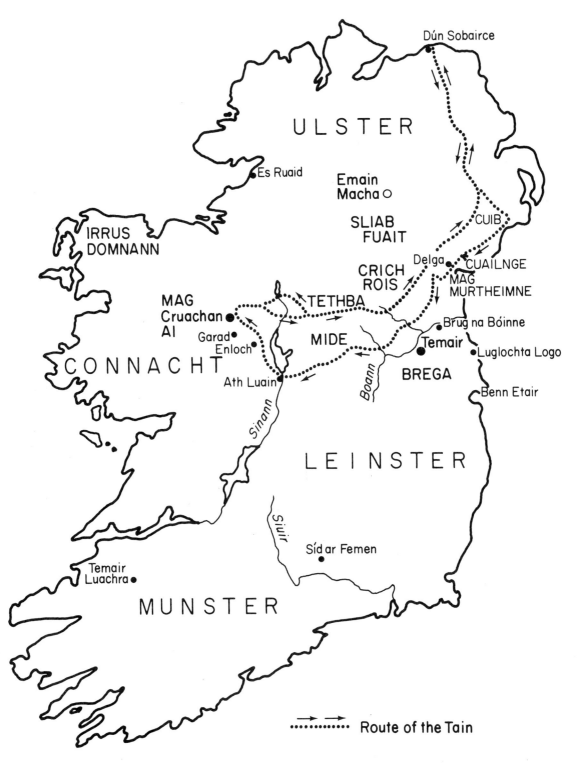

THE IRELAND OF CUCHULAINN

Dún Sobairce

ULSTER

Es Ruaid

Emain Macha ○

SLIAB FUAIT

CUIB

CRICH ROIS

Delga

CUAILNGE

MAG MURTHEIMNE

IRRUS DOMNANN

MAG Cruachan Ai

TETHBA

Brug na Bóinne

Garad Enloch

MIDE

Temair

Luglochta Logo

CONNACHT

Ath Luain

Boann

BREGA

Benn Etair

Sinann

LEINSTER

Siuir

Síd ar Femen

Temair Luachra

MUNSTER

············▸ Route of the Tain

The Cuchulainn Saga

To examine Cuchulainn in depth has been the task of many great Irish language and Celtic scholars over the last century or more. In this simple retelling of those adventures are selected insights into the cultural background wherever facts can be confirmed. To look at Cuchulainn's culture, weapons, battles, and mythical or magical origins is to combine evidence from a number of sources.

First and foremost, the early Irish texts in which this great champion features are extensive and very complex. So, in looking at the basic, important themes and adventures, many of the lesser stories have to be omitted.

The Cuchulainn texts do not stand alone; they are related to a number of other Celtic legendary sources, many of which are not Irish but British. Thus we have to look at comparisons between themes in Cuchulainn and those in the legends of King Arthur as they arise in discussion of the champion and his adventures. As with the warriors of Arthur, or the ancient Greek heroes, we find the dim echoes of divinity in these legends of the origins of our hero; whoever or whatever Cuchulainn was originally, by the time the great tales and sagas had been built around the astonishing exploits of himself and his men, he was of magical and semi-divine proportions and ability.

The feats of the warriors of Ulster were indeed magical; they were able to kill hundreds of men with ease, they ate entire oxen and drank vats of alcohol; they cut the tops of hills away with their mighty swords, and boiled their bath water with their furious body heat.

The tales of Cuchulainn also consist of a rich complex of magical and pagan religious symbols, found as adventures, mysterious locations, curious taboos, and a host of other specific and often rather startling features within the structure of the epic tales. Clearly, there is far more to Cuchulainn than his superhuman strength and skill in arms. These abilities and natural gifts may be one of the main reasons why his adventures have survived. Yet underneath these heroic deeds runs a deeper and more enduring layer of high adventure, transformation and growth, and the perilous mysteries of the Otherworld or Underworld.

Finally, there is hard physical archaeological evidence that corresponds to material in the Cuchulainn texts. This includes physical locations such as the fortress of Emain Macha (now called Navan Fort), many early finds of weaponry and armour, and the most significant use of natural locations such as islands, rivers, and countries in the development of the legends.

It soon becomes clear that Cuchulainn moved not merely in a localised circuit of Ulster in Northern Ireland, but upon a broader basis to Britain in general. This ease of movement from Ireland to Scotland reveals a culture in which an overall unity – loosely defined as Celtic – seems to have existed. Such a unity is supported by the writings of classical authorities, such as Julius Caesar, who took some care to describe the religion of the Celts, certain aspects of druidism, and the fact that the culture had a type of religious unity, despite being decentralised politically or geographically. We find exactly this same picture in the Cuchulainn tales; the unity was found through religious and magical practices and beliefs, which transcended tribal boundaries; yet powerful kingdoms made war upon one another within this overall unity. This last aspects of conflict out of deep unity is a typically Celtic characteristic, and persists even today.

Origins of the Saga
The preservation of the Cuchulainn saga is as remarkable as its origins; the extended story-cycle comes from a bardic or oral tradition of great sophistication. The complexity of the descriptions, the cultural ambience, and the vast body of material that corresponds to historical and archaeological or early literary parallels leaves us in no doubt that this is the product of a civilised and complex people. That the original culture was heroic, consisted of head-hunters and warriors and had a strict magical–religious foundation does not in any way debar us from calling the pagan Irish sources for Cuchulainn civilised. They had central locations, such as Emain Macha, now known as Navan Fort, a highly organised governmental structure, and extremely well defined rules of behaviour for all aspects of life.

The origins of the translated material used here are even more curious than our speculations and knowledge about pagan Celtic civilisation. They were transcribed by monks, probably from oral tradition, and preserved in monastic libraries. The oldest example of Cuchulainn tales is the *Book of the Dun Cow* from the monastry of Clonmacnoise. *The Book of Leinster* was transcribed by Finn mac Gorman, the Bishop of Kildare. When we examine the broader spectrum of preserved material, it is clear that monastic chroniclers and transcribers took great care to set out the oral tradition. This was still maintained in the days of the early Church in Britain and Ireland by bards and poets, the descendants of the same druidic caste system which plays such an important role in the adventures of Cuchulainn and the Red Branch warriors.

Curiously, the overt pagan and magical elements were not written out of the Cuchulainn material, as we might expect. The short examples quoted here might have been enlarged by a significant number of extracts which clearly demonstrate magical arts, pagan religion, and druidic lore. Those included tend to bear directly upon the skills, adventures, and doom, of

Bronze brooch from Emain Macha, now in the British Museum.

warriors; but they reveal this totally un-Christian element. There are, of course, Christian interpolations and deliberate alterations of chronology in the full body of the Cuchulainn texts. But it is clear that the Irish monks held the Hound of Ulster and his not so distant pagan world in great respect; so much so that they did not suppress or rewrite or destroy, as many other Christians have done through the centuries.

In the context of this account of the hero, literary and historical comparisons are unimportant other than to show the drama and power of the basic character and tales. The reader who wishes to go into the subject in depth will find an immense wealth of other reference material, scholarship, and speculation. The most recent detailed annotated translation is *The Tain* by Thomas Kinsella.

Weapons and Warrior Training

The weapons of Cuchulainn's culture were basically those of the early Celts, with a number of very specific and individual items unique to certain characters. In addition to the actual hardware, we may also include a number of other less usual but certainly very prominent and important weapons used in

Late Bronze Age sword, now in the British Museum. This weapon is probably very close to the kind carried by Cuchulainn.

the various conflicts in which the Champion of Ulster was engaged. These are, of course, the magical weapons, skills, and illusions which abound through the Cuchulainn legends.

Basic weapons were the spear, sword, sling – and the shield which could be used as an offensive weapon with sharpened rims. Many of these weapons were famed in themselves.

Spears

The Gapped spear of King Conchobar.

The Venomous spear of King Conchobar.

The *Culghlas* or blue-green spear of Conall the Victorious.

The *Cual gae* or grouping of spears and swords; perhaps similar to the medieval *chevaux de frise*.

Swords

Caladcholg, the sword of Fergus Mac Roich (Roy) which stretched to the length of a rainbow; this was a sword from the *sidhe* or Otherworld.

The sword of Manannan mac Lir which left no sign of stroke or blow behind.

The *Cruaiden cadatchenn*, Cuchulainn's hereditary sword; the name means something like 'dear little hard one'.

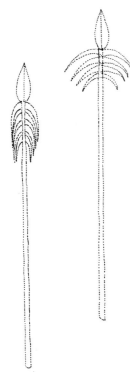

Reconstruction of the gae bulga, Cuchulainn's barbed spear which was thrown with the feet.

Shields

The Bright Rim of King Conchobar.

Cuchulainn's shield of dark crimson with a pure white silver rim.

Missive or throwing shields with sharp edges, used as offensive weapons.

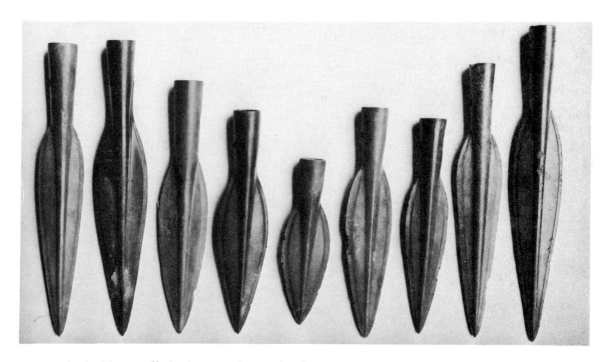

One such shield cut off the hero Sualtam's head in a mysterious accident
   leading to a magical prophecy.

The large bossed shield of Fergus Mac Roich, with fifty bosses that could each
   bear the weight of a hog, and a great central boss of red gold.

Celtic bronze socketed spearheads of about 700 B.C., showing typical leaf-shaped design.

*   *   *

Body armour was worn by certain heroes, sometimes in conjunction with
chariots with scythe bearing wheels, trained war horses and special spears
such as five-pointed weapons and the *gae bulga*.

This curious and highly individual weapon was a type of harpoon with
retractable barbs, similar to a number of tearing or lodging spears and arrows
used in historical warfare. The *gae bulga* was originally given by Scathach the
warrior woman to Aoife, who Cuchulainn conquered as a test and task in
service of Scathach. Therefore, it seems that it was passed from the second
warrior woman to the Champion of Ulster at the time of her defeat. This is
significant, as an indication of the powers of fate, for it was Aoife's son (by
Cuchulainn) who was tragically slain by his father, using the *gae bulga*. It is
worth quoting in full the technique described for throwing this deadly
weapon, from the duel between Cuchulainn and Ferdiad:

Then Cuchulainn asked Laeg [his charioteer] for the *gae bulga*. The manner of the weapon
was this; it had to be set down the stream, and cast from between the toes. It made the
wound of one spear entering the body, but it had thirty barbs to open and could not be withdrawn from the body but must be cut out . . . the servant set the spear down the stream and
Cuchulainn caught it between the toes of his foot and threw an unerring cast at
Ferdiad. . . .

The *gae bulga* passed through Ferdiad's firm deep apron of wrought iron, and broke the great stone as large as a mill stone (set over his lower body as a shield) into three parts. It passed through these protective coverings into his body, so that every crevice and every cavity of him was filled with its barbs.

The standard techniques and motifs of fighting included single combat (rather than multiple pitched battles), seen later to good effect in the context of the Cattle Raid of Cooley. Champion charioteers and chariots were used as fighting units and there were formalised or ritualised modes of combat and challenge. Raiding and stealing over tribal boundaries were common sources of combat.

Unusual techniques of deliberate conflict, widespread in all tales, included magical attacks such as weakening or debilitating sleep, illusions of great armies, monstrous beasts and opponents from the Otherworld. There were also the druidic techniques of satire, undeniable requests, music and poetry, and *geasa*, a system of unavoidable taboos which were often used as weapons or tactical devices to gain power or control situations.

Divine intervention, the continual and essential intervention of gods and goddesses or other supernatural beings occurs very often in the legends. Indeed most of the tales hinge upon such intervention, often through a complex chain of events, *geasa*, parentage, meetings, challenges, tests and dedications.

The Duel

The duel between the Hound of Ulster and Ferdiad provides us with another detailed and colourful description of heroic combat techniques:

'Do you remember, the throwing weapons that we used to practise with Scathach?' said Ferdiad.
   'I remember them indeed,' replied Cuchulainn.
   'Then let us use them against one another,' said Ferdiad.

The account then continues:

So they took their throwing shields in their hands, and their eight turned handled spears, and their eight little quill spears, and their eight ivory hilted swords, and their eight sharp ivory handled spears. The weapons flew back and forward between them like bees on the wing on a sunny day. Till midday they fought with these weapons. . . .

Warrior Training

During the scene described above, both champions referred to their training together under the instruction of the warrior woman Scathach. During this part of the Cuchulainn saga, we find once again some interesting detailed observations upon the traditional techniques taught to the ancient Celtic warrior:

At last, when the full lore of soldierly arts had been mastered by Cuchulainn; the apple-feat, the thunder-feat, the blade-feat, the supine-feat, the spear-feat, the rope-feat, the body-feat, the cat's-feat, the salmon-feat of a chariot chief, the throw of the staff, the whirl of a brace

Typical bronze helmet from a Celtic grave. The use of bronze for armour and weaponry appears to have persisted among Celtic tribes long after the appearance of iron.

chariot chief, the spear of the bellows (*gae bulga*), the *boi* of swiftness, the wheel-feat, the breath-feat, the *brud geme*, the hero's whoop, the blow, the counter blow, running up a lance and righting the body upon its point; the scythe chariot and the twisting around spear points . . . when he had learned all this a message came to him to return to his own land, and so he took his leave.

This list is extremely detailed, and derives from a precise tradition of combat techniques.

Cuchulainn – Man and Legend

According to Irish tradition Cuchulainn, as leader of the great hero band of Ulster, lived at the beginning of the Christian era. Indeed, his king Conchobar MacNessa, is said to have died of fury upon hearing of the death of Christ. This interesting rationalisation of early Irish history is likely to be religious propaganda, but like many traditions may have some element of truth within it. We may reasonably date a historical Cuchulainn to the first century B.C. at the very latest. As we shall soon discover, many elements of his story and his culture obviously come from a much earlier period.

It seems likely, as with many legendary heroes (such as King Arthur and the Knights of the Round Table) that a fusion of historical tradition and magical or mythical tradition surrounds Cuchulainn and the band of warriors of Ulster. In such cases, a real hero becomes part of a myth, such as that of the victorious sun. This occurs not merely because he seems to be a brightly-shining and divine person, when tales and songs are woven around him, but because such heroes and kings, even as real persons, were part of a pagan culture in which they held a semi-divine status. Cuchulainn is said to have been a son of the Gaelic sun-god; this may be myth or a poetic memory of the fact that such warriors were dedicated body and soul to the early gods and goddesses of pagan Ireland.

Lineage of Cuchulainn
On his mother's side Cuchulainn was the grandson of the Dagda, whose name simply means 'the good god'. The Dagda was a primal giant figure, one of the dimly remembered but extremely potent first deities of the Celts; humorous and scurrilous tales were told about this lusty, powerful, hungry giant. As if this grandparentage was not sufficient, Cuchulainn was also said to be the son of Lugh Long Hand, whose name means 'Light', a very direct image of the ancient Celtic sun god.

The mother of Cuchulainn was Dechtire, daughter of Maga, grand-daughter of Angus 'Son of the Young', and half-sister to King Conchobar. Thus the King and his hero were related.

Bronze scabbard from Co. Antrim, Ireland; a typical weapon from the sagas.

13

King Conchobar and his Court

King Conchobar MacNessa, blood relative and ruler of Cuchulainn held court at Emain Macha. As with so many apparently mythical sagas, there is a physical location attached to the tradition of Conchobar and his court. Near Armagh, the extensive prehistoric fortress, Navan Fort is imposing and atmospheric to this day. Archaeologists are still investigating this ancient and impressive site, which ceased to be used around 90 B.C.

From here, Conchobar ruled the kingdom of Ulster which extended southwards as far as the Boyne. It was at this location that the astonishing band of heroes assembled, under the undisputed leadership of Cuchulainn.

The relationship between Cuchulainn and his mythical or divine father and grandfather becomes all the more apparent when we study the descriptions of his nature and his physical attributes. He was small and insignificant in size, yet no one could look full upon him in his glory without blinking. The very heat of his burning body could melt snow and ice for yards around; he glowed red and when he dipped his body to bathe in the sea, the waters hissed and steamed. Perhaps the most dramatic description of Cuchulainn is his battle fury, which was the most ferocious ever known among the many Celtic heroes and warriors:

Among the clouds over his head could be seen seething pouring showers and sparks of red fire, which his savage wrath caused to mount upwards above him. His hair became tangled about his head, as if it had been branches of a red thorn bush stuffed into a strongly fenced gap. . . . Taller thicker and more rigid than the mast of a great ship was the jet of dusky blood which shot upwards out of the very centre of his scalp, to be scattered to the four cardinal points (of east, south, west, and north). From this fountain was formed a magical mist of gloom, resembling the smoky pall which drapes a royal hall, at nightfall of a winters day.

(Tain Bo Chuailgne)

Birth of Cuchulainn

Like many heroes with a curious semi-magical or divine origin, Cuchulainn had a miraculous birth. His mother Dechtire was sitting at her wedding feast, about to be married to the Ulster chieftain Sualtam. Into her cup of wine flew a mayfly, which she swallowed without noticing its presence. Soon she fell into a deep sleep in which the sun-god Lugh appeared to her as if in a dream. Lugh told her that it had been no mere mayfly that she had swallowed, but himself.

After delivering this revelation, Lugh transformed Dechtire and her fifty maidens into the shape of a beautiful flock of birds, and so they disappeared without trace. After months had passed, the warriors of Emain Macha were lured out to hunt, drawn by the appearance of a flock of birds.

Riding in their chariots until nightfall, pursuing the elusive flock, the men of Ulster suddenly realised that they had been lured to the Brugh na Boyne which was the home of the gods and goddesses of the land. Before the warriors arose a splendid hall, of a beauty and size such as they had never before seen. A tall, handsome chieftain, very richly attired, came out of the hall and welcomed them, offering them hospitality. When the warriors

The Court House in modern Dundalk, the town traditionally cited as the home of Cuchulainn.

entered this marvellous place, they found seated there a beautiful woman and fifty lovely maidens; upon the tables was set a feast of meat and wine such as would grace the hall of a great king.

The Ulster warriors rested for the night, and during their rest they heard the cry of a new born babe. In the morning, Lugh revealed his true name to them, and told them that the woman was no other than the half-sister of Conchobar, and that she had given birth to a child who was to be taken back to grow up among the warriors at the Ulster court. Thus the mother, the baby boy and maidens returned; all the heroes, Druids, poets, and lawgivers of Ulster gave the best of their skills and wisdom to the infant as instructed.

Naming of Cuchulainn

At first the baby boy was called Setanta but this was to change in that most magical manner by which heroes acquire their true names, i.e. through unusual and highly symbolic circumstances. As a child, Setanta was the

15

strongest boy in Emain Macha, champion of all sports. One day, while playing hurley single-handed against a team of the other boys, and beating them, he was summoned by King Conchobar. The king who had watched his skill and was impressed by the child's ability, commanded him to come to a feast at the house of Culann the chief blacksmith. Setanta promised to come as soon as he had finished the game.

When the Ulster champions entered the smith's hall, the king gave permission for Culann to let loose his terrible watch hound, fiercer than any hundred other dogs. But they had forgotten that the child was following them (after winning his game of hurley). When the savage hound attacked Setanta, he threw his ball into its mouth, and grabbing it by the legs, dashed out its brains against a rock.

Culann the chief smith was enraged at the loss of his guard hound, but the child promised to find him another and train it for him. He also undertook to guard the hall of the smith himself, just as the hound would have done, until a replacement was fully trained. Thus Setanta became Cuchulainn, which means 'The Hound of Culann'.

The Druid of the royal court, Cathbad, prophesied that this child's name would one day be known and spoken by every man in Ireland; which was not surprising with such a remarkable parentage and childhood promise of skill and strength.

One day, Cuchulainn overheard Cathbad giving instruction in the lore of druidism, and one of the pupils asked for what would the day be propitious. The answer was that any young man taking arms that day would gain a greater name than any other hero, but that his life would be short. Cuchulainn immediately asked King Conchobar for arms and a chariot, declaring that the Druid had predicted this to be a day for the arming of a hero.

On this first day of bearing arms, and commanding his own chariot and charioteer, the young Cuchulainn went into battle and killed three champions who had long harassed the warriors of Ulster. He brought back their heads to the hall of the King. At this time he was reputedly only seven years old.

Cuchulainn and Love

It is hardly surprising that such a miraculous youth should grow at a rate faster than that of any normal child. So it was not long before the women of Ulster paid so much attention to the young Cuchulainn that the other warriors became extremely jealous. They demanded that his youthful exploits be tamed by his taking of a wife; but he was not an easy person to please in the choice of a prospective bride. Cuchulainn swore that he would have only one maiden as his bride, Emer, the daughter of Forgal the Wily. She was the maiden in all of Ireland who had the best of the six gifts of maidenhood; chastity, wisdom, needlework, sweet speech, singing, and of course beauty. No other young woman was her equal. But when Cuchulainn went to court her, she laughed at him, saying that he was merely a boy. He swore a great oath that he would make his name known wherever the deeds of heroes were

Driven by Laeg, 'king of charioteers', the youthful Cuchulainn rides to battle and makes a chariot charge upon the hosts of Ireland. Such use of chariots and other weapons suggests that the Cuchulainn sagas come from an early Celtic heroic culture.

related . . . and Emer finally promised that she would marry him if he could take her away from her warlike family.

Scathach the Warrior Woman

However, Forgal the Wily lived up to his name, and devised a plan by which he hoped to be rid of this troublesome suitor. Deliberately, he went to visit Emain Macha, pretending never to have heard of Cuchulainn. When he saw this remarkable youth win at every game, challenge, test, and feat of arms or skill, Forgal declared that such a hero should go to the island of Scathach the Warrior Woman, situated in Alba (Scotland). This curious stronghold, usually identified as the Isle of Skye (Scathach is pronounced 'Sca-hah') was difficult to reach, and even more difficult to escape from unscathed. Forgal hoped that rather than gain training in arms from the fearsome Scathach, Cuchulainn would meet his death.

The tradition of Celtic warrior women is not limited to this reference to Scathach, for women were accustomed and sometimes obliged to bear arms as late as the sixth century. That the great heroes should go for arms training to a warrior woman living on an isolated island is not so unusual when we

The boy hero killed the huge hound of Culann with his hurley stick, thus earning his name Cuchulainn, which means 'Hound of Culann'.

remember that the most terrible and warlike of the Celtic deities were always female.

Cuchulainn's travel to the isle of Scathach is particularly magical; it is an Otherworld journey undertaken by the hero to gain wisdom, skill, and most important of all, to be transformed. Cuchulainn left behind his two closest friends, Laegaire Battle Winner and Conall the Victorious; they lost heart and returned to Ulster.

First he crossed the Plain of Ill Luck; here the feet of men could stick fast and be pierced by razor-sharp grass blades; he entered the Perilous Glens filled with devouring beasts; then he came to the Bridge of the Cliff. This bridge tilted upwards whenever anyone tried to cross, throwing all comers to their death. Three times Cuchulainn tried to cross this bridge, which would give him access to the stronghold of Scathach, and three times he failed to cross. Finally, his heroic fervour came upon him, causing his face to shine like the sun (who was his father). Taking a great leap – the salmon leap – of the hero which involves twisting and turning against the flow – Cuchulainn landed in the middle of the tilting bridge. As it rose up vertically, he slid down to the other side.

At last he gained access to the stronghold of Scathach, and threatened her with his sword until she agreed to teach him all her famous skill in arms. Like so many hero sagas, this tuition, part of a bargain or test (for the hand of Emer) involved Cuchulainn in yet another task, for he fought and conquered Aoife, another warrior Queen as part of his bargain with Scathach. The curious wooing and winning of Emer is a primal version of a myth known all over Europe, rooted in pagan religious belief, in which a young power or hero must win the beautiful maiden from her ogre-like father or guardian.

Cuchulainn Marries Emer

When the newly skilled Cuchulainn returned to Ireland, he attacked the stronghold of Forgal the Wily in his scythed chariot. The fortress had triple walls, typical of the threefold symbolism of the Otherworld which repeatedly occurs in the tales about Cuchulainn.

Cuchulainn slew the defenders of the stronghold and finally killed Forgal. Pursued by the remaining warriors, whom he killed whenever they drew too close, Cuchulainn reached Emain Macha. There, after such a violent courtship and meeting, he married Emer. This remarkable couple, the ultimate hero and the most beautiful and skilled maiden in Ireland, were given honour and precedence in the court of King Conchobar MacNessa.

It seems unlikely that much of the above tale of Cuchulainn's wooing and marriage is based upon historical truth, yet there are many aspects to it which seem to be borne out by early Celtic tradition, custom, and evidence from literature and archaeology.

Once again we encounter a mixture of genuine cultural material; the tradition of warrior women, with idealised figures of the hero and his lover, fused into a myth of good overcoming evil, or perfection overcoming chaos.

The Cattle Raid of Cooley

The most famous and extensive of the adventures of Cuchulainn is the tale of the war fought over the Brown Bull of Cualgne (pronounced 'Cooley').

The legend tells of two bulls of fairy or immortal lineage that were in Ireland at that time. When we use the word fairy in this context, we are not dealing with the weak tinsel creatures found in Victorian fantasies, but with the true fairies of Celtic tradition. These are powerful, terrible and beautiful immortal beings, similar to gods and goddesses, who are tall and fair to look upon. As late as the eighteenth and nineteenth century in Ireland and Scotland, Gaelic speakers still confirmed their belief in the people of the *sidhe* or fairy mound, and could still see them with the 'second sight'. The story goes on to say how the bulls were each transformed from other shapes and origins. First they were the swineherds of the gods Bodb (King of the Sidhe of Munster) and Ochne (King of the Sidhe of Connaught).

The two swineherds were in rivalry with one another, changing shape in pursuit of their endless quarrel. They became ravens to battle for a year, then water creatures, then they fought as human champions, and finally changed into eels. One of these magical eels swam into the River Cruind in Cualgne in Ulster, and was swallowed by a cow belonging to Daire of Cualgne. The other swam into the spring of Uaran Garad, in Connaught, where it was swallowed by a cow belonging to Queen Medb.

From this curious origin were born two bulls, the Brown Bull of Ulster, and the White Horned Bull of Connaught.

The Dispute

The White Bull was proud and scornful; he did not want to be the property of a woman, so he left the herds of Queen Medb and went into those of her husband Ailill. When the King and Queen counted their possessions one day, having nothing better to do, they found that they were equal in all things but one. Queen Medb had no bull to equal the White Bull in the herd of her husband Ailill.

So Medb sent bards with flattering gifts and words of praise to Daire, asking him to lend her the Brown Bull for the space of one year. Daire was about to agree to this request, when he overheard one of the Queen's men boasting that if the Bull was not lent freely, then the Queen would command her champions to take it by force. Naturally, Daire swore that under no circumstances would Queen Medb have the great Brown Bull.

So did the great war of the Cattle Raid begin; Queen Medb of Connaught raised all the armies of Ireland to fight against Ulster on account of the refusal of the loan of the Brown Bull. She made Fergus Mac Roich, an Ulster warrior who had previously quarrelled with King Conchobar MacNessa, the leader of this great host.

It was assumed that the war would be easy; the heroes of Ulster were suffering a magical sickness which came upon them each year as a result of an

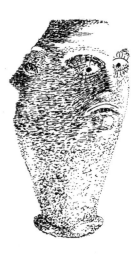

The head was a sacred object to all the early Celts. This three-headed urn dates from the third century B.C. and is now in the Landesmuseum, Klagenfurt, Austria.

19

ancient curse laid upon them by a goddess who had once been insulted by an ancestor of King Conchobar. Queen Medb called up a prophetess and asked her what she saw of the warriors of Ulster. The account which follows is from a translation of the saga, edited by E. Hull, and the spelling of Irish names is thus not standardised:

So that night they pitched and encamped, and between the four fords of Aei – Athmaga, Athbercna, Athslisen, and Athcoltna – there was a mass of smoke and fire. Until the far end of a fortnight they tarried in Rath-Cruachan of Connacht, with quaffing and all pleasure, so that all the more lightly anon they should face their travel and their hosting. At which time it was that Meave bade her charioteer to put-to her horses for her; to the end she should go and confer with her wizard, to require of him foreknowledge and prophecy.

When she had gained the place where her magician was, she required of him foreknowledge and prediction accordingly, saying: 'Many there be which this day, and here, do part from their familiars and their friends, from their country and from their lands, from father and from mother. Now if so it be that not all of them return safe and sound, upon me it is that they will discharge their lamentation and their curses. For all which, however, there neither goes forth, nor yet stays there behind, any that to us is dearer than are we ourselves. Thou therefore find out for us whether we come back or not. The wizard answered: 'Whosoever comes or comes not, thou thyself shalt come.'

The driver wheels round the chariot, and the queen returns. But lo, she saw a thing that was a marvel to her: a woman close to her, on the chariot's shaft and facing her. The damsel's manner was this: in her right hand she held a weaver's sword of white bronze with seven beadings of red gold on its ends, and wove a bordering. A spot-pied cloak of green enveloped her, and in it at her breast there was a bulging massive brooch. She had a high-coloured, rich-blooded face; a blue and laughing eye; lips red and thin; glistening pearly teeth, which indeed you might have taken for a shower of white pearls fallen and packed into her head. Like unto fresh coral were her lips. Sweeter than strings of peaked harps played by long-practised masters' hands was the sweet sound of her voice, of her gentle utterance. Whiter than snow shed during a single night was the lustre of her skin and flesh, filtered through and past her raiment. Feet she had that were long and most white; nails pink and even, arched and pointed; fair-yellow gold-glittering hair: three tresses of it wound round her head, while yet another fell downwards and cast its shade below her knee.

Meave scanned her, and she said, 'Girl, at this time, and here, what doest thou?'

The young woman answered: 'I reveal thy chances and thy fortunes, and Ireland's four great provinces I gather up and muster against the Raid for the Kine of Cuailgne.'

'And for me wherefore dost thou this?'

'Great cause I have,' the girl explained; 'for I am a woman bondmaid of thy people.'

'And who art thou of my people?'

'I am Feidelm the prophetess, out of Cruachan's fairy hill.'

'Well, then, O prophetess Feidelm, how seest thou our host?'

'I see them all in red, I see them all becrimsoned.'

'Yet in Emania, Conachar for sure lies in his pangs,' said Meave; 'my messengers have been to him, and nought there is which we need fear from Ulster. But, Feidelm, tell us the truth of the matter: O woman-prophet Feidelm, how seest thou our host?'

'I see all red on them, I see crimson.'

'But Cuscraidh Menn Macha, Conachar's son, is in Iniscuscraidh in his pains; my messengers have been to him, and nought there is which we need dread from Ulster. But, Feidelm, tell us the truth of it: O Feidelm, O prophetess, how seest thou our host?'

'I see red on them, I see crimson.'

'But at Rathairthir, Eoghan mac Durthacht is in his pains: my messengers have been to him; nought is there which we need fear from Ulster. But, Feidelm, tell us true: Feidelm, thou woman-seer, how seest thou our host?'

'I see all red on them, I see all crimson.'

'Why, Celtchar mac Uitechar within his fort lies in his pangs: my messengers have been to him; nought is there which we need to fear from Ulster. But, O Feidelm, tell us true; woman-seer Feidelm, how seest thou our host?'

'I see red on them, I see crimson.'

'The manner in which thou deducest all this I approve not,' said Meave. 'For when the men of Erin shall have congregated to one place, among them doubtless will be quarrels and affrays and broils and onslaughts: as regards either taking the lead or bringing up the rear, concerning precedence at ford or river, concerning priority in killing a swine, a cow, a stag, or other game. But, Feidelm, tell me true: O prophetess Feidelm, how seest thou our host?'

'I see red on them, I see crimson. I see a small man who shall demonstrate weapon-feats,' . . . and here now she began to foretell and to foreshow Cuchulainn to the men of Erin, and she made a lay:

A small man I see, one who shall demonstrate weapon-feats, but at the price of many wounds in his smooth skin; the 'hero's light' is on his brow, and victory's arena his forehead is. The seven gems of an heroic champion are in the midst of both his eyes; his understanding is plain to perceive, and a red mantle, clasped, wraps him round. A face he has that is the noblest, best, and towards a woman-bevy great modesty he does observe; a stripling young and of complexion beautiful, but to the battle he shows a dragon's form. Like to Cuchulainn of Muirthemne his semblance and his valour are; who this Cú of Culann's from Muirthemne may be, I indeed know not, but this much full well I know: that by him the present host will all be red. In either one of both his hands, four small swords belonging to superlative sleight-feats he holds; he will attain to ply them on the host, an extraordinary act which drives men to eschew him. When, over and above his sword and spear, his *gae bulga* as

The sword was an important weapon of the Celts. This bronze hilt is from the second century B.C. and was found at North Grimston in Yorshire, England.

21

well he brings into play – he, the man who clad in scarlet mantle acts the sentinel – on all spaces he puts down his foot. His two spears point over the chariot's left; the frenzied one lets himself go: as to the form which to me hitherto has been revealed as worn by him, to me 'tis certain that his fashion he will change. For the battle now he sets forth, who unless he be provided against will prove to be a bane; for the combat 'tis he comes towards you, even Sualtach's son Cuchulainn. Your hosts now safe he will hew down, and make your slain to thickly lie: by him ye shall lose all your heads – she-prophet Feidelm conceals it not. From skins of heroes blood will pour, the memory of which shall be lasting, long; there shall be mangled bodies, women shall lamentation make, all by the 'Hound of the Forge,' whom now I see.

Thus far then the prediction and prognostication and the head and front of the story; with the occasion of its being found and made, and with the bolster-conversation which Ailell and Meave held in Cruachan.' (*The Cuchullin Saga* edited: E. Hall)

Cuchulainn was the only man in Ulster not affected by the curse of weakness; it was his task to defend almost single handed the Ulstermen against the hosts of Queen Medb.

Although Fergus had been insulted by King Conchobar, he sent a message warning the warriors of Ulster that the host of Medb was about to march upon them. Thus, Cuchulainn was keeping watch, forewarned, when the opposing army arrived.

Single Combat

Although an army set out to do battle, combat was primarily undertaken on a single basis; chosen warriors fought one another rather than an all-out pitched or mobile battle between all concerned. We find similar single combats in ancient poems such as the *Iliad* where the Greek warriors attacking Troy undertook selected duels to the death in order to settle specific aspects of the war. Equally, such single combat was seen as preferable to debilitating, all-out combat which would render both sides useless regardless of whoever gained the ultimate victory.

This economy of manpower is perhaps the basis of the ancient heroic single combat, for such fighting comes from times and cultures where manpower was scarce. Furthermore, it was regarded as the height of barbarism to waste many lives when allotted and specifically chosen champions were an integral part of the culture. It was the primary role of such champions to act for many men; this was their reason for living, fighting, and dying. In this sense, we might say that heroic warfare was more civilised than modern warfare in which thousands of lives are heedlessly wasted. The ancient concept of heroic combat persisted until as late as the Great War of 1914–18, in which early aerial combat retained some of this chivalric or heroic duelling quality. Paradoxically, this was also the war in which the modern concept of wasting many lives for the sake of relatively unimportant objectives was so strong a feature.

So we find the champion Cuchulainn as the sole defender of Ulster, while his companions are stricken by a magical weakness and sleep. Instead of merely overwhelming him by strength of numbers, as we might expect, the army of Queen Medb engages the hero in single combats, one after the other.

None of the warriors who challenged Cuchulainn returned; he killed them one by one. Between duels, he harassed the great army with his sling, slaying many men each day. He also killed the totem beasts belonging to the Queen; the dog, the bird, the squirrel. He generated such fear that no one dared to leave the camp. When one of the Queen's serving women wore her mistress's golden headdress, she was immediately slain by a well aimed stone from Cuchulainn's sling.

Eventually, Queen Medb, wanting to see this astonishing champion of Ulster face to face, sent a bard to ask Cuchulainn to parley. He agreed, and at the meeting Medb was amazed at his youth and seeming innocence. There he was, a mere seventeen years old, without a beard, yet destroying her vast army day after day. In the time honoured manner of powerful women, she offered the hero her own love and friendship, with great honour and possessions, if only he would come over to the side of Connaught and forsake Ulster. Despite his refusals, she repeated her offer over and over, until Cuchulainn warned that any further messengers of temptation would be slain.

In the end, he offered curious terms of battle, which the Queen was forced to accept. He agreed to fight one of the heroes of Ireland every day, and as long as the combat ensued, the main army was allowed to march forwards to gain ground. But as soon as the combat was over, the army must cease to move. Medb thought this a better bargain than to lose many men daily and gain no ground at all.

As an incentive to her warriors, Medb offered the love of her daughter Findabair (or Finnavar) who eventually died of maidenly shame on discovering that she had been the object of such a bargain. Yet despite the hand of the Queen's daughter as an incentive to do great deeds, not one hero of the army could kill Cuchulainn. However they did distract him sufficiently and Medb's men managed to steal the Brown Bull and fifty heifers while the hero was engaged in the series of combats.

The Morrigan

As with all ancient sagas or hero-cycles, the Cattle Raid of Cooley is a complex sequence combining myth and cultural history. After his remarkable exploits in single combat, reflecting actual styles of combat used by the ancient Celts, Cuchulainn next encountered a supernatural adversary.

So great were the warlike achievements of the Champion of Ulster that he attracted the attention of none other than the primal great goddess of war herself, known in Irish tradition as the Morrigan or Morrigu. It may be significant that in another legend altogether, Cuchulainn's grandfather, the Dagda, makes love to the Morrigan in an explicitly lusty creation and conflict myth. In other words, the Morrigu is concerned with the powers of life and death; as such she would be the natural patroness of heroes such as

Cuchulainn. While sleeping deeply and resting from his series of single combats, Cuchulainn was awakened by a great shout from the north, which in Celtic legend is the realm or region of the dead, justice and of the primal element of Earth. He ordered his driver Laeg to make the chariot ready and seek out the source of such a miraculous shout.

Travelling northwards, Cuchulainn met with a woman riding towards him in another chariot. She wore a red dress, a long red cloak, had red hair and eyebrows and carried a long grey spear. Courteous as all such heroes were, the Champion of Ulster hailed this apparition and asked her who she might be; she replied that she was a king's daughter who had fallen in love with him as a result of his wonderful exploits. This motif, in which a goddess seeks out a hero and declares her love for him is found in a number of myths world-wide, and has direct parallels in British and Greek tales from heroic cultures.

While Cuchulainn was adept at martial arts, he seems to have been rather naive when it came to recognising and dealing with supernatural beings, a failing common to many heroes. He told the red haired woman that he had more important things to concern himself with than a woman's love. The Morrigan then replied that she had been helping him throughout the battle, through her love for him, and that she would still continue to help him in return for his love. Unfortunately, Cuchulainn replied that he did not need any female help in battle. Despite the extremely broad clues as to her true identity, the Champion failed to recognise the goddess.

'If you will not have my love and help, then you shall have my hatred and enmity,' she said. 'When you are in combat with a warrior as good as yourself, I shall come against you in many shapes and hinder you, until your opponent has the advantage.'

Cuchulainn drew his sword to attack this threatening woman, but saw only a crow sitting upon a branch. The crow was the totem bird of the goddess, and then the Champion finally understood that he had rejected the help of the great goddess.

On the following day, a great warrior called Loch came to meet Cuchulainn in battle. Scornfully, he refused to fight a beardless youth, so Cuchulainn rubbed blackberry juice into his chin until it appeared darkened with a growing beard. Then the Champion discovered what it meant to have the goddess against him rather than for him; while he was in combat with Loch, she came against him three times. The first time she came in the shape of a heifer which tried to knock him over; the second time she came in the shape of an eel which wrapped around his legs as he stood in running water; the third time she came against him as a wolf that seized his sword arm.

But Cuchulainn broke the heifer's leg, trampled upon the eel, and poked out one of the eyes of the wolf. Yet every time he was hindered by these beasts, the warrior Loch wounded him deeply. Despite the worsening odds, Cuchulainn finally killed Loch with a cast of his magical spear, the thirty barbed *gae bulga* made from the bones of a sea monster.

After this threefold conflict and the hero's success against both goddess and champion, the Morrigan appeared again to Cuchulainn in the shape of an aged crone. She requested that he heal the wounds that he had inflicted upon her in her animal shapes, and finally a true pact was made between mortal and immortal.

Lugh and Cuchulainn

Just as the goddess appeared to Cuchulainn and ultimately helped him after conflict in which he was made fully aware that she was his patroness, so did his father the god Lugh appear. This sequence of apparitions and divine intervention is not merely a whim or trick of the story-teller's art; it is central both to the historical culture of the ancient Celts and to the magical, mythical and transformative adventures which the hero undertakes.

Cuchulainn's qualities are partly hereditary, from his parentage, and partly through training and support by the feminine personae of the warrior woman Scathach and the great goddess the Morrigan. Nevertheless, in some respects, he is still extremely young, and while showing natural strength and speed, trained skill, and remarkable qualities of endurance, he seems to be emotionally immature. Much of the hidden aspect of this sequence of tales leads the hero towards emotional and spiritual maturity. In this sense the hero sagas of the Celts are not dissimilar to the educational or exemplary tales connected to the martial arts in Eastern cultures; no matter how fast, strong or deadly the warrior is, it is ultimately his spiritual maturity that is at stake, not merely the winning and losing of battles.

Exhausted by continual combat, Cuchulainn suffered from lack of sleep; he could only snatch short rests, with his head on his hand, his hand on his spear, and his spear on his knee. Finally, his father Lugh the Long Handed took pity upon the champion, and appeared to him in the shape of a tall, handsome man in a green cloak, golden silk shirt covered with embroidery and carrying a black shield and five pointed spear. He cast his son into a magical sleep for three days and nights. While Cuchulainn slept, Lugh healed his many wounds with magical herbs; and when he awoke the Champion was completely refreshed and whole.

During this magical sleep, the boy troop of youthful warriors from Emain Macha came to fight against the army of Medb. Although they slew three times their own number, they were wiped out entirely.

Fergus and Cuchulainn

The next champion set against Cuchulainn in the war over the Brown Bull was his foster father Fergus. After much persuasion from Queen Medb, Fergus set out against the Champion, but without his famous sword. The two warriors made a remarkable agreement on the field of combat. For the sake of their years together when Cuchulainn was a child, Fergus asked Cuchulainn to only pretend to fight, and then to run away. Naturally, Cuchulainn declared that he was unwilling to be seen running away from

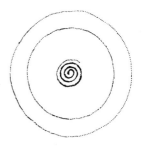

Impression of sharp-edged throwing shield as described in the Cuchulainn sagas.

anyone, even his own foster father. Fergus promised Cuchulainn that if he ran away on this occasion, then Fergus would, in turn, run away at some future time of Cuchulainn's choice. In this way, the Champion of Ulster showed some beginnings of wisdom, for he agreed to this trick, knowing that a future benefit might be superior to a momentary triumph, or even to the momentary shame of fleeing from combat. So during the man-to-man combat, Cuchulainn ran off and Fergus was able to return to the army and claim that he had fulfilled his duty.

Cuchulainn and Calatin

Next to be sent against the Champion of Ulster was the magician or Druid Calatin. Queen Medb ordered him to fight Cuchulainn with the assistance of his twenty seven sons and his grandson. This she justified by declaring that they were all of one body, that of Calatin, and that therefore she was not breaking the agreement to send only one man into combat.

The sons of Calatin had the notorious reputation of using poisoned spears which never missed their mark; any man wounded by such spears was soon certain to die. When Fergus heard of this dishonourable trick, he sent another Ulster exile called Fiacha to watch the combat and report back to him. Fiacha could not restrain himself from helping the outnumbered Cuchulainn, and between them the two warriors killed Calatin and his family.

Cuchulainn and Ferdiad

Medb now called upon the warrior Ferdiad who had been senior to Cuchulainn during the time of arms training on the island of Scathach. This provides an interesting insight into the manner in which such training schools were run, for Cuchulainn was Ferdiad's junior and servant during the early part of his training. Also the hero had been fostered to Fergus, a common practice among the Celtic tribes, leading to a stable structure of relationships between various families or clans. So another bond now appeared in the context of Ferdiad, who had a role similar to that of elder brother or senior student in arms.

At first Ferdiad refused to fight Cuchulainn, on account of their time together training under the instruction of Scathach. Queen Medb threatened that if he refused this combat, she would have him satirized so terribly that he would die of shame, and his name would be notorious for ever. This is a curious insight into the culture, for satire was not the weak concept of idle humour that it has become today. One thing that was feared by all champions, no matter how strong, was to be satirized by a poet. In a culture in which oral tradition held everything together (there being little or no written word) a satire would long outlast the memory of a living man. Satires were rapidly spread about the land, and any man who had been satirized was soon known to everyone as an object of insult and shame. Medb also offered a carrot with her stick, for she promised Ferdiad great rewards, and bound herself by a six-fold oath of surety that he would indeed be rewarded as promised.

So Ferdiad went reluctantly to combat. Cuchulainn met him with a warm welcome, but was told that his old companion had come to do battle rather than to celebrate friendship. They fought all day with neither gaining any advantage. At sunset, they retired to rest, and Cuchulainn sent half of his healing herbs to Ferdiad, while Ferdiad sent half of his food to Cuchulainn. Their horses were tended in the same stable, and their charioteers slept by the same fireside. This pattern was repeated on the second and third days, when they parted in great sorrow, knowing that on the next day one of them would die. This time the horses did not share a stall nor the charioteers share a fire; on the fourth day Cuchulainn killed his old companion with a low cast from his spear, the *gae bulga*.

When he saw Ferdiad dying, the battle frenzy faded from Cuchulainn. He took up the warrior into his arms, carrying him across the river so that he might die with the men of Ulster rather than with the army of Ireland as was the ancient custom. He made a lament over the body of Ferdiad, declaring that all had been a mere game and sport until this moment . . . 'yesterday Ferdiad was greater than a mountain, today he is less than a shadow.'

By this point in the conflict, the Champion of Ulster was so covered in wounds that he could not let his clothes touch his body, holding them off with hazel twigs and padding the spaces in between with moss and grass. The only part of his body not covered in wounds was the left hand which held his shield.

The Summoning of the Men of Ulster

Cuchulainn lay in this terribly wounded state, his groans of agony heard at great distance by his *human* father, Sualtam. The Champion persuaded his human father not to tend his wounds, but to ride immediately to the stronghold of Emain Macha and try to arouse the sleeping men of Ulster from their magical lethargy.

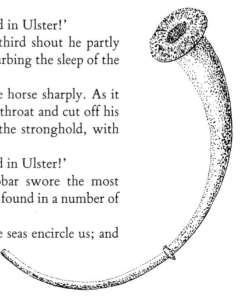

Bronze trumpet from Lough-na-Shade, Co. Armagh, Ireland.

Sualtam mounted upon Cuchulainn's great war horse Gray of Battle and made haste for the stronghold of King Conchobar. There, he gave three great shouts:

'Men are being killed, women stolen, and cattle lifted in Ulster!'

But no one heeded the first two shouts. With his third shout he partly awakened the Druid Cathbad, who cursed him for disturbing the sleep of the King.

So great was the rage of Sualtam, that he turned the horse sharply. As it reared, the sharp shield edge pressed against the rider's throat and cut off his head. The uncontrolled battle horse charged through the stronghold, with Sualtam's severed head still crying out:

'Men are being killed, women stolen, and cattle lifted in Ulster!'

Now the host truly awakened, and King Conchobar swore the most powerful oath known to the Celtic world, one which is found in a number of ancient tales, histories, and in oral tradition even today:

'The heavens are over us, the earth is beneath us, the seas encircle us; and unless the heavens with all their stars fall upon us or the earth gives way beneath us, or the seas flood in to drown the land, I will restore every cow to her stable and every woman to her rightful home!'

Messengers were sent to rally Ulster, and soon a battle was being fought such as had never before been seen in Ireland. Cuchulainn heard the noise of this great conflict, and despite his terrible wounds, arose to challenge Fergus as he led the army of Queen Medb. But rather than fight again, the Champion of Ulster reminded Fergus of his oath to run away when asked to do so; then Fergus ran from Cuchulainn, and when the great hosts saw their leader running, they ran also.

The Last Combat
The Brown Bull of Cualgne had travelled with the army into Connaught, where he challenged the White Bull of King Ailill. During the terrible battle which fell out between them, the Brown ripped the White to pieces, tossing his loins as far as Athlone and the liver to Trim. After this fight, the Brown Bull returned to Cualgne, where he became maddened with rage and killed all that moved before him. Finally, his heart burst with the power of his great bellowing, and so he died.

Thus ended the remarkable exploits of Cuchulainn during the Cattle Raid of Cooley.

Tragedy and Death

Like so many great heroic characters, the life of Cuchulainn is bound up not merely with stupendous feats of strength and martial skill, but also with unavoidable doom and tragedy. We found earlier how he had received his training in arms from the formidable warrior woman Scathach, and that during this training period he agreed to fight another warrior princess, Aoife, who he defeated and forced to bear him a son.

Cuchulainn Kills his Son
Cuchulainn's son Conlaoch (pronounced 'Connla') was the cause of tragedy through a subtle but inevitable process. When Aoife heard the news that Cuchulainn had married Emer, she decided to make the son into a weapon against his father. She taught him all her considerable skill in arms and sent him to Ireland; but before taking leave of her son, she put three *geasa* or immutable taboos upon him. The first was that he should not turn back, the second that he should never refuse a challenge, and the third was that he should never tell anyone his name.

When Conlaoch arrived at his father's home in Dundalk, he was met by the warrior Conall, who, according to most ancient custom asked him his name and lineage. Normally, he would have replied with his name, his father's name, and a list of his illustrious ancestors and relatives. This was an essential formality in the heroic culture of early Britain and Ireland; any man refusing to give such a lineage would have been highly suspect. Conlaoch's refusal, according to the *geas* laid upon him by his mother, caused Conall to challenge him to a duel, which of course Conall lost.

Next Cuchulainn himself came and asked the strange young man to reveal his lineage; Conlaoch replied:

'If I was not under a *geas* there would be no man in the world whom I would rather tell my lineage to, for I love your face.'

But the magical prohibitions of Aoife his mother had done their work, and father was forced to challenge son. In the terrible battle that followed, Cuchulainn shone with his famous hero light. Then Conlaoch realised that by a cruel twist of events he was fighting his own father, who he had come to find. He flung his spear sideways deliberately to miss the glowing hero, but Cuchulainn had already cast his terrible *gae bulga* which could not be withstood. The hero's son died, but not before he had identified himself to his father.

Cuchulainn's grief was terrible, and the men of Ulster were afraid that his madness would be turned violently upon them. In an attempt to save both the hero and his companions from further tragedy, the Druid Cathbad cast a spell upon Cuchulainn, such that he saw the waves of the sea as armed opponents. He battled with the waves until he collapsed from exhaustion.

The Final Battle

As might be expected in such a remarkable hero, Cuchulainn's death was brought about by a woman. Queen Medb, after her defeat in the Cattle Raid, held meetings with all the families who had had relatives killed by Cuchulainn. She worked upon them continually to seek revenge for their loved ones against the Champion of Ulster.

However, her deadliest weapons were the three daughters of Calatin the magician. She sent these three to Alba (Scotland) and to Babylon to learn magical arts.

When the three daughters returned from their training, they were able in every aspect of the magical arts, and could summon illusions of battle hosts with their formidable skills. Finally, Queen Medb waited until the period of weakness and lethargy fell upon the men of Ulster, just as she had done during the Cattle Raid. Thus, Cuchulainn faced alone her combined forces, both human and non-human.

As the massed forces of Queen Medb and her associates marched into Ulster and ravaged the land, King Conchobar MacNessa called a council of war. His warriors and Druids were too weak to fight, yet the King did not wish Cuchulainn to battle single-handed, for it was known that if the Champion fell, then the land would be luckless forever.

To keep the Champion from entering into battle until his fellow warriors were fit and active enough to assist him, the King ordered the women, the

An early Celtic bronze scabbard from Scotland, showing the grace and skill lavished upon their weapons by the early Celts of the Cuchulainn era.

bards, and the poets to divert Cuchulainn in every possible way, keeping him idle at Emain Macha. But while this desperate ploy was under way and Cuchulainn was feasting and talking, the three daughters of Calatin appeared. They created an illusory army out of grass, thistles and withered leaves, and caused the sound of trumpets and the roar and scream of battle to be heard all about Emain Macha.

Only when Cuchulainn was convinced by Conchobar's Druids that it was all an illusion did he restrain himself from rushing into battle. But it was clear to Conchobar that his Champion would soon be lured out into death unless he was further protected from enticements and tricks. The Champion was moved to the magical valley of Glean-na-Bodhar (Glen na Mower) which means 'Deaf Valley'; even if all the men in Ireland were to shout at once around this valley, no one inside would hear them.

Once again, the daughters of Calatin worked their arts of illusion, until it seemed that a vast host surrounded the valley, with fires raging and women shrieking. This noise reached even into the magical Deaf Valley, and although the women and Druids attending Cuchulainn tried to drown it, the Champion was certain that battle had come to his very resting place. Finally, Cathbad the Druid convinced Cuchulainn that it was still an illusion and that he need not venture out to battle.

But the last attempt to trick the champion into combat succeeded. One of the daughters of Calatin took the shape of a lover of Cuchulainn, crying out that Ulster was being ravaged. Despite all attempts to restrain him, Cuchulainn had his chariot harnessed and rode out to find the invading army. The omens for this last battle were bad; the Gray of Macha refused to be bridled and wept tears of blood; the Champion's mother Dechtire brought him wine three times, and each time it turned to blood when it touched his lips. When he crossed the first ford, he saw an Otherworld maiden washing clothes and armour, an important death vision. Just as if he was a stranger, or as if she did not recognise him in person, she told him that she washed the armour of Cuchulainn, who would shortly die.

Next the champion met three ancient hags roasting a hound on rowan spits. This apparition was an aspect of the Morrigan, the death goddess, and the hound was Cuchulainn's own totem animal as his name meant Hound of Culann. The three hags asked the Champion to share their feast, but it was taboo for him to eat the flesh of hound. Finally, they shamed him into eating, by saying that he was too proud to eat the humble food of three poor old women, yet was only too willing to spend his time idly feasting in the halls of chieftains and kings. It is significant that Cuchulainn failed to recognise what was happening, for he ate the meat, and by so doing half of his body was paralysed.

Cuchulainn carried three spears into battle, and each one, it was predicted, would kill a king. The first tactic used against the Champion of Ulster was that three Druids were sent to ask for the three spears; it was considered highly unlucky and dishonourable to refuse any request from a Druid.

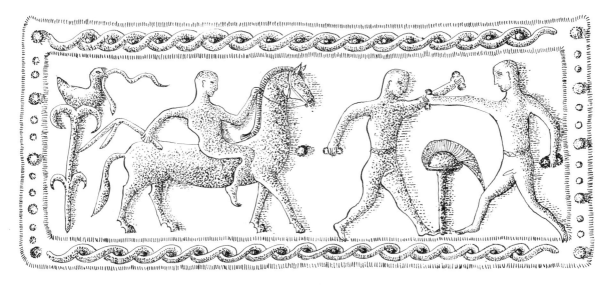

When the Champion was in the midst of conflict, fighting the ravaging army single handed, the first Druid came up to him and asked him for his spear.

'Give me one of your spears, or I will satirize you . . .'

'Take it,' said the champion, 'Never have I been satirized for lack of generosity . . .' So saying he cast the spear at the Druid and killed him. But an opposing champion, Lugaid son of Curoi, took the spear and killed Laeg the charioteer. The loss of his charioteer was a desperate blow indeed, and with it the second Druid came to Cuchulainn and asked for a spear, saying that he would lampoon the province of Ulster if he was refused the gift.

'I need not give more than one gift in a day,' said Cuchulainn, 'But never let it be said that Ulster was satirized on my account . . .' and he threw the spear through the head of the Druid. But Erc the King of Leinster snatched the spear, and killed the Gray of Macha with it.

'Give me your spear,' asked the third and last Druid sent to Cuchulainn by his enemies, 'or I will satirize your kindred . . .' Once again, the champion speared the Druid, but this time Lugaid son of Curoi threw the spear back at Cuchulainn himself, wounding him to the death. Thus was the prophesy of the spears fulfilled, for Laeg had been king of the charioteers, and the Gray of Macha had been king of the horses, while Cuchulainn was the king of all champions.

In his death throes, Cuchulainn asked his enemies to allow him to reach a lake to drink and then return to the battle. He bound himself to a standing stone by the lakeside, so that he could fight and die standing up, for he had lost the ability to walk. Before its death, his horse, the Gray of Macha, supported him in battle, and killed fifty men with its teeth, and thirty with each of its hooves. But the hero light was fading from the Champion of Ulster and his face became as pale as snow. Finally, a crow, the death bird of the Morrigan, came and perched upon his shoulder.

A fine Celtic clasp showing a rider and two warriors fighting. If typifies both the attention to detail and the story telling elements frequently found in early Celtic culture and art across Europe.

Certain now that the Champion was dead, his enemies cut off his head.

With the death of Cuchulainn the power and prosperity of Emain Macha failed, as did the warriors of the Red Branch of Ulster.

Extracts from the Saga

Having described the main adventures of Cuchulainn, and examined the primal heroic culture in which the warriors of Ulster lived, we can consider some examples from the early poems that preserve their legendary history.

The extracts which follow are taken from *The Cuchullin Saga* edited by Eleanor Hull in 1898, published by David Nutt of London. Spellings of Celtic language names were not standardised at this time, and the various translators who contributed used variant spellings, including the hero's name. The translations quoted have been selected to follow the main theme of our earlier chapters, and to demonstrate the rich colourful language and imagery of the sagas.

Firstly, we have a description of *The Hero*, which is both dramatic, powerful, and fantastic. Clearly, we are not being told of a human figure, but of a divine hero. Cuchulainn was the son of Lugh, the Sun God, and many of the features of our extract seem to indicate a magical image or god-form. The varying colours of his hair, multi-faceted eyes, and other attributes that seem bizarre to the modern reader are all associated with themes such as The Four Elements, the Seven Planets, and the mysterious powers of the Sun God. By way of contrast, we have a description of Ferdiad, Cuchulainn's heroic adversary; his appearance is more human, but clearly his arms and armour are of a magical and marvellous nature.

Our second example is a description of the famous *Battle Fury* of Cuchulainn. Once again, the imagery is full of magical potency, and terrible transformations. The historical Celts were noted by Greek and Roman historians for charging naked into battle, driven by a mystical frenzy that seemed to make them invincible; such behaviour persisted well into later centuries. Clansmen as late as the medieval period shunned armour, carried only small shields and the long Celtic sword, and even at that late period were still prone to charging naked into combat! The spirit of the Champion of Ulster was shared by many lesser heroes. In this quotation we also have a description of the armoured, spiked, and scythed chariot sometimes used by Cuchulainn.

The third extract is of a very different nature, being *Cuchulainn's Instructions to a Prince*. It is easy to forget, amidst the heroics and wonders, that the early Celts had a complex sophisticated culture. There were many rules of conduct rooted in an oral tradition of honour, religion, and tribal unity. The set of instructions reflect some of the concepts that underpinned Celtic culture for many centuries.

In *Cuchulainn and the Morrigan* we return to the supernatural theme that

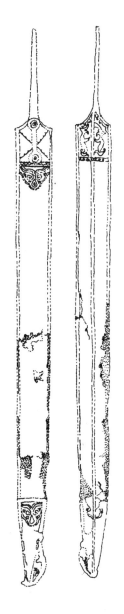

Decorated swords of the late Iron Age, from the La Tene Celtic culture of around the fourth century B.C.

While still a beardless boy, Cuchulainn slew three great champions and cut off their heads. Primal Celtic culture regarded the head as a sacred object of power, and head hunting was part of the ritual of war.

The modern, romantic statue of Cuchulainn which stands in Dublin Post Office, Eire.

underpins his adventures. It is partly through his relationship to this primal Celtic goddess of death, procreation, and life, that Cuchulainn is so successful, for she is also goddess of war. Only after she withdraws her support can the Champion of Ulster be defeated.

Our last translation is *The Death of Cuchulainn* in which the desperate and in many ways ritualised end of the hero is described in detail.

The Hero

'A handsome lad truly was he that stood there; Cuchulainn son of Sualtam. Three colours of hair had he; next to the skin of his head the hair was brown; in the middle it was crimson; on the outside it was like a diadem of gold; comparable to yellow gold was each glittering long curling splendid beautiful thread of hair, falling freely down between his two shoulders.

About his neck were a hundred tiny links of red gold flashing, with pendants hung from them. His headgear was adorned with a hundred differ-

The Morrigan – the terrifying Irish goddess of war, death, and procreation – confronts Cuchulainn. During his combats with the warriors of Queen Medb, Cuchulainn was first aided by the Morrigan; then through his own ignorance of her divinity, he caused her to turn against him.

ent jewels. On either cheek he had four moles, a yellow, a green, a blue and a red. In either eye he had seven pupils, sparkling like seven gems. Each of his feet had seven toes, each of his hands seven fingers; his hands and feet were endowed with the clutching power of hawk's talons and hedgehog's claws.

He wore his gorgeous raiment for great gatherings; a fair crimson tunic of five plies all fringed, with a long pin of white silver gold encased and patterned, shining like a luminous torch with a brilliance that men could not endure to look upon. Next to his skin was a body vestment of silk, bordered and fringed all around with gold, silver and white bronze braided together. His silken vestment came to the upper edge of his russet coloured kilt.

The champion carried a trusty special shield coloured dark crimson with a pure white silver rim all around its circumference; at his left side hung a long golden hilted sword. Beside him in his chariot was a lengthy spear, together with a keen aggressive javelin fitted with a hurling thong and rivets of white bronze. In one hand he carried nine heads, and nine more in the other; he held these heads as emblems of his valour and skill in arms, and at the sight of him the opposing army shook with terror.'

'And Ferdiad put on his battle suit of armour before the coming of Cuchulainn. It was a kilt of striped silk with a border of spangled gold next to his white skin. Outside, well sown over it was an apron of brown leather over the lower part of his body. Over that again he placed a stone as big as a millstone to defend his body below. And above all he put on his firm, deep apron of purified iron over the great stone, through dread of the *gae bulga* on that day.

Upon his head he wore his crested helmet of battle on which were four gems flashing in each quarter; it was studded all over with crystals and precious stones and *cruan* and with the brilliant rubies of the eastern world. In his right hand he took his destructive sharp pointed strong spear, and on his left side hung his curved sword of battle with a golden hilt and red pommel of gold. He slung upon his back his huge large bossed beautiful shield on which were fifty bosses each of which would bear the weight of a full grown hog, and with a great central boss of red gold.'

Cuchulainn in Battle Fury

'Then it was that he suffered his *riastradh* or paroxysm, whereby he became a fearsome and multiform and wondrous and hitherto unknown being. All over him, from his crown to the ground, his flesh and every limb and joint and point and articulation of him quivered as does a tree, yea a bulrush, in mid-current.

Within in his skin he put forth an unnatural effort of his body: his feet, his shins, and his knees shifted themselves and were behind him; his heels and calves and hams were displaced to the front of his leg-bones, in condition such that their knotted muscles stood up in lumps large as the clenched fist of a fighting man. The frontal sinews of his head were dragged to the back of his neck, where they showed in lumps bigger than the head of a man-child aged

one month. Then his face underwent an extraordinary transformation: one eye became engulfed in his head so far that 'tis a question whether a wild heron could have got at it where it lay against his occiput, to drag it out upon the surface of his cheek; the other eye on the contrary protruded suddenly, and of itself so rested upon the cheek. His mouth was twisted awry till it met his ears. His lion's gnashings caused flakes of fire, each one larger than fleece of three-year-old wether, to stream from his throat into his mouth and so outwards. The sounding blows of the heart that panted within him were as the howl of a ban-dog doing his office, or of a lion in the act of charging bears.

Among the clouds over his head were visible the virulent pouring showers and sparks of ruddy fire which the seething of his savage wrath caused to mount up above him. His hair became tangled about his head, as it had been branches of a red thorn-bush stuffed into a strongly fenced gap to block it; over the which though a prime apple-tree had been shaken, yet may we surmise that never an apple of them would have reached the ground, but rather that all would have been held impaled each on an individual hair as it bristled on him for fury.

His hero's paroxysm projected itself out of his forehead, and showed longer than the whet-stone of a first-rate man-at-arms. Taller, thicker, more rigid, longer than mast of a great ship was the perpendicular jet of dusky blood which out of his scalp's very central point shot upwards and then was scattered to the four cardinal points; whereby was formed a magic mist of gloom resembling the smoky pall that drapes a regal dwelling, what time a king at night-fall of a winter's day draws near to it.'

The Battle Chariot

'This distortion being now past which had been operated in Cuchulainn, he leaped into the scythed chariot that was equipped with iron points, with thin edges, with hooks, with hard spit-spikes, with machinery for opening it, with sharp nails that studded over its axles and straps and curved parts and

Three-headed deity, a recurrent theme, on a Celtic vase from Bavay, France. Cuchulainn himself is described as transforming his face during fits of frenzy, linking human and divine powers.

35

Gold bracelet (La Tène style) typical of the type of adornments worn by Cuchulainn. This is from the Celtic region of Bad Durkheim, Germany. Celtic jewellery spread across Europe with movement of tribes and through trade.

tackle. Then he delivered a thunder-feat of a hundred, one of two hundred, one of three hundred, one of four hundred, and stood at a thunder-feat of five hundred; and he went so far, because he felt it to be obligatory on him that in this his first set-to and grappling with the four provinces of Erin, even such a number must fall by his hand. In which guise then he goes forward to assault his enemies, lending the chariot such impulse that its iron shod wheels sank in the earth and made ruts which well might have served as earth-works of defence; for both stones and rocks, both flags and the earth's bottom-gravel on either hand were heaped up outside the wheels and to an equal height with them.

The reason which moved him this day to make such hostile demonstration round about the men of Erin for he careered round them in a circle was that he designed thus to ensure that they should not escape him, neither should dissolve away from him, before he should have avenged the boy-corps on them. Then he charged them, and all round the host on their outer side he drew a fence built up of his enemies' carcasses. An onfall of a foeman on foemen indeed was this attack of his, for they fell sole to sole and trunk to trunk. Thrice in this wise he made the circuit of them, thereby leaving them laid in slaughter: the soles of three against the headless bodies of three more.'

Instructions from Cuchulainn to a Prince
The detailed instructions which follow – in their originally translated style – are a curious mixture of pagan Celtic ritual and belief, and of a code of conduct which is most familiar to the modern reader as that of King Arthur and the Knights of the Round Table. It is likely that the material was drawn from an enduring oral tradition, preserved by bards or poets, but elaborated and refined through repeated transcription and commentary by monastic chroniclers who finally set the Cuchulainn tales into written form:

36

'A meeting of the four great provinces of Erin was held at this time, to seek out a person on whom should be bestowed the sovereignty of Erin; because it was deemed an evil that the Hill of Supremacy and Lordship of Erin, Tara namely; should be without the rule of a king; moreover, they deemed it an evil that the tribes should be without a king's government to judge their houses. For a period of seven years the men of Erin had been without the government of a king over them; that is, from the death of Conaire at Bruidhen da Derga to the time of this great meeting of the four provinces of Erin in the court of Erc, son of Cairbre at Tara of the Kings.

Now these were the princes that were gathered to that meeting: Meave and Ailell, Curói, Tighernach son of Luchta, and Finn Mac Rossa. These would not admit the Ultonians to their council in the election of a king, because they were of one accord opposed to Ulster.

A bull-feast was prepared by them, that by its means they might discover on whom the sovereignty should be bestowed.

This was the manner in which the bull-feast was prepared. A white bull was killed, and one man ate his sufficiency of the flesh and of the broth; and he slept after having partaken of that meal, and a charm of truth was pronounced upon him by four druids. Then in a dream was shown to him the form of the man who should be made king, and his appearance and manner, with the sort of work that he was engaged in. Out of his sleep the man uttered a cry and he described to the kings the thing he saw, namely, a young man strong and noble, with two red streaks around him, and he sitting over the pillow of a man in a decline in Emain Macha.

Then was a message sent with this description to Emain Macha. Now the men of Ulster were at that time gathered round Conachar in Emania, where Cuchulainn lay upon his bed of sickness. The messenger told his story to the king and to the nobles of Ulster also. Then said Conachar, 'There is with us a free and nobly descended youth of that description, namely Lugaid, the son of

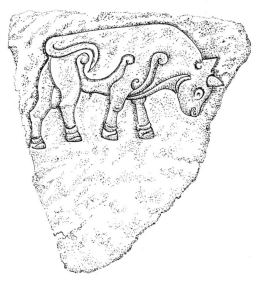

Typical Pictish/Celtic style bull, as shown in many carvings and manuscripts, and one of the great magical or sacred animals of the Celts.

37

Iron and bronze linchpin from a chariot wheel (La Tene style). The chariot was one of the principle weapons used by the early Celts, and features prominently in the Cuchulainn sagas.

the Three Fair Twins: the pupil of Cuchulainn; over whose pillow he sits alone within, solacing his tutor, that is Cuchulainn, who is in his bed of decline.

Suddenly Cuchulainn arose and began to instruct his pupil. These are his words:

"Stir not up sharp and ignoble contests. Be not flighty, inaccessible, haughty. Be not intractable, proud, precipitate, passionate. Be not bent down by the intoxication of much wealth.

Be not like a flea who fouls the ale in the house of a provincial king. Make not long sojourn on the frontiers of strangers. Do not visit obscure persons and those without power. Let not prescription close on illegal possession. Let witnesses be examined as to who is rightful heir of the land. Let the historians combine to act uprightly before you. Let the lands of the brethren, and their increase, be ascertained in their lifetime. Let the genealogical trees be added to as children are born. Let the living be called to their possessions; on the security of their oaths let the habitations of their ancestors be revived. Let the heir be established in his lawful patrimony. Let strangers be driven out by force of arms.

Speak not haughtily. Discourse not noisily. Mock not, insult not, deride not the old. Think not ill of any. Make no demands that cannot be met. [Grant nothing, refuse nothing, lend nothing without good cause.] Receive submissively the instructions of the wise. Be mindful of the admonitions of the old. Follow the decrees of your fathers.

Be not cold-hearted to friends, but against your foes be vigorous. Avoid dishonourable disputes in your many contests. Be not a tattler and abuser. Waste not, hoard not, alienate not. Submit to reproof for unbecoming deeds. Do not sacrifice justice to the passions of men. Lay not hands on the possessions of others, lest you repent it. Compete not, that you may not excite jealousy; be not lazy, lest you become weakened; be not importunate, lest you become contemptible. Do you consent to follow these counsels my son?"

Then Lugaid answered Cuchulainn in these words: "These precepts are worthy to observed without exception. All men shall see that none of them shall be neglected. They shall be executed if it be possible."

Lugaid then returned to Tara with the messengers. He was proclaimed King. That night he slept at Tara, after which all of the assembly returned to their own homes.'

(trans: *Book of the Dun Cow*)

Cuchulainn and the Morrigan

When Cuchulainn lay in sleep in Dún Imrid, he heard a cry sounding out of the north, a cry terrible and fearful to his ears. Out of a deep slumber he was aroused by it so suddenly, that he fell out of his bed upon the ground like a sack, in the east wing of the house.

He rushed forth without weapons, until he gained the open air, his wife following him with his armour and his garments. He perceived Laegh in his harnessed chariot coming towards him from Ferta Laig in the North. 'What brings thee here?' said Cuchulainn. 'A cry that I heard sounding across the plain,' said Laegh. 'From which direction?' said Cuchulainn. 'From the north-west,' said Laegh, 'across the great highway leading to Caill Cuan.' 'Let us follow the sound,' said Cuchulainn.

They go forward as far as Ath da Ferta. When they arrived there, they heard the rattle of a chariot from the loamy district of Culgaire. They saw before them a chariot harnessed with a chestnut horse. The horse had (but) one leg, and the pole of the chariot passed through its body, so that the peg in front met the halter passing across its forehead. Within the chariot sat a woman, her eye-brows red, and a crimson mantle round her. Her mantle fell behind her between the wheels of the chariot so that it swept along the ground. A big man went along beside the chariot. He also wore a coat of crimson, and on his back he carried a forked staff of hazelwood, while he drove a cow before him.

'The cow is not pleased to be driven on by you,' said Cuchulainn. 'She does not belong to you,' said the woman; 'the cow is not owned by any of your friends or associates.' 'The cows of Ulster belong to me,' said Cuchulainn. 'You would give a decision about the cow!' said the woman; 'you are taking too much upon yourself, O Cuchulainn!'

'Why is it the woman who accosts me?' said Cuchulainn. 'Why is it not the man?' 'It is not the man to whom you addressed yourself,' said the woman. 'Oh yes,' said Cuchulainn, 'but it is you who answer for him.' 'He is Uar-gaeth-sceo Luachair-sceo.' 'Well, to be sure, the length of the name is astonishing!' said Cuchulainn. 'Talk to me then yourself, for the man does not answer. What is your own name?' 'The woman to whom you speak,' said the man, 'is called Faebor beg-beoil cuimdiuir folt scenb-gairit sceo uath.'

'You are making a fool of me!' said Cuchulainn. And he made a leap into the chariot. He put his two feet on her two shoulders, and his spear on the parting of her hair.

The Sheela-na-gig *a primal goddess of sexuality, found in various carvings in Britain and Ireland. The savage Morrigan may be related to this type of image.*

'Do not play your sharp weapons on me!' she said. 'Then tell your true name,' said Cuchulainn. 'Go further off from me then,' said she. 'I am a female satirist, and he is Daire mac Fiachna of Cuailgne; I carry off this cow as a reward for a poem.' 'Let us hear your poem,' said Cuchulainn. 'Only move further off,' said the woman. 'Your shaking over my head will not influence me.' Then he moved off until he was between the two wheels of the chariot. Then she sang to him. . . .

Cuchulainn prepared to spring again into the chariot; but horse, woman, chariot, man, and cow, all had disappeared.

Then he perceived that she had been transformed into a black bird on a branch close by him. 'A dangerous enchanted woman you are!' said Cuchulainn. 'Henceforth this Grellach shall bear the name of the 'enchanted place'' (*dolluid*),' said the woman; and Grellach Dolluid was it called.

'If I had only known that it was you,' said Cuchulainn, 'we should not have parted thus.' 'Whatever you have done,' said she, 'will bring you ill-luck.' 'You cannot harm me,' said he. 'Certainly I can,' said the woman. 'I am guarding your death-bed, and I shall be guarding it henceforth. I brought this cow out of the *Sidh* of Cruachan so that she might breed by the bull of Daire mac Fiachna, namely the Donn of Cuailgne. So long as her calf shall be a yearling, so long shall thy life be; and it is this that shall cause the Táin Bó Cuailgne.'

'My name shall be all the more renowned in consequence of this Táin,' said the hero:

> I shall strike down their warriors
> I shall fight their battles
> I shall survive the Táin!

'How wilt thou manage that?' said the woman; 'for, when thou art engaged in a combat with a man as strong, as victorious, as dexterous, as terrible, as untiring, as noble, as brave, as great as thyself, I will become an eel, and I will throw a noose round they feet in the ford, so that heavy odds will be against thee.'

'I swear by the God by whom the Ultonians swear,' said Cuchulainn, 'that I will bruise thee against a green stone of the ford; and thou never shalt have any remedy from me if thou leavest me not.' 'I shall also become a grey wolf for thee, and I will take from thy right hand, as far as to thy left arm.'

'I will encounter thee with my spear,' said he, 'until thy left or right eye is forced out; and thou shalt never have help from me, if thou leavest me not.'

'I will become a white red-eared cow,' said she, 'and I will go into the pond beside the ford, in which thou art in deadly combat with a man, as skilful in feats as thyself, and an hundred white red-eared cows behind me; and I and all behind me will rush into the ford, and the ''Faithfulness of men'' will be brought to a test that day, and thy head shall be cut off from thee.'

'I will with my sling make a cast against thee,' said he, 'so that thy right or thy left leg will be broken, and thou shalt never have help from me, if thou dost not leave me.'

Thereupon the Morrigu departed into the *Sidh* of Cruachan in Connacht, and Cuchulainn returned to his dwelling.

Cuchulainn's Death (from the *Book of Leinster*)

When Cuchulainn's foes came for the last time against him, the land was filled with smoke and flame; weapons fell from their racks, and the day of his death drew nigh.

The evil tidings were brought to him, and the maiden Levarcham bade him arise, though he was foreworn with fighting in defence of the plain of Muirthemne. Niamh, wife of Conall the Victorious, also urged him, so that he sprang to his arms, and flung his mantle about him; but the brooch fell and pierced his foot, forewarning him.

Then he took his shield, and ordered his charioteer, Laegh, to harness his horse, the Gray of Macha. But Laegh said: 'I swear by the God by whom my

people swear, that though all the men of Conchobar's fifth were round the Gray of Macha, they could not bring him to the chariot. I never gainsaid thee until to-day. Come, then, if thou wilt, and speak with the Gray himself.'

Cuchulainn went to him. And thrice did the horse turn his left side to his master. On the night before, the Morrigu had unyoked the chariot, for she liked not Cuchulainn going to the battle, for she knew that he would not come again to Emain Macha.

Then Cuchulainn reproached his steed, saying that he was not wont to deal thus with his master. Thereat the Gray of Macha came, and let his big round tears of blood fall on Cuchulainn's feet. And Cuchulainn leaped into the chariot, and started southwards along the road of Mid-Luachair.

And Levarcham met him, and besought him not to leave them; and the thrice fifty queens who were in Emain Macha, and who loved him, cried to him with a great cry. But he turned his chariot to the right, and they gave a scream of wailing and lamentation, and smote their hands, for they knew that he could not come to them again.

The house of his nurse that had fostered him was on this road. He used to go to it whenever he went driving past from the north or south, and she kept for him always a vessel, with drink therein. He drank a drink and fared forth, bidding his nurse farewell. Then he saw somewhat, the Three Crones blind of the left eye, before him on the road.

They had cooked a hound with poisons and spells on spits of the rowan-tree. Now, one of the things that Cuchulainn was bound not to do, was to go to a cooking-hearth and consume the food. Another of the things that he must not do, was to eat his namesake's flesh. He speeds on, and was about to pass them, for he knew that they were not there for his good.

The triple goddess on a Roman-Celtic carving from Cirencester, England. This persistent theme emphasises multiple head and eyes as Celtic symbols of divine power.

41

Then said the Crone to him, 'Stay with us a while, O Cuchulainn.'

'I will not stay with you, in sooth,' said Cuchulainn.

'That is because the food is only a hound,' quoth she. 'Were this a great cooking-hearth thou wouldst have visited us. But, because what is here is little, thou comest not. Unseemly is it for the great to despise the small.'

Then he drew nigh to her, and the Crone gave him the shoulder-blade of the hound out of her left hand. Then Cuchulainn ate it out of his (left) hand, and put it under his left thigh. The hand that took it, and the thigh under which he put it, were stricken from trunk to end, so that their former strength abode not in them.

Then he drove along the road of Mid-Luachair around Sliab Fuad; and his enemy, Erc son of Cairpre, saw him in his chariot, with his sword shining redly in his hand and the light of valour hovering over him, and his three-hued hair like strings of golden thread over an anvil's edge beneath some cunning craftsman's hand.

'That man is coming towards us, O men of Erin!' said Erc. 'Await him.' So they made a fence of their linked shields, and at each corner Erc made them place two of their bravest, feigning to fight each other, and a satirist with each of these pairs; and he told the satirists to ask Cuchulainn for his spear, for the sons of Calatin had prophesied of his spear that a king should be slain thereby unless it were given when demanded.

And he made the men of Erin utter a great cry, and Cuchulainn rushed against him in his chariot, performing his three thunder-feats; and he plied his spear and sword so that the halves of their heads and skulls and hands and feet, and their red bones were scattered broadcast throughout the plain of Muirthemne, in number like unto the sand of the sea, and the stars of heaven; like dewdrops in May, and flakes of snow and hailstones; like leaves of the forests and buttercups on Magh Breagh and grass under the feet of the herds on a summer's day. And grey was that field with their brains after the onslaught and plying of weapons which Cuchulainn dealt out to them.

Then he saw one of the pairs of warriors contending together, and the satirist called on him to intervene, and Cuchulainn leaped at them, and with two blows of his fist dashed out their brains.

'Thy spear to me!' says the satirist.

'I swear by the oath of my people,' said Cuchulainn, 'thou dost not need it more than I myself do. The men of Erin are upon me here, and I too am upon them.'

'I will revile thee if thou givest it not,' says the satirist.

'I have never yet been reviled because of my niggardliness or my churlishness,' said Cuchulainn, and with that he flung the spear at him with its handle foremost; and it passed through his head and killed nine on the other side of him. And Cuchulainn drove through the host, but Lugaid son of Curói got the spear.

'What will fall by this spear, O sons of Calatin?' said Lugaid.

'A king will fall by that spear,' say they.

42

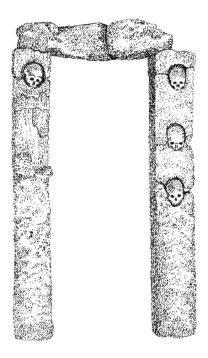

Then Lugaid flung the spear at Cuchulainn's chariot and it reached the charioteer, Laegh son of Riangabar, and all his bowels came forth on the cushion of the chariot.

'Then,' said Laegh, 'bitterly have I been wounded, etc.'

Thereupon Cuchulainn drew out the spear and Laegh bade him farewell. Then said Cuchulainn, 'Today I shall be champion and I shall also be charioteer.'

Then he saw the second pair contending, and one of them said it was a shame for him not to intervene. And Cuchulainn sprang upon them and dashed them into pieces against a rock.

'That spear to me, O Cuchulainn!' said the satirist.

'I swear by the oath of my people, thou dost not need the spear more than I do. On my head and my valour and my weapons it rests to-day to sweep the four provinces of Erin from the plain of Muirthemne.'

'I will revile thee,' says the satirist.

'I am not bound to grant more than one request in one day; and moreover, I have already saved my honour by payment.'

'Then I will revile Ulster for thy default,' says the satirist.

'Never yet hath Ulster been reviled on account of any refusal or churlishness of mine. Though little of my life remains to me, Ulster shall not be reviled this day.'

Then Cuchulainn cast the spear at him by the handle, and it went through his head and killed nine behind him, and Cuchulainn passed through the host even as we said before. But Erc son of Cairpre took the spear.

'What shall fall by this spear, O sons of Calatin?' says Erc, son of Cairpre.

Niches for sacred heads were a feature of Celtic sites, as in this reconstruction of the religious sanctuary at Roquepertuse, Bouches du Rhône, France.

43

'A king falls by that spear,' say the sons of Calatin.

'I heard you say that a king would fall by the spear which Lugaid long since cast,' he replied.

'And that is true,' say the sons of Calatin, 'thereby fell the King of the Charioteers of Erin, namely Cuchulainn's charioteeer, Laegh mac Riangabra.'

Thereupon Erc cast the spear at him and it lighted on the Gray of Macha. Cuchulainn snatched out the spear, and each of them bade the other farewell. Thereat the Gray of Macha left him with half the yoke hanging from his neck, and went into Gray's Linn in Sliab Fuad. Then Cuchulainn drove through the host, and saw the third pair contending, and he intervened as he had done before. The satirist demanded his spear, and Cuchulainn at first refused it.

'I will revile thee,' quoth the satirist.

'I have paid for mine honour to-day. I am not bound to grant more than one request in one day.'

'Then I will revile Ulster for thy default.'

'I have paid for the honour of Ulster,' said Cuchulainn.

'I will then revile thy race,' said the satirist.

'Tidings that I have been defamed shall not go back to the land to which I myself shall never return; for little of my life remains to me,' said the hero. So Cuchulainn flung the spear to him, handle foremost, and it went through his head and through thrice nine other men.

' 'Tis grace with wrath, O Cuchulainn,' says the satirist.

Then Cuchulainn for the last time drove through the host, and Lugaid took the spear and said, 'What shall fall by this spear, O sons of Calatin?'

'A king will fall thereby,' say the sons of Calatin.

'I heard you say that a king would fall by the spear that Erc cast this morning.'

'That is true,' say they; 'the King of the Steeds of Erin fell by it, namely the Gray of Macha.'

Then Lugaid flung the spear and struck Cuchulainn, and his bowels came forth on the cushion of the chariot, and his only horse, the Black Sainglend, fled away, with half the yoke hanging to him, and left the chariot and his master, the King of the Heroes of Erin, dying alone upon the plain.

Then said Cuchulainn, 'I would fain go as far as that loch to drink a drink thereout.'

'We give thee leave,' said they; 'provided that thou come to us again.'

'I will bid you come for me,' said Cuchulainn, 'unless I shall return to you myself.'

Then he gathered his bowels into his breast, and went on to the loch. And he drank his drink, and washed himself, and came forth to die, calling on his foes to come and meet him.

Now a great mearing went westwards from the loch, and his eye lit upon it, and he went to the pillar-stone that is in the plain, and he put his

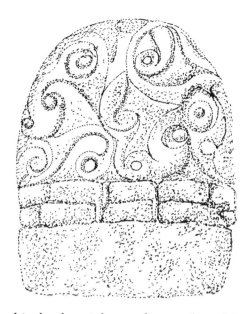

The Turoe Stone, a late Iron Age cult stone from Ireland.

breast-girdle round it that he might not die seated nor lying down, but that he might die standing up. Then came the men around him, but they durst not go to him, for they thought he was alive.

'It is a shame for you,' said Erc, son of Cairpre, 'not to take that man's head in revenge for my father's head that was taken by him.'

Then came to Cuchulainn the Gray of Macha to protect him, so long as his soul was in him, and the 'hero's light' out of his forehead shone above him. And the Gray of Macha wrought the three red onsets around him. And fifty fell by his teeth and thirty by each of his hoofs. Hence is the saying: 'Not keener were the victorious courses of the Gray of Macha after Cuchulainn's slaughter.'

Then came the birds and settled on his shoulder.

'There were not wont to be birds about that pillar,' said Erc, son of Cairpre. Then Lugaid arranged Cuchulainn's hair over his shoulder, and cut off his head. And the sword fell from Cuchulainn's hand, and it smote off Lugaid's right hand, so that it fell to the ground. And they struck off Cuchulainn's right hand in revenge for this. Then Lugaid and the hosts marched away, carrying with them Cuchulainn's head and his right hand, and they came to Tara, and there is the grave of his head and his right hand, and the full of the cover of the shield of mould.

From Tara they marched southward to the river Liffey. But meanwhile the hosts of Ulster were hurrying to attack their foes, and Conall the Victorious, driving forward in front of them, met the Gray of Macha streaming with blood. Then Conall knew that Cuchulainn had been slain. Together he and the Gray of Macha sought Cuchulainn's body. They saw the corpse of Cuchulainn at the pillar-stone. Then went the Gray of Macha and laid his head on Cuchulainn's breast. And Conall said, 'A heavy care is that corpse to the Gray of Macha.'

*Celtic helmet, from fourth cen-
tury Italy. Made of iron with
bronze and coral decorations, it
is typical of the highly decorated
arms and armour described as
being important in the
Cuchulainn poems.*

Then Conall followed the hosts, meditating vengeance, for he was bound
to avenge Cuchulainn. For there was a comrade's covenant between
Cuchulainn and Conall the Victorious, namely, that whichever of them was
first killed should be avenged by the other.

'And if I be the first killed,' said Cuchulainn, 'how soon wilt thou avenge
me?'

'On thy death-day,' said Conall, 'before its evening I will avenge thee.
And if I be the first slain,' says Conall, 'how soon wilt thou avenge me?'

'They blood will not be cold upon the earth,' says Cuchulainn, 'before I
shall avenge thee.'

So Conall pursued Lugaid to the Liffey.

There was Lugaid bathing. 'Keep a look-out over the plain,' he said to his
charioteer, 'that no one come upon us without being seen.'

The charioteer looked past him.

'A single horseman is coming to us,' said he, 'and great are the speed and
swiftness with which he comes.

Thou wouldst deem that all the ravens of Erin were above him. Thou
wouldst deem that flakes of snow were specking the plain before him.'

'Unbeloved is the horseman that comes there,' says Lugaid. 'It is Conall
the Victorious mounted on Dewy-Red. The birds thou sawest above him are
the sods from the horse's hoofs. The snow-flakes thou sawest specking the
plain before him are the foam from the horse's lips and from the bits of the
bridle. Look again,' says Lugaid, 'by what road is he coming?'

'He is coming to the ford, the path that the hosts have taken,' answered
the charioteer.

'Let that horse pass us,' said Lugaid; 'we desire not to fight against him.'

But when Conall reached the middle of the ford he spied Lugaid and his
charioteer and went to them.

'Welcome is a debtor's face!' said Conall. 'He to whom thou owest debts
demands them of thee. I am thy creditor,' continues Conall, 'for the slaying
of my comrade Cuchulainn, and here I stand suing thee for it.'

Then it was agreed to fight on the plain of Argetros, and there Conall

46

wounded Lugaid with his javelin. Thence they went to a place called Ferta Lugdach.

'I wish,' said Lugaid, 'to have men's truth from thee.'

'What is that?' said Conall the Victorious.

'That thou shouldst use only one hand against me, for one hand only have I.'

'Thou shalt have that,' says Conall the Victorious.

So Conall's hand was bound to his side with a cord. There, for the space between two watches of the day, they fought, and neither of them prevailed over the other.

When Conall found that he prevailed not, he saw his steed the Dewy-Red by Lugaid. And the steed came close to Lugaid and tore a piece out of his side.

'Woe is me!' said Lugaid, 'that is not men's truth, O Conall.'

'I gave it thee only on my own behalf,' said Conall; 'I gave it not on behalf of savage beasts and senseless things.'

'I know now,' said Lugaid, 'that thou wilt not go till thou takest my head with thee, since we took Cuchulainn's head from him. Take therefore my head in addition to thine own, and add my realm to thy realm, and my valour to thy valour. For I prefer that thou shouldst be the best hero in Erin.'

Then Conall the Victorious cut off Lugaid's head. And Conall and his Ulstermen returned to Emain Macha. That week they made no triumphal entry.

But the soul of Cuchulainn appeared there to the thrice fifty queens who had loved him, and they saw him floating in his spirit-chariot over Emain Macha, and they heard him chant a mystic song of the Coming of Christ and the Day of Doom.

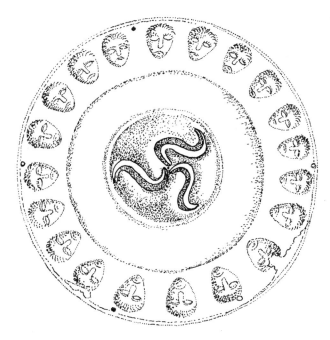

Early Celtic silver horse decoration, showing severed heads and the triskele or triple symbol of divinity.

47

Emain Macha

Emain Macha, now known as Navan Fort, is situated in Northern Ireland a few miles west of Armagh. It is the ancient royal capital of Ulster and is associated with Celtic culture, both through the Cuchulainn saga and from the evidence of archaeology. Its present condition is that of a large mound inside an immense circular hilltop enclosure. The term 'fort' is an unfortunate hangover from early days of archaeology, for like the royal enclosure of Tara in Meath (once seat of the High Kings of Ireland), Emain Macha is more likely to have been a ritual site rather than a defensive one. The site forms part of a complex in the area, which includes Lough na Shade nearby, where skulls, bones, and a remarkable bronze trumpet were found in the eighteenth century.

There is evidence of use from the Neolithic period, four to five thousand years ago, and occupation from around 600–100 B.C. It is this last period that is likely to connect to the tales of Cuchulainn, King Conchobar, and the warriors of Ulster, though some of the material preserved in the sagas could equally apply to much earlier Celtic culture. Excavation has shown that around 100 B.C., the site was considerably enlarged; a complex and sophisticated structure approximately 120 feet in diameter was built, consisting of five concentric circles of about 275 posts, with a large central post approximately 36 feet in height. With its original roof, this structure formed a huge conical building, very similar to those described in the sagas. Clearly, the poems preserved by later Christian monks echoed oral tradition and collective or family memory of this impressive period of development. The vast building is likely to have been a ritual centre for the people of the region.

Within a short period of its building, boulders were piled between the posts and the entire structure set alight. The remains were then covered with earth and turf, eventually creating the grassy mound which can still be seen today. Archaeologists suggest that this burning and mound-building was of religious rather than of military significance; destructive invaders would not be likely to commemorate their victory with such careful cairn building and covering of the remains.

Although some excavation was made as early as 1963, research was not completed until 1971, and has not yet been published. Certain famous artefacts have found their way to museums from earlier discoveries in the region.

Emain Macha, Navan Fort, associated with the warriors of Ulster in Irish tradition.

Character Names

This is a short list of names occuring in the narrative, with their role or function briefly described.

Aoife A warrior woman defeated by Cuchulainn
Brugh Na Boyne Prehistoric site; dwelling place of gods
Calatin Evil magician serving Queen Medb
Cathbad Druid serving King Conchobar
Conchobar King of Ulster
Conlaoch The son of Cuchulainn
Cuchulainn The Champion of Ulster
Dechtire Mother of Cuchulainn
Emain Macha Navan Fort, seat of King Conchobar
Emer Wife of Cuchulainn

Ferdiad Hero, brother in arms to Cuchulainn
Fergus Mac Roich Foster father of Cuchulainn
Fiacha An Ulster exile in Medb's army
gae bulga A thirty-barbed spear
Laeg Charioteer to Cuchulainn
Loch A champion of Queen Medb
Lugh The Sun God (father of Cuchulainn)
Medb Queen of Connaught
Morrigan or Morrigu Goddess of war, death, life, sexuality
Scathach Warrior woman who trains Cuchulainn
Setanta Original name of Cuchulainn
Sualtam Human father of Cuchulainn
Tain Bo Chuailnge The Cattle Raid of Cooley, the epic poem

Further Reading

Gantz, J. (trans.) *The Mabinogion* Penguin, Harmondsworth, 1976
Hull, E. *The Cuchulainn Saga* London, 1898
Kinsella, T. (trans.) *The Tain* London, 1970
McCana, P. *Celtic Mythology* London, 1970
Meyer, K. and Nutt, A. *The Voyage of Bran* London, 1898

Newark, T. *Celtic Warriors* Blandford Press, Poole, 1986
Rees, A. and B. *Celtic Heritage* London, 1961
Ross, A. *Pagan Celtic Britain* London, 1974
Stewart, B. and Matthews, J. *Warriors of Arthur* Blandford Press, London, 1987

BOADICEA
WARRIOR QUEEN OF THE CELTS

In adopting the more traditional, but possibly now unfashionable, spelling of Boadicea for the great Celtic Queen's name, perhaps one should recall the preference of that noted British archaeologist Sir Mortimer Wheeler. He stated clearly that 'Boadicea' sounded like the sort of lady one would dine with, but never with someone called 'Boudicca'!

ROMAN BRITAIN

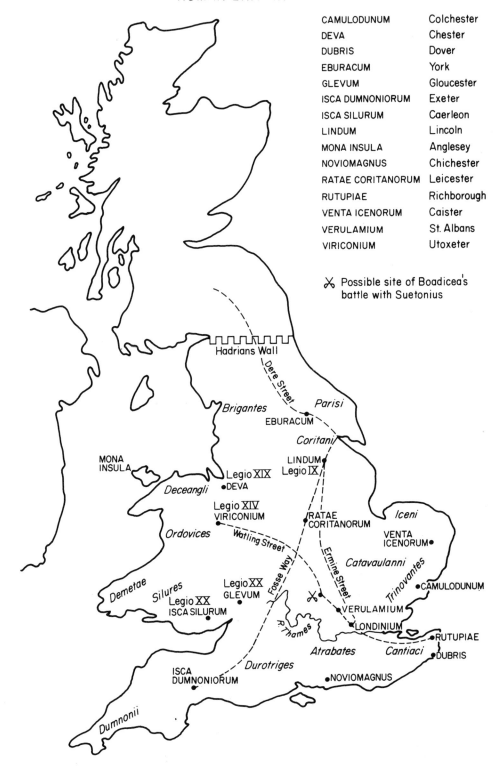

CAMULODUNUM	Colchester
DEVA	Chester
DUBRIS	Dover
EBURACUM	York
GLEVUM	Gloucester
ISCA DUMNONIORUM	Exeter
ISCA SILURUM	Caerleon
LINDUM	Lincoln
MONA INSULA	Anglesey
NOVIOMAGNUS	Chichester
RATAE CORITANORUM	Leicester
RUTUPIAE	Richborough
VENTA ICENORUM	Caister
VERULAMIUM	St. Albans
VIRICONIUM	Utoxeter

✄ Possible site of Boadicea's battle with Suetonius

Hadrians Wall

Dere Street

Brigantes
EBURACUM

Parisi

Coritani

MONA
INSULA

LINDUM
Legio IX

Deceangli

Legio XIX
●DEVA

Legio XIV
VIRICONIUM

RATAE
CORITANORUM

Iceni

Ordovices

Watling Street

VENTA
ICENORUM ●

Catavaulanni

Fosse Way

Ermine Street

Trinovantes

Demetae

Silures
Legio XX
ISCA SILURUM

Legio XX
GLEVUM

R. Thames

VERULAMIUM

● CAMULODUNUM

LONDINIUM

RUTUPIAE

Atrabates

Cantiaci

●DUBRIS

ISCA
DUMNONIORUM

Durotriges

● NOVIOMAGNUS

Dumnonii

The British Celts

In 50 A.D. Ostorius Scapula, the Roman governor of the province of Brittannia, declared confidently that with the capture and transportation to Rome of Caractacus, already termed 'the last of the Celts', Celtic opposition to the Roman occupation would soon cease. Ten years later, he was proved drastically wrong when a violent revolt exploded in the territory of the Iceni, one of the largest tribes in Britain. Led by their Queen, Boadicea, they swiftly overwhelmed and massacred the populations of Camulodunum (Colchester) and Verulamium (St Albans), decimated a large part of the IX Legion, and went on to capture and burn London. Before she was finally defeated by the XX and XIV Legions under the command of Suetonius Paulinus, the name of Boadicea had become synonymous with terror and savage attack. She has ever since kept her place in the forefront of a small band of British heroes whose names have become part of a national heritage.

Yet who was this woman, who achieved such remarkable feats of war? What kind of warriors did she lead into battle with such resounding success? The story is a complex one and there are few reliable sources. Yet, a coherent picture does emerge if first we look at the kind of people from which she sprang.

The Celts

Our earliest impressions of the Celts come from classical sources. Posidonius, Strabo and Polybius described the Celts as tall, fair and ruddy-complexioned, loving the arts of war, feasting and drinking, famous hunters and fighters. To the Greeks, and later to the Romans, they seemed savage and barbaric: headhunters who tattooed themselves with strange patterns and went naked into battle. Yet their culture was far from backward. They loved literature and the arts, decorating everything – pots, mirrors, drinking vessels, weapons and horse-harnesses – with intricate and beautiful designs. Their sense of justice was almost as pronounced as their pride, which was considerable, and they were amongst the first people in Europe to develop a sophisticated system of laws to govern daily living.

Their religion, under the guidance of a druidic priesthood, was complex and highly mystical. They were close to the earth and its natural forces to a

The famous Gundestrup cauldron from Denmark shows Celtic warriors with long shields and spears, mounted men, and trumpeters – the latter must have added to the frightening noise produced by the warriors themselves.

degree unusual even for an ancient people. Their pantheon of gods was every bit as developed as those of Rome or Greece.

Diodorus Siculus, writing in the first century B.C. describes them as:

Terrifying in appearence, with deep-sounding very harsh voices. In conversation they use few words and speak in riddles, for the most part hinting at things and leaving a great deal to be understood. They frequently exaggerate with the aim of extolling themselves and diminishing the status of others. They are boasters and threateners and given to bombastic self-dramatization, and yet they are quick of mind and with good natural ability for learning.

While all of this is undoubtedly true as far as it goes, it is also something of a generalization. The classical writers tended to gloss over certain details, lumping *all* Celts together as one nation, irrespective of tribal differences. However, Tacitus did go so far as to distinguish racial types within the various areas of Britain. Thus the Caledonians were described as large and red-haired; the Silures or Welsh as shorter and with black curly hair, and the inhabitants of the South as resembling the Gauls.

This is an important distinction, which one has to keep in mind when discussing the Celts. The term 'Celtic' is itself really a linguistic or archaeological term for a people of very mixed origin. They seem to have come from an area in what is now the Steppelands of Russia, and to have migrated north and west in search of better lands and a warmer climate. Somewhere about 400 B.C., they settled in areas of Europe which today correspond to parts of Italy, Switzerland, Germany and Eastern France. They spoke a language which is the ancestor of contemporary Irish, Welsh, Gaelic and Breton, but they were so loosely confederated that to call them 'a people' is really something of a misnomer. It would be more accurate to see them as a large number of fiercely independent tribes, who settled wherever they could find land suitable for farming and grazing their herds of cattle.

Though they were called *Keloi* or *Galatai* by the Greeks, and *Celtae* or *Galatae* by the Romans, we do not know for certain what they called themselves. *Cymru* 'the companions', is one possibility, which may also be translated more simply as 'the People'.

Tribal Society

The Celtic tribe, or *Tuath*, consisted of a number of families which according to Welsh and Irish laws extended back four generations. But, while a family was legally defined as man and wife (or wives, the Celts were polygamous) and their children, this could be further extended to include descendants of a common grandparent on the male or the female side.

The basic family unit was known as the *gelfine*, the larger as the *derbfine*, and within these two groups there was a shared responsibility for the apportioning of land and goods.

Wealth was calculated in terms of cattle and slaves. If a nobleman had a large herd of cattle, he hired out beasts to clients in return for a fee, and most important, for service. This meant that if a man owned a large herd, he also had more clients; the more clients he had the larger was the force of men he could put in the field in time of war, or to raid neighbouring tribes for more cattle, thus enabling him to raise more clients, and so on . . .

Caesar makes much of this in his description of the Celtic peoples, stressing a clear dividing-line between nobility and client. In reality, this was probably less distinct that it appeared to be. In a warrior society like that of the Celts, there were many opportunities for people to raise themselves to the status of the nobility, and with so much interrelatedness there was always a family tie of some kind to call upon.

To be a client did not imply curtailment of freedom. Class was defined according to whether or not one was free or unfree. The unfree, or slaves, consisted of men and women taken in raids, or of conquered people from earlier native races. The client gave service to a nobleman in return for cattle or goods: it was not uncommon for a chieftain to give a gold arm ring or torque to a warrior who had served him particularly well. Indeed, freedom was so very particularly important to the Celts, that it was doubly hard for them to accept Roman rule. After all, such rule meant disarming and paying fines for any insurrection, as well as involving a substantial loss of lands, which were given piecemeal to retired Roman army veterans. When the time came for Boadicea to raise her clan, as well as those of her neighbours, her first cry was one of 'freedom!'. It made her task far easier, even without the already powerful circumstances of her own treatment at the hands of corrupt Roman officials.

The overall ruler of the tribe, the patriarchal or matriarchal head of the most senior family, was known as a King, or *Ri*. There were thus many kings

This bronze figurine found near Rome gives a splendid idea of the warrior Celt as he appeared in battle – naked except for helm, belt and neck torque, he is poised in the act of throwing a spear.

and queens in the Britain of Boadicea's time, a fact which made it extremely difficult to form any kind of united front against the Romans; each petty ruler was fiercely independent of the others. Getting them to fight side-by-side was like trying to get two neighbouring dogs to fight for a single piece of territory.

The main tribes in Boadicea's time were – in the south of Britain – the Coritani, the Dobunni, the Catavellauni, the Atrabates, the Belgae, the Durotriges, the Trinovantes and her own Iceni. Their territory was probably bounded by the Wash on the east coast, and the Devil's Dyke, and what are now the towns of Stowmarket and Peterborough, taking in most of the fenland between. Since there were no such things as boundary markers – or if there were they are long-since vanished – it is virtually impossible to tell where the lands of one tribe and another met or divided. Nevertheless, reference to the map will give a general idea of the positions of the various tribes.

Warfare

We shall have good reason to look again at the way in which Boadicea fought her rapacious rebellion, but it is worth making a few preliminary remarks about the Celtic way of war, and to consider the (perhaps inevitable) reason why it repeatedly foundered against the disciplined wall of the Roman Legions.

The Celts were probably among the finest natural warriors in the world at that time, but they certainly knew nothing of discipline. Every warrior fought for himself, for his personal glory (which tended to be further exaggerated afterwards) and for booty – which comprised heads as much as weapons or jewelry. Again and again, we see the truth of Caesar's remark that only the first charge of a Celtic force was of any note – after that it was easy for the legionaries to mop up the remains! Yet, that first charge was certainly something to be feared. Here is Polybius' description:

> . . . the noise of the Celtic host terrified the Romans; for there were countless trumpeters and horn blowers and since the whole army was shouting its war cries at the same time there was such a confused sound that the noise seemed to come not only from the trumpeters and the soldiers but also from the countryside which was joining in the echo. No less terrifying were the appearance and gestures of the naked warriors in front, all of whom were in the prime of life and of excellent physique.

(trans: Ritchie)

The head and mouth of a bronze Celtic trumpet found in Scotland. Accounts of Celtic warfare abound with descriptions of their war trumpets and the terror they inspired in their enemies.

The nakedness was in part caused by sheer bravado; in part a lack of sufficient body armour except among the rich and noble. Celtic blacksmiths were skilled workers, but never seem to have considered mass-producing armour or weapons for the ordinary warriors, who had to depend on the magical protection of the patterns painted on their bodies.

This certainly made them of striking appearance, with their limed hair combed into fantastic spikes or ruffs. Strabo tells us that it was socially unacceptable for a warrior to put on more than a certain amount of weight, and that there was a belt-tax levied whenever expansion went beyond a certain hole on the belt!

But by far the most feared and practical weapon ever used by the Celts must be the chariot. These light, two-wheeled carts, pulled by two strong and agile horses, had a single driver, and a warrior mounted behind him with a clutch of deadly throwing spears. Together they made a fighting team which was the scourge of the Roman legions.

But we must rid ourselves of one striking error which still lingers in the minds of many people even today. This is that Boadicea thundered onto the battlefield in a chariot with scythes on the wheels. No single example of such an equipped chariot has ever been unearthed in Britain, nor does Caesar mention them, despite having a good deal to say on the subject of chariots in general. Finally, as has often been wryly pointed out, a scythed chariot would have been as likely to inflict damage upon Boadicea's own warriors as on the Romans.

This being said, there is little doubt of the effectiveness of these vehicles in war. The Celts had certainly developed special skills when it came to fighting from a chariot – typically, perhaps, considering the nature of the Celtic personality, there was an element of bravado and sport about the whole thing. Thus, the warrior would often run out along the central pole, between the galloping horses, fling his spears at the enemy and then retreat to the bucking and careering platform in order to use it as base from which to fight with sword and mace.

Apart from mobility, which enabled the warriors to attack and retire at speed, the sheer noise of the chariot wheels thundering over the ground, mixed with the screams of the horses and the shouted war cries, must have been a shocking and terrifying sight.

Caesar certainly seems to have thought so, since he devoted several pages to the skills of the Celtic charioteers in his description of the fighting Britons. But just what they were pitting themselves against we must now examine.

The Roman Invaders

Julius Caesar had probably been receiving secret reports about Britain for some time before he made his first visit in 55 B.C. Certainly, he seems to have had a very good idea of what to expect when he arrived there. His account of the country is included in his history of the *Conquest of Gaul*, and is detailed and reasonably accurate. When it comes to describing the island he had this to say:

The island is triangular with one side facing Gaul. One corner of this side, on the coast of [now] Kent, is the landing place for nearly all the ships from Gaul, and points east; the lower

Bronze decorations from an Icenian chariot horse harness show the heights which the artistic abilities of the tribes could attain.

This reconstructed chariot is based on fragments discovered in a bog at Anglesey (Mona). It is of the kind that both the defenders of the island against Suetonius Paulinus and Boadicea's own warriors would probably have used.

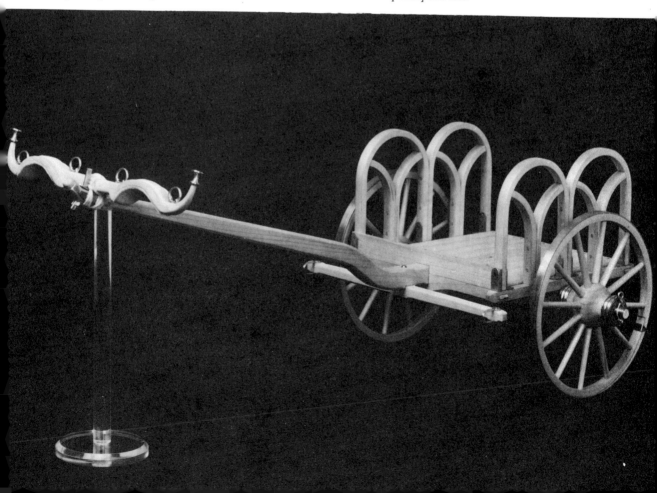

corner points south. The length of this side is about 475 miles. Another side faces west, towards Spain. In this direction is Ireland which is supposed to be half the size of Britain, and lies at the same distance from it as Gaul. Mid-way across is the Isle of Man, and it is believed that there are also a number of smaller islands, in which according to some writers there is a month of perpetual darkness at the summer solstice. Our inquiries on this subject were always fruitless, but we found by accurate measurements with a water-clock that the nights are shorter than on the continent. This side of Britain, according to the natives' estimate is 665 miles long. The third side faces north; no land land lies opposite it, but its eastern corner points roughly in the direction of Germany. Its length is estimated at 760 miles. And thus the whole island is 1,900 miles in circumference.

(trans: S. A. Handford)

It seems probable that this detailed, if rather baroque, description of the island, which Caesar had not seen and which indeed he never saw in anything like its entirety, is drawn in part from reports and from the works of earlier writers. The point being that, although this first attempt at invasion (as well as the one that followed it in 54 B.C.) were failures, Britain was very firmly established in Roman consciousness as a rich, fertile and ill-defended land which should clearly be a part of the Empire. It meant that however many years might elapse between, the Romans were bound to return.

And return they did, almost 100 years later, led by a very different commander – the remarkable Emperor Claudius. His campaign was staggeringly effective, and within two years Britain had become another province of Rome, with a large army of occupation installed in a growing network of forts strung out across the country.

Yet between the two invasion attempts, the one successful and the other not, links between Britain and Rome remained. On his second visit Caesar had negotiated a treaty which included an annual tribute and hostages. This

This aureus (sovereign) was issued around 51–2 A.D. to celebrate the Emperor Claudius' victory over the Britons and shows a triumphal arch bearing the word DEBRITTAN.

60

soon ceased after Caesar's assassination in 44 B.C. and with all the upheavals and civil wars that followed, it was some time before Rome again turned towards Britain with thoughts of conquest. Links of another kind, those of trading and political alliance, continued to be built up, thus affording Claudius, when the time came, both additional information for his campaign and a firmer foothold among the natives.

Claudius arrived in 43 A.D. – or rather his general Allus Plautius, whom he had commanded to go ahead and win every battle except the last – to which Claudius himself was to be summoned to take command – arrived with II, IX, XIV and XX Legions (some 24,000 men). They landed on a tiny island off the larger mass of Thanet, in what is now the south eastern county of Kent.

At first, they met with little resistance beyond the odd raiding party as they marched through the dark forest of the Kentish weald. But at the River Medway, they met a fully fledged war-band under the leadership of two brothers, Togodumnus and Caractacus, sons of the redoubtable King Cunobelinus (whom Shakespeare later made famous as Cymbeline). Cunobelinus had reigned over the powerful Catavellauni tribe as well as several tributary tribes for a number of years, and had left a strong and well-established kingdom to his sons' rule.

A long and ferocious battle took place at the mouth of the Medway estuary. But once the Romans had succeeded in crossing the stretch of water, victory followed. Against the splendidly carefree tactics of the Britons, the Romans were hard, ruthless and subject to an iron discipline which made them virtually undefeatable in battle. Again and again we hear of battle-maddened Celts hurling themselves against the Roman shield-wall, only to be repulsed. In contrast, the iron-shod boots of the legionaries pressed ever forward, step by step, until their adversaries were either exhausted or overwhelmed.

This gilded bronze eagle, discovered during the excavation of the Roman basilica at Silchester, may be part of a military standard. The eagles were carried into battle before each Legion and were regarded almost as gods. To lose such a standard brought disgrace and ill-luck to the legion it represented.

61

A model of the magnificent temple at Colchester dedicated to the Claudius, as it must have looked at the time of the revolt. It was never completed, and Boadicea destroyed it utterly when the defenders of Colchester took refuge there.

At London – then only a small trading post – a second battle ensued, in which Togodumnus fell and the Britains were routed. Plautius pushed on towards Camulodunum (Colchester), the Catavellauni capital, where he expected to stage a final victory.

Plautius sent word to Claudius in Gaul, and the Emperor – with reserve troops, elephants, and a sweating baggage train – proceeded there with full speed. Caractacus, desperate by now, and unable to raise any support from neighbouring tribes, fell back before the advancing Roman army and finally fled to Wales, where he could count on the help of wild Silures.

After this, British defence virtually collapsed; several chieftains, among them Prasutagus, Boadicea's husband, made haste to capitulate, and became tributaries of the invader in the hope of better terms of settlement. They became official allies of Rome with the status of vassal, and were allowed to continue nominal rule over their lands and people. Indeed, Cogidumnus of the Regnenses, became so romanized that an inscription found at Chichester in Sussex reads:

To Neptune and Minerva this temple is dedicated for the welfare of the divine house by the authority of Tiberius Claudius Cogidumnus king and legate of Augustus in Britain. . . .

62

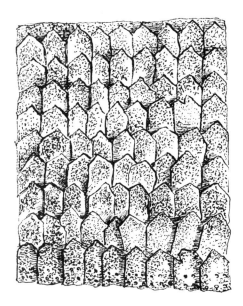

Though Britain could by no means be described as conquered, it was forthwith declared a province. Camulodunum, former capital of the Catavellauni, became the official centre of government, with Allus Plautius as governor and a procurator under him to handle tax-collection and civil affairs.

Work began at once on the building of a great temple to the gods of Britain and Rome, and after the death of Claudius in 54 A.D., it was dedicated to him as *Divus Claudius*, awarded, as were most emperors of the time, the status of godhead.

Fragment of Roman scale armour from Northumberland. Only officers or the more heavily armoured cavalry units would have possessed this kind of protection.

Britannia

This was far from the end of the story. In the ensuing four years, Plautius established bases at Ratae (Leicester) and on the borders of Wales. He sent his most able commander Vespasian (later to become Emperor himself) in command of the II Legion to subdue the Belgae and the Durotriges, who occupied regions roughly equivalent to the modern counties of Somerset and Dorset.

Vespasian fought thirteen battles against the natives including a massive assault against Maiden Castle in Dorset, where subsequent archaeological evidence suggests a massacre of men, women and children.

By the time Allus Plautius departed, handing over the governorship to Ostorius Scapula, all of Britain south of a line drawn across from Bath to London and including most of Essex had been subdued. The IX Legion was established at Colonia (Lincoln), the II at Isca (Caerleon) and the XIV and XX as Viroconium (Wroxeter).

The capture of Caractacus took another two years and was only accomplished by the treachery of Queen Cartimandua of the Brigantes, who handed him over together with his family into Roman hands. He was taken to Rome

63

itself, where he so impressed Claudius that he was awarded a pension and allowed to live out his life there. He is said to have looked at the buildings of the eternal city and remarked: 'And yet the owners of these must needs covet our poor huts?'

It was shortly after this that Ostorius Scapula made his confident statement about the end of British resistance, which was to be proved so dramatically wrong. However, something like a *Pax Romana* did exist in Britain for a time, and the new province began to experience some of the more welcome effects of Roman rule. The countryside became more settled, and the steady flow of trade goods, pottery, wine and cloth, began to enter the country. The pro-Roman dignataries were encouraged to adopt the ways of their conquerors, building houses for themselves in the style of Roman villas, complete with hypercaust (underfloor heating) and vineyards.

Though the tendancy thus begun was not to reach fruition for 100 years after the initial period of conquest, it began almost as soon as the last active resistance ended – or was thought to have ended – with the capture of Caractacus.

There was also a move to bring in settlers, mostly legionary veterans who were granted allotments of land in return for which they were expected to keep an eye on the native population in case of any signs of revolt. The first of these was established in the old British capital of Camulodunum, and thus became one of Boadicea's first targets when she began her revolt against the conquerors. Ostorius' hope seems to have been that while the regular legions were away policing less-settled areas, the presence of the veterans at Camulodunum would keep things stable in the south – another error for which the Romans were to pay dearly.

Thus stood matters at the beginning of 59 A.D. when Suetonius Paulinus arrived to become the new military governor of Britain.

Power of the Druids

It has been stated by more that one commentator on Roman Britain that the Druids had a great deal to do with the forging and fuelling of the revolt – partly because of their natural animosity towards the invaders, but mostly in retaliation for the destruction of the great Druid college on Anglesey.

This may be partly true, but the situation was considerably more complex than it would at first appear. Much of this complexity stems from previous misconceptions about the nature of druidism and the activities of the Druids in Celtic Britain.

Indeed, so much has been written about the Druids that is *total* fiction that it is now extremely hard to extract the truth. Yet they were certainly a power

Before the battle which ended the Icenian revolt, Boadicea harangued her troops from the step of her chariot. Flourishing a spear, she demanded vengence for the wrong done to her.

in Britain (as in Gaul) and the classical accounts we do possess tell us a certain amount.

The Druids did not, as is still commonly believed, build Stonehenge, or indeed any of the great megalithic monuments with which Britain is so liberally littered. Indeed, though they may have used these sites on certain occasions, they seem generally to have worshipped (or at any rate gathered) in groves of sacred trees. The idea that these were primarily oak trees may stem from the connection made by Greek lexicographers between their word for oak, *drus* and the Celtic (Irish) word *druïd*.

The Origin of the Druids

We do not know the origin of the Druids, though it is possible that they migrated to Gaul and later Britain from the area of the Mediterranean or North Africa, sometime during the Bronze Age.

This has lead in turn to speculation as to whether they were influenced by the teachings of Pythagoras (around 500 B.C.) which spread from classical Greece into Alexandria and thence to the rest of the Western world. They seem to have shared a belief in reincarnation, the transmigration of souls and the sacredness of all life, animal as well as human. There are also tantalizing references to a Greek traveller named Aristeas of Proconnesus, who visited Britain (or a country which may have been Britain) and found there a place where men worshipped Hyperborean Apollo in a circular stone temple in the midst of a plain. Stonehenge? Possibly. But were these the Druids? They do indeed seem to have worshipped the sun – or at least to have taken care to observe its risings and settings. But there is no specifically solar deity in the Celtic religion – despite a number of solar heroes whose strength increased and decreased with the rising and setting of the sun.

Diogenes Laertius (200–250 A.D. records a meeting between Alexander the Great and a wandering Celt, who may or may not have been a Druid. It has been pointed out by at least one commentator that when asked if he feared anything, his reply: 'Not so long as the sky never falls or the sea does not burst its bounds' does have a familiar ring to it. The same formula is repeated several times throughout Celtic literature, almost as a kind of invocation, though whether it was of Druid origin we cannot say.

Shamanism

Another Greek, Pliny the Elder, in a dissertation on the medicinal properties of mistletoe, gives us the famous connection of this plant with the Druids, who were said to hold it in the highest esteem: so much so that any tree on which it grew – it is a parasite – was at once regarded as sacred.

The reasons for this may well lead us to a very important factor in our understanding of druidism. One of the properties of mistletoe not mentioned by Pliny is the hallucinogenic drink which is distilled from it. The method by which this was attained is long since lost – mistletoe is deadly poison in its natural state – but it may have given the Druids their means of entry to the

Before her triumphal compaign, Boadicea sought the guidance of Andraste, the goddess of victory in Celtic Britain. Boadicea released a hare from beneath her cloak; according to which path it ran, so was victory or defeat determined.

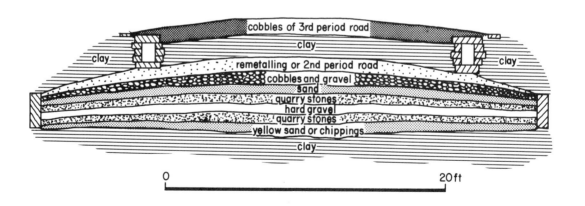

Typical construction of a Roman road. The system of roads built by the Romans enabled messages to be delivered speedily and troops to be moved more effectively. This lonely stretch crosses Wheedale Moor in Yorkshire.

inner realms of the spirit where they could learn remarkable truths and make prophecies for the future of the people.

This puts them on a par with the shamans of other ancient people, who were the preservers of tradition and the inspirers of the tribes in their care as well as guarding their religious truths and knowledge. This seems precisely the function of the Druids in Britain and Gaul.

A bronze boar, possibly from a Celtic war-helm. It was recognised as a symbol of strength, fierceness and potency. Helmets and chariots bore decorations in the shape of the boar to give their wearers added strength and protection. The clan totem of the Iceni was either a horse or a boar.

Druids and Druidism

Even assuming this to be true, there is still a basic confusion between the Druids themselves and druidism. It would probably be a mistake to view this as in any way the 'official religion' of Britain, either during Boadicea's reign or at any other time. The druidic colleges, like the one despoiled by Suetonius Paulinus on Anglesey, was one of several such establishments both in Britain and Ireland. But the Druids who ran these were historians, archivists, lawgivers and teachers rather than priests in the properly understood meaning of the word.

If we see them in this light, much of the speculation and fantasy concerning the Druids fall away. They taught the arts of poetry and song, compiled genealogies and generally preserved the history of the people. Much of this they kept in their heads, expecting their pupils to learn immense amounts of poetry and lore by heart. They were also lawgivers, as Caesar's testimony shows:

They act as judges in practically all disputes whether between tribes or between individuals; when any crime is committed, or a murder takes place or a dispute arises about an inheritance or about a boundary, it is they who adjudicate the matter and appoint the compensation to be paid and received by the parties concerned.

67

These three Celtic shields from different periods and places show the consistency of design over the years. Made from wood or leather, and covered with decorations in bronze, they protected the warrior from shoulder to knees.

All this seems a very far cry from the usual image invoked by the word 'Druid'; that of blood-soaked rituals performed at dawn over stone altars, or for that matter the traditional cloaked, white-bearded patriarch who seems to belong rather in a Biblical scene than in a picture of ancient Celtic life.

In retrospect it seems probable that the blood sacrifices talked of frequently by commentators, though they may indeed have taken place, were presided over by a native priesthood which had little or nothing to do with the Druids. Certainly the Celts were a war-like, often savage people (as indeed were the Romans, despite their much-vaunted civilization) but they were no more or less so than any other ancient tribal society. The picture sometimes presented of Druid sacrifices with men held in wicker cages which were then set on fire, is almost certainly far from the truth.

What we should try to see is a body of enlightened men and women, to which membership was a highly sought honour, who endeavoured to preserve and educate, and who above all sought to hold in trust the sacred heritage of the people.

Thus, we have on the one hand the 'Druids-as-known', and on the other 'Druids-as-wished-for' – the former being of a very different tenor from the latter.

Rebellion

Teachers then, guardians of wisdom and tradition, poets, historians and genealogists; these were the primary functions of the Druids, all of them important within the Celtic world. This would indeed have given them

68

considerable power and influence, and had they chosen to give support to Boadicea it would have been more than sufficient to tip the scales in her favour. That they did indeed give her this support seems likely. Equally likely is the effect that news of Suetonius Paulinus' attack upon Anglesey would have had. Tacitus gives a vivid portrait of the event – though it should be noted that he does not designate the Druids as targets.

On the beach stood the adverse array, a serried mass of arms and men, with women slipping between the ranks in the style of furies in robes of deathly black and with disheveled hair they brandished their torches; while a circle of druids, lifting their hands to heaven and showering imprecations, struck the troops with such an awe at the extraordinary spectacle that, as though their limbs were paralyzed, they exposed their bodies to wounds without an attempt at movement. Then, reassured by their general, and inciting each other neer to flinch before a band of females and fanatics they charged behind the standards, cut down all who met them, and enveloped the enemy in his own flames.

(trans: John Jackson)

Queen of the Iceni

For many years she was called Bunduica and believed to have a co-regnant named Voadicia. Then, for a while, she became Bonducca and later still the familiar Boudica or Boadicea. Whatever, her real name means 'victory', the early spellings resulting from poor mediaeval manuscript transcription and inaccurate Elizabethan versions of Tacitus, whose account of her story was unknown at all until the sixteenth century.

We can follow the mutations of her name far more easily than we can put flesh onto the bones of her life. We know much about the military details of the revolt of 61 A.D.; we know her end; and we know something of what drove her to begin. Yet, though her name is widely known, we really know very little more.

How old she was when she died we can infer only from the fact that she had two teenage daughters (thus making her between thirty and forty); we know from Dio Cassius what she looked like:

In stature she was very tall, in appearance most terrifying, in the glance of her eye most fierce, and her voice was harsh; a great mass of the tawniest hair fell to her hips; around her neck was a large golden necklace; and she wore a tunic of divers colours over which a thick mantle was fastened with a brooch. This was her invariable attire.

(trans: E. Cary)

Beyond this there is little to add. Imagination suggests a strong and stubborn woman married to a weak husband. Prasutagus' haste to bend the knee to Roman rule must have gone hard with his wife, who was almost certainly of equally royal blood, but had no love for the conquerers. Even if she had not at first felt animosity, her later treatment at the hands of greedy and unscrupulous officials would only have increased her dislike to full hatred.

The Celtic warrior and his chari_teer. In pitched battle they were an unbeatable team – fast, manoeuvrable and deadly. Drawn by two swift and sturdy ponies, they would hurl themselves against the opposing force and discharge their spears. Then the warrior would leap down and engage the enemy directly, while the charioteer withdrew to the fringes of the battle.

We can speculate that she received warrior training which fitted her for the battles to come. The Celts made no distinction between men and women when it came to fighting, and many ran training schools for teaching warriors of both sexes. Certainly, the Romans had a healthy regard for them as adversaries, as the historian Ammianus Marcellinus tells us:

A whole troop . . . would not be able to withstand a single Gaul if he called his wife to his assistance. Swelling her neck, gnashing her teeth and brandishing her sallow arms of enormous size, she begins to strike blows mingled with kicks as if they were so many missiles sent from the string of a catapult.

The Iceni

Of the tribe which came to be at the middle of the revolt, we know only that it appears to have been made up of two distinct groups of people, whose arrival in Britain dates from between 500 B.C. and 150 B.C. The first influx probably came from the area of Europe now occupied by the Netherlands and Belgium, the second from the Marne Valley area in France. The first were a peaceable people, who mixed with the earlier native population and taught them the skills of iron smelting. The second were of a more militant, warrior class who were better armed and accoutred than their forbears, and soon overran large tracts of what are now Lincolnshire and Essex, setting up places from which they ruled over the former inhabitants as a military elite.

In time, these elements blurred into a more homogenous whole which is recognizable in the Iceni as they appear at the time of Prasutagus and Boadicea.

Judging by treasure and quantities of coins discovered in the areas known to have been occupied by them, the Iceni seem to have been a wealthy tribe. This fact must have contributed both to Prasutagus' desire not to lose out to the Romans, and the strong desire of the latter to acquire as much as they could.

There seems to have been a well established Icenian coinage from as early as 10 B.C. and this has given us a clue to their probable totem animal – the tribal guardian who protected them from ill-luck, monsters or attack. This is a curious beast which at once bears a strong resemblance to a boar and a horse. Depending upon which period one examines, this seems to alter from generation to generation, almost as though the coiners themselves were unsure – though doubtless this was a matter of style rather than uncertainty.

There are no coins from the period of Prasutagus' reign, a fact which has led some commentators to believe that client-kings were not allowed to mint their own coinage once the Romans had established theirs. Perhaps Prasutagus was simply being cautious and trying to retain a hold over his considerable wealth in order to provide for an always uncertain future. On his death, he was found to have willed half his kingdom to the Emperor – an undoubted contributory factor in the causes of the revolt.

The Horse Breeders

The Iceni seem to have possessed another kind of wealth – horses. There are persistent rumours of their being horse breeders, though on the face of it this would seem unlikely due to the large areas of marshland in the Iceni country of eastern Britain.

Boadicea's army certainly contained a significant number of chariots. These required a special kind of horse; small, compact, powerful and agile.

The romantic image of Boadicea and her daughters as portrayed in this nineteenth century group which stands in the Civic Hall, Cardiff.

In fact, the kind of horse which archaeological evidence has found most frequently in Britain. They may have been a cross breed of the cold-blooded beasts found in much of Northern Europe, and the Arab 'barb'.

There is really no firm evidence to point to the Iceni as the possessors of large herds of horses, but we are allowed to speculate. Perhaps the shrewd Prasutagus chose this means of conserving his wealth, while at the same time providing the chariot beasts necessary for sudden or unexpected warfare. So, to this kingdom, suddenly in 60 A.D., Boadicea ascended as queen; Prasutagus' death had sown the seeds of the rebellion soon to follow.

In the Runs of the Iceni

We have little or no evidence of the Icenian situation prior to and after the death of Prasutagus. All that we can do is surmise and draw parallels from the prevailing Celtic society which was shortly to fragment in Britain.

At the death of Prasutagus, Britain had been nominally subdued to the Roman yoke some eighteen years. The idea was still new enough and repugnant enough for tribes to think of revolt, but there is no evidence that Prasutagus personally desired this. With the steady encroachment of the Romans upon tribal territory, from the south-west northwards, any local king would have realised the inevitability of having either to totally defeat the Roman army, or of coming to terms with the fact of Imperial control. By becoming a client king, sworn to be federate to Rome, Prasutagus wisely took the most reasonable alternative. Tribes to the south of him had already realised the impossibility of military superiority; other tribal kings had discovered cultural and political benefits from peaceful secession and alliance.

Such a decision would not have pleased the more traditional of his followers who, inculcated with generations of ancestral pride in their battle prowess and respect for the royal bloodlines of their race, would have urged a fight to the death. Older men, perhaps retired war veterans themselves, would have urged younger relatives to vaunt their prowess and make ready for war. They would have roused their blood with daring deeds of past glory – rival tribes being raided, women carried off, insults avenged. This was contrary to Prasutagus' policy.

We have no knowledge of Prasutagus' age at his death. He is unlikely to have been a young or middle-aged man. The description of Boadicea suggests a mature woman, and it was usual for a woman to be up to one or two generations younger than her husband in an age where women frequently died in childbirth. Prasutagus was probably an elderly man or at least one who had the best part of his active life behind him. The city of Camulodunum was at the borders of his territory, steadily developing in testimony of Rome's conquering magnificence. Knowing himself to be near the end of his life and wanting to ensure the future existence of his tribe, he acceded to the rationalist's way out: he swore allegiance. How he restrained his hot-headed tribesmen – all of whom would have voiced their very strong objection to his decision in open council – is not known. But restrain them he did, keeping himself and his tribe within the *Pax Romana*.

The Honour of the Tribe

This peaceful solution was dear bought. Icenian honour was brought low. Whatever obvious resistance and opposition might have been voiced was countered by the sheer order and organisation of Roman conquest. This insidious web of bureaucracy soon wound its way into every aspect of Icenian life. Taxes had to be paid and where Icenian families would doubtless have groaned at tribute owed to their overlord in any case, giving tribute to Rome via him was a worse case. Roman officials would have been attached to Prasutagus' court as subtle reminders of conquest and their different standards of elegance and behaviour would have been resented.

What struck at the heart of Icenian honour was the reading of Prasutagus' will, leaving half his kingdom to the Emperor. While this document was obviously drawn up in secret, and probably under a good deal of political duress (Prasutagus doubtless had Roman officials who dropped hints on the correct form in such matters), the shock to Boadicea must have been considerable.

We only know that Boadicea was governing in the name of her daughters, who were Prasutagus' legal heirs under British law, though not the only likely or possible ones under Celtic custom. It is possible that the girls were as yet unmarried and that suitable husbands had to be found for them from within the prescribed royal branches of the family: men who were mature and able enough to rule in the name of their wives and carry on the good name of the Iceni in battle. It is on this point of the viability of female heirs that the subsequent outrages should be balanced. Roman law did not make allowance for such inheritance of mere females; British law made no distinction.

As Boadicea was herself mature and able, she assumed the throne in their name and thus held the tribe together. There is no thought of her being a cipher in tribal policy. She may have sternly and privately disagreed with her husband's policies, while supporting him publicly in his seemingly cautious regime of submission to Rome. Her subsequent behaviour leads one to believe that she was his chief wife; used to issuing orders, to being obeyed and capable of laying down the law to her husband. Her anger at his betrayal of their life's work must have been extreme. But, while she later gave rein to her anger, there is no suspicion that she was uncontrolled or unprincipled. Her duty was clear: to bind the tribe to her and to protect her daughters' rights.

It was Rome's mistake that its commanders did not take Boadicea seriously – either as a royal woman or as a mother. Female rulers were risible to them. They had the standing joke of Cleopatra in Egypt, with whom Julius, that erstwhile conqueror of Britain, had a brief dalliance. Queens were for seducing, for manipulating. Rome should have been warned: queens were also treacherous, dextrous in attack and ruthless when cornered. Cleopatra took poison to avoid the inevitable Roman triumph in which she would have been dragged when Augustus Caesar finally caught up with her.

No one thought of seducing Boadicea or marrying her off to another pliant client king: she was a woman of maturity, her character was indissolubly formed, her years of political sexuality behind her. She was not a commodity. But her daughters were.

These unnamed girls were probably in their early teens. They were a dangerous factor in the political balance. To the Roman mind, virgin daughters of a dead king might be as hazardous as a massed army of Icenian tribesmen – let only one man of power marry one of them and power could be focused and the flame of revolt be fanned.

The Treacherous Lioness

When the officials finally came to strip Boadicea of her governing rights, they clumsily drew all the wrong conclusions. The Icenian queen's righteous anger could be cooled by the scourge. The daughters could be conveniently deflowered and made less desirable to a nobleman of discernment. It was customary for the public executioner to deflower virgins before their deaths, lest the gods be offended, within Roman tradition. The young daughters of attainted consuls were inevitably raped before being thrown to their deaths or strangled.

That Boadicea might have bided quietly at home after such treatment was not to be countenanced. While she might not care on her own behalf, she had her daughters to fight for. Rome had raped the sovereignty of Britain; now it had raped the daughters of an Icenian king, women of the royal kingmaking blood. The Romans would have done better to kill all three women. A directionless battle might have ensued: one easily won by Rome. As it was, the Iceni rose on the command of an outraged mother. The 'treacherous lioness' as the chronicler Gildas called her, was aptly named by him. 'The lion may look proud and disdainful in his tree, but it is the lioness who hunts and brings home prey for her cubs'. The Icenian queen was now ready to rend any who harmed her offspring.

The Face of Revolt

It is never easy to judge the exact measure of cause and effect, especially long after the events in question. In the case of the British revolt of 61 A.D., there are two clear contributory factors, but far more that lay beneath the surface. The temporary *Pax Romana* was only superficial; beneath it the native population seethed with unrest and anger. In many cases, their lands had been taken

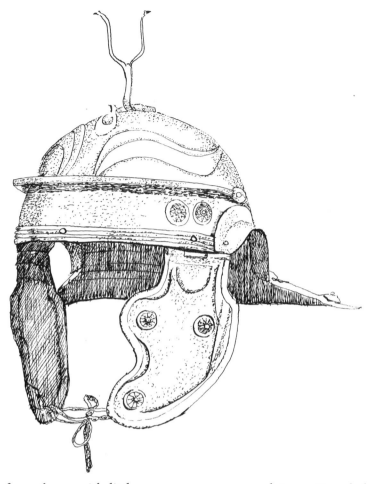

away from them, with little or no recompense, and (as at Camulodunum) given out in parcel form to retired Roman army veterans. Added to this was the very nature of the petty Roman officials placed over them for the task of collecting taxes and tributes and seeing that everything conformed to Roman neatness. In effect, it was the behaviour of some of these officials which touched off the smouldering fuse which was to ignite the south under Boadicea's leadership. Given the nature of Prasutagus' will, the government officials moved in to collect the extraordinary tribute to the Emperor. Finding only Boadicea and her daughters to oppose them, they went about their business as crudely as possible – in the hope, we may assume, of getting all.

At least, this is how things seem to have been. The current Procurator, Catus Decianius, seems to have been a greedy man, not above taking a large share of any goods that were to hand – as were his officers, mostly retired army men and slaves.

Thus, given the treatment she received and the seemingly pre-planned rape of her daughters, small wonder at Boadicea's rage. She and her family had been outraged in every way possible and her tribe made to suffer. She herself, as Queen of the Iceni, had been publicly humiliated.

This Roman helmet of the Imperial-Gallic type from a reconstruction by H. Russell-Robinson dates from roughly the period of the Icenian rebellion and is the kind that would have been worn by the Legionaries. It is made of iron and would have borne a crest.

75

BRIGANTIAE

Goddess of War

Before the revolt was even properly under way, Dio Cassius puts into the mouth of Boadicea a noble speech worthy of the greatest Roman orators, with metaphors ransacked from classical literature in which she compares herself favourably with Nitocris, Semiramis and Messalina. It is here that we read of her invocation to the Icenian goddess Andraste, to whom she speaks as a woman to a woman.

The goddess Andraste is only mentioned in Dio Cassius: we have no other information about her attributes or mythos. It seems reasonable, since Celtic scholars give the meaning of Andraste as 'Invincible', that she was a goddess of battle. She may well have been akin to Brigantia, the titulary goddess of the Brigantian tribes of northern Britain.

Dio Cassius tells how Boadicea let a hare out of a fold of her garments and set it speeding towards the oncoming enemy as a means of divining the battle's outcome. Whichever side it ran on was considered the auspicious side. The hare has ever been a beast of the shapeshifter, a creature of the moon. The nature of Boadicea's invocation to Andraste leaves us in no doubt what she is said to have thought of the Romans. She impunes their soft comforts, their pederasty and their womanish emperors (particularly Nero). She takes to herself the attributes of the goddess and invokes her protection upon her tribe: 'Mistress, be thou alone our leader!'

It is possible that the wholesale slaughter of civilians which followed was in the nature of a ritual sacrifice to propitiate Andraste in her sacred groves. Certainly, Andraste's hare ran before the chariots of the Iceni for a good many months before her protection expired.

Paulinus and the Druids

Meanwhile, Suetonius Paulinus as military governor, a hard and dedicated soldier with experience of fighting natives in Spain and Gaul, and a knowledge of mountain terrain which may have influenced his choice, began an action which was to antagonize further the already angry Britons.

He had already spent the first two years of his office, from his arrival in 59 A.D. to the spring of 61 A.D., familiarizing himself with the particular problems facing him in Britain. It was clearly not a 'settled' province, and at the end of this time he was convinced that the main backbone of native resistance centred on the Druids, and in particular their college on Mona (Anglesey).

He was probably only partially correct in this belief; but apart from any Druid involvement, Mona had certainly become a sanctuary for a considerable number of refugees and dissidents, who remained there awaiting an opportunity to stir up trouble against their oppressors.

At least, this is how Suetonius Paulinus saw matters, and thus, in the spring of 61 A.D., not long before Catus Decianius sent his collection squad into Iceni territory, Suetonius marched on Anglesey with every intention of laying it waste.

It seems safe to assume that the Roman general had already secured large areas of the territory occupied by the Silures and the Deceangli, and that he had wintered at Deva (Chester) on the River Dee. From there, he had overseen the building of large numbers of flat-bottomed boats with which to cross the Menai Strait. As Tacitus' laconic narrative tells us:

By this method the infantry crossed; the cavalry, who followed, did so by fording or, in deeper water, by swimming at the side of their horses.

Yet even as Suetonius' army celebrated its victory by cutting down the sacred

trees on the island, news came that the Queen of the Iceni had risen in revolt and that the Trinovantes had joined with her. The south was in flames.

The Fall of Camulodunum

Suetonius immediately sent orders to Cerealis Petillius, the commander of the IX Legion, to quell the rebellion. However, it took this general precious time to gather a large enough force from the scattered forts and camps in which they were billeted. In that time, Boadicea marched on the city of Camulodunum (Colchester) and totally destroyed it.

Had Cerealis moved more quickly, or had the Procurator Catus Decianius been able to send more than the meagre 200 ill-armed veterans he managed to scrape together in response to a panic-stricken call from the citizens of

78

On this sword blade found at South Shields is the image of the legionary eagle and standards inlaid in bronze. This kind of weapon probably belonged to a high-ranking officer and would have been jealously guarded.

Camulodunum, things might have been very different. As it was, the Britons met with virtually no resistance until they reached the temple of Claudius, hated symbol of their subjugation and a permanent reminder of the man who had conquered them.

In fact, the temple, which had been dedicated to Claudius shortly before his death in 54 A.D., was still incomplete. However, its massive walls were the only defensible area in the city, since the walls of the earlier Roman fort had been pulled down to make room for the expanding township.

Here, then, the desperate defenders, men, women and children, gathered to make their last stand, hoping to hold out long enough for relief to arrive from the IXth Legion. They were not to know that Boadicea had laid a carefully prepared ambush in the woods along the road towards Camulodunum. There, her army cut the Legion to pieces, leaving only a handful of cavalry, with which Petillius ignominiously escaped.

Thus, no help was forthcoming, and effectively the citizens of Camulodunum were doomed. The Iceni and the Trinovantes, who had been forced to contribute to the cost of building the Claudian temple, destroyed it utterly, along with the entire population, estimated at some 2,000 people, including army veterans and pro-Roman Britons living in the town.

Suetonius Strikes

Two things then happened. The Britons, elated to a point of madness by their success, began rampaging across the country, looting and burning any settlement of Roman or pro-Roman standing they could find. Suetonius Paulinus, with news of the fall of Camulodunum ringing in his ears, took a fast galley to Deva and pushed on at full speed with a detachment of cavalry towards Londinium (London) which lay directly in the path of Boadicea's victorious army.

Fortunately for the governor, the Celts were still celebrating their success and had scattered across the country, otherwise they might have been waiting for him as they had for Petillius outside Camulodunum – when events would probably have been very different. As it was, the Governor of Britain arrived to find the people of Londinium in a state of petrified fear. The Procurator, Catus Decianius, whose actions had helped fuel the rebellion, had fled to Gaul from where he disappears in recorded history.

The only hope for London was in Suetonius Paulinus. Having grasped the gravity of the situation, he realized that his only hope lay in abandoning London to its fate, in the hope that it would hold up Boadicea long enough for him to gather sufficient troops to face her on ground of his own choosing.

Therefore, he did the only thing possible in the circumstances – offered his protection to any refugees who wished to accompany him on the road south. There he could billet them on the still pro-Roman king Cogidumnus, who seems to have willingly promised his support. (He must have had to make a swift decision on which side to back: had Boadicea triumphed he would

Camulodunum (Colchester) was the centre of Roman government in Britain. It was here that Boadicea first struck, overwhelming the city and reducing it to rubble and ashes.

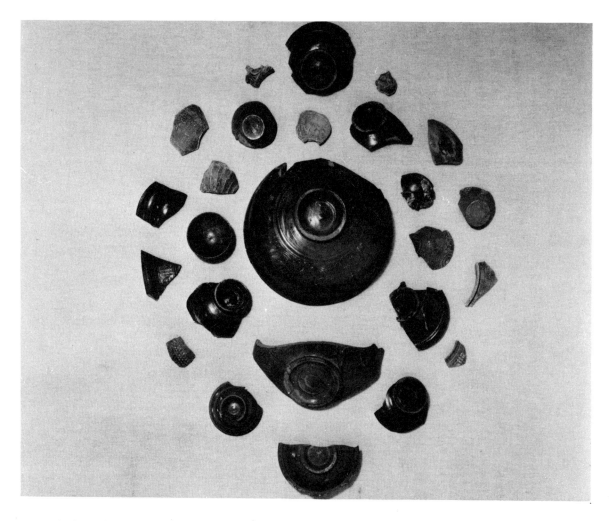

A selection of pottery from the period of the rebellion. They are blackened and burned from the holocaust which struck the city in 65 A.D.

certainly have been killed; had he backed her and Rome become the victor, his comfortable career would have been swiftly over.)

A number of citizens elected to travel with Suetonius and straggled south. It was now early July of 61 A.D. Nothing stood between Boadicea and the huddle of houses and official buildings shambling beside the River Thames.

The Sack of London

Dig anywhere within the compass of the earliest Roman settlement in London and at a certain level – about twenty feet down – you are bound to encounter a layer of ash and blackened pottery-shards. This is the legacy of Boadicea's sack of Londinium. She left it a smoking ruin scarcely days after Suetonius had withdrawn.

In those days, London extended barely two miles from its centre – the crossing-place of the River Thames at (now) London Bridge, where two roads

The Roman army, led by Suetonius Paulinus, met the Iceni at Mancetter, near Watling Street, and defeated them utterly. Boadicea took a fatal dose of poison after the battle, rather than suffer the ignominy of capture.

met which lead north-east to Camulodunum and north-west to Veralamium (St Albans) and Silchester.

Londinium had been founded by the Romans around 43 A.D. on two hills either side of the Walbrook stream where it issued into the Thames on its northern bank. Shortly afterwards they erected a bridge across the river at more or less the same point of the present day London Bridge, and began making roads to connect with the Channel port of Rutupiae (Richborough). This at once made Londinium an important supply depot for incoming ships supplying the armies in the North, South and West. However, its importance at this juncture was subsidiary to that of Camulodunum, which had become, to all intents and purposes, the centre of Roman government in the South of the country. After the revolt, when both sites had been levelled, emphasis shifted from Camulodunum to Londinium, which rapidly became the most important commercial and administrative centre in Britain. A new governor's palace was erected, which rivalled all previous structures, and soon bath houses and a magnificent basilica followed.

In Boadicea's time, however, none of this existed; only a scatter of tumbledown houses, some villas owned by rich merchants, a temple and a few shops and warehouses. Yet despite its size, London was undoubtedly busy and crowded with merchants, traders and the inevitable population which nearly always grows up around such commercial and mercantile centres.

Lewis Spence, in his book on the rebellion, describes the probable appearance of Londinium at this time as follows:

. . . on the whole, with the exception of a few shrines and executive buildings the 'architecture' of the Londinium of this phase . . . seems mostly to have been composed of timber plastered over and dwellings of Romano-Celtic type, mainly constructed from that wattle-and-daub material of the Britons . . . The general aspect must have been that of a somewhat irregular and impermanent-looking straggle of comparatively small buildings, villas, booths, shacks and hutments falling riverwards down the slope from the present site of Leadenhall to the mouth of the Walbrook . . .

Moreover, there seem to have been no defences at all – archaeological investigation has revealed no evidence of any walls – even of timber – until after the rebellion. Neither was there any military presence, so that it must have seemed to Boadicea that she was about to harvest a fruit over-ripe for the picking.

Why did the majority of the citizens of Londinium – an estimated 20,000 – remain behind when Suetonius offered them his protection? Firstly, it is by no means easy to pack up all one's goods and follow the swift pace of a Roman cavalry unit whose commander is anxious to make good time. Secondly, there were a great many women and children in the township, who were unable to travel far or fast. Thirdly, many simply refused to believe their danger.

Rumour of the sack of Camulodunum had certainly reached them, but there were many who believed that Boadicea would come no further south, or that she would bypass Londinium and attack Verulamium instead. One

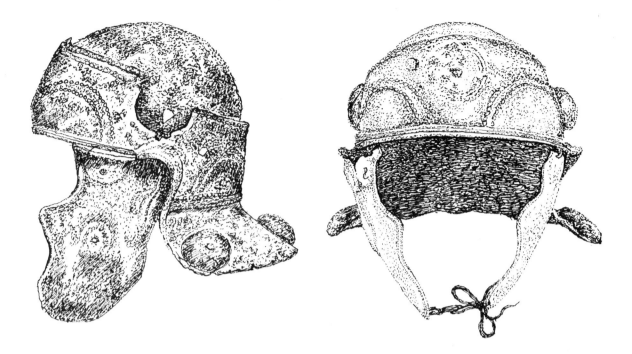

suspects that many did not believe in the seriousness of the situation, even after Suetonius had made his brief, dramatic appearance and withdrawal. The rest simply accepted the end as inevitable, and while a few made hasty preparations to defend the township, others simply waited.

Two views of a Roman helmet of the Auxiliary cavalry type, dating from the period of the rebellion: the left side with its distinctive cheek-piece; and the front view of a reconstruction by H. Russell-Robinson.

The End of Londinium

The defenders almost certainly never knew what hit them. Boadicea's host now numbered around 20,000 and they simply overwhelmed the township, putting its community to the sword and burning all the buildings to the ground. Doubtless the citizens gave their lives dearly, but they had no chance against the battle-crazed Britons, being ill-armed and ill-prepared for the devastation that was to come.

Dio Cassius' account of what happened is precise, though it makes grim reading:

Those who were taken captive by the Britons were subjected to every form of outrage. The worst and most bestial atrocity committed by their captors was the following. They hung up naked the noblest and most distinguished women and then cut off their breasts and sewed them to their mouths, in order to make the victims appear to be eating them; afterwards they impaled the women on sharp skewers run lengthwise through the entire body. All this they did to the accompaniment of sacrifices, banquets and wanton behaviour . . .

(trans: E. Cary)

Exaggeration? Perhaps; though atrocities of this kind were not unknown at the time, and the Britons had by this time been fuelled by hatred and success to a point where they were less a host than a deadly machine which destroyed everything in its path. Dio Cassius was a Roman and wrote some time after

83

the events, so there may well be an element of exaggeration. But Boadicea clearly felt no regrets. She led the sacrifices to the goddess Andraste, whose name appears to mean Victory, but who surprisingly enough appears nowhere else in the history of the Celts.

Boadicea must already have been planning the next stage in her campaign, for though she had little control over the warriors who wanted to spend time exacting a full recompense for past wrongs done to them, she knew that ahead lay Verulamium, and somewhere beyond it Suetonius Paulinus and the Legions. Time was against her and she may have chafed at the delay caused by the excesses of her tribesmen. She also knew the impossibility of trying to do more than direct them, in their own time, towards the next objective. It was this delay which cost her the rebellion and, untimately, her own life.

Suetonius and the Legions

What kind of man was it that Boadicea faced in her battle to free Britain from Roman domination? Giaus Suetonius Paulinus was a hardened soldier with several campaigns behind him. He had fought in North Africa against the Moors some years previously, leading an army as far as the Atlas Mountains in his urge to quell an incipient rebellion. It was probably at this time that he attained consular rank, though he had to wait a further seventeen years before being given the military governorship of Britain.

He arrived to find the province in a state of some confusion. The previous governor, Quintus Verianius, had lived less than a year before succumbing to the climate. Though the south seemed peaceful, the northern tribes, especially the Brigantes, were a constant threat to Roman security in the island.

Verianius had been a milder man, though still an able soldier, whose brief had been to take a more conciliatory attitude to the native population. Suetonius set out to crush any revolt and to police the island with his Legions in such a way as to allow no opportunity for insurrection. His first major campaign, as we have seen, was against the Druid sanctuary on Anglesey, which was carried out with typical military precision and iron determination. Suetonius was, in short, a professional and typically Roman soldier.

The Legions in Britain
The Legions within Suetonius' command at this time were the II Augusta, IX Hispana, XIV Gemina and XX Valeria. The II was probably stationed at Isca (Caerleon) and in the Severn and Wye valleys; the IX at Lindum (Lincoln); while the XX was ranged along the borders of Brigantia. The XIV was first of all stationed at Viroconium (Wroxeter) but moved to Deva (Chester) at the start of the campaign against the Silures and the attack on Mona (Anglesey). It had, in all probability, been drafted from the Rhine

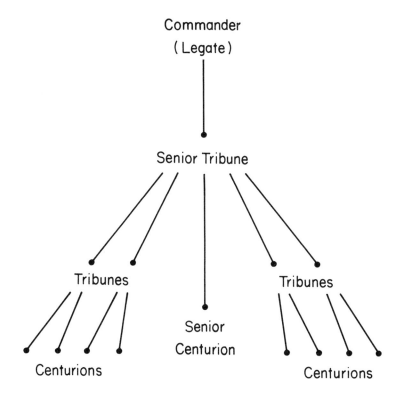

```
                    Commander
                     (Legate)


                        |
                        |
                        |

                  Senior Tribune



        Tribunes              Tribunes


                     Senior
Centurions          Centurion          Centurions
```

Staff structure within the Roman Legions.

army, which had already the greatest experience in fighting Celtic peoples in Gaul and Germania.

In general, a legion consisted of 6,000 men. These were divided into ten cohorts, further divided into eight centuries. Nine of the cohorts were normal, with the tenth, 'double' century forming the elite core of the legion under the command of a senior centurion.

Initially, only those born into Roman citizenship were permitted to join the army, but this soon became impracticable and it became normal to confer citizenship along with a commission. Thereafter, the legions consisted of people from many nations, and one might find within any one legion Goths, Gauls, Scythians, Samartians or Asturians from Spain. In the same way, Celtic warriors from Britain were sent to fight on Rome's furthest frontiers.

Each legionary served a term of 20 years, during which time it was possible for him to rise through the ranks to the position of centurion, commanding eighty men and answering directly to a prefect or tribune. There were five of these tribunes, four of equal rank and a fifth who answered directly to a commander.

In addition, a number of prefects commanded several cohorts of auxiliaries, which normally consisted of native militia, fighting in native dress and with their own weapons, rather than the mailed uniform of the regular legionary. Unlike the legions, they were regarded as irregular troops, and though they served five years longer than the legionaries, they received lower pay and seem to have been given the hardest and most arduous tours of duty.

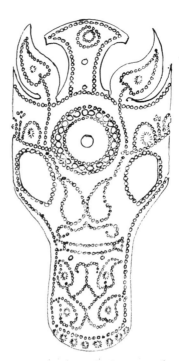

Though the Romans made little use of cavalry in Boadicea's day, it was an important part of the Legions' strength. This leather horse mask was probably used for parade wear rather than daily use. It gives an idea of the splendour of which they were capable.

Any soldier could re-enlist at the end of an initial term of duty – but there was no discharge from the Legion except in exceptional circumstances, or because of severe wounds. Men who had lost limbs or were otherwise incapacitated were often kept on as camp servants, but there was no official pension until they had served for a number of years. Of course, it was the apportioning of native lands to retired veterans which caused such ill-feeling among the tribes at the time of the rebellion.

The regular soldiers were trained to a standard which stands comparison with modern day commando or special forces. They had to be able to scale embankments, leap ditches and swim rivers and straits – as well as marching for twenty miles in five hours carrying a full pack, which might contain three days' rations and a mess tin, together with a saw, axe and shovel. This last item, along with a wicker-work basket, was used to throw up an earthen bank around their camp at night. This was standard procedure whether the stopping time was one night or ten.

Of course, each man also had to carry his weapons and the armour he wore. This was usually of leather strengthened with strips of iron, though some senior officers wore mail shirts of overlapping scales.

Their weapons consisted of two, six-foot throwing spears, with hardened wooden shafts and iron heads. It was this *pilum* which was to inflict such terrible havoc among the close-packed Celtic warriors in the final battle of the rebellion. Additionally the legionary carried a short stabbing sword called a *spatha*, and a dagger. These were intended for close work, and the typical action of a Roman unit was to form a shield-wall behind which they advanced, step by inexorable step, striking between swiftly raised shields and then rapidly recovering themselves. Their long shields, made of several layers

86

Typical image of a Roman officer, so hated by the Celts. From the tomb of Marcus Favonius Facilis, Colchester.

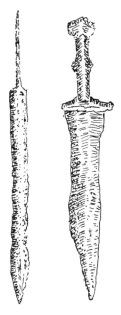

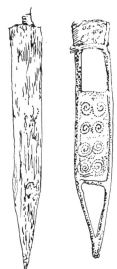

of wood, were designed to protect the body from neck to thigh, and were thus ideal for such work.

Their only really weak spot was their legs and feet, which were virtually undefended in order to give them better mobility; there must have been many casualties with wounds in these areas. Otherwise they were virtually invulnerable, with their hard leather helmets protecting their heads and necks. Once a powerful wedge of legionaries moved forward against an enemy, there was little that could stop them short of a head-on cavalry charge.

Rome's own use of cavalry was still limited at this time – the usual tactic being for the mounted units to remain on the wings, while the infantry did the hardest part of the work. Then they would fling into the fray to mop up the remaining enemies or those who tried to flee.

Within the Legions were positions for masons, surveyors, engineers and sappers, as well as signallers, medical orderlies, armourers and clerks. Some of these specialized troops were present in every Legion, which had to be self-sufficient and self-governing during its long months away from base.

Once a foothold had been established in Britain by Allus Plautius in 43 A.D., immediate building was instituted to set up an expanding network of forts and armed camps throughout the country. These were connected by a system of roads which were still recognised as being one of the finest achievements of their day and whose remains as highways can still be seen.

Against such disciplined, well-armed and highly trained soldiers, moving at speed along a growing system of roads, the wild tribesmen had little chance when it came to direct conflict. On the one hand, Britons were experts at guerrilla tactics, as they demonstrated in their destruction of the XX Legion

Weapons carried by every legionary included the spatha *(two-edged sword),* pugio *(dagger) and* gladius *(broad-bladed sword), here shown with a decorated scabbard.*

outside Verulamium. On the other hand, the Romans were past masters of the art of flexible movement in battle, with a complex system of signals which enabled a commander to move units of force at will.

A fast system of couriers with connecting post stations along the whole length of the roads enabled messages to be sent at great speed. Hence, the way that Suetonius was able to get word of the rebellion while he was still far away in Wales.

All of this made the Roman Legions probably the best army in the world. So Boadicea's initial success is all the more impressive – though she had elements of surprise on her side, as well as a feeling of moral indignation which acted as fuel to her already enraged followers. Let us look now at the final act in the drama, and at the meeting between these two implacable foes.

The End of the Revolt

Finally succeeding in gathering her battle-sated warriors around her, Boadicea now pressed on towards Verulamium (St Albans), the third important township on which she unleashed her fury. However, unlike both Camulodonum and Londinium, Verulamium was almost totally British, its population consisting almost entirely of Catavelaunii, a tribe so staunchly pro-Roman they had earned the hatred of their neighbours. There was probably also an element of tribal rivalry present in this, which the general atmosphere of slaughter and warfare restimulated.

Whatever the reasons, Verulamium met the same fate as the other towns. The fine Roman-style houses, the basilica and other public buildings were burned to the ground and the inhabitants wiped out with as much savagery as had been meted out to the Roman citizenry of the other townships.

Classical accounts of the revolt estimate the number of dead at 70,000. This is almost certainly an exaggeration, given substance by the passage of time; but enough evidence exists to suggest a truly frightful slaughter of men, women and children. It seemed that nothing could stop Boadicea from sweeping across the country and either killing or driving out every Roman in Britain. Only Suetonius Paulinus now stood between her and this objective, and he still lacked the forces to meet the Iceni and Trinovantes in direct conflict with any real hope of winning.

Therefore, he continued to withdraw, and according to Dio Cassius began to grow short of food – a reasonable supposition if his base was still in Wales and his supplies correspondingly far removed. By now, he had been joined by the rest of the XIV Legion, as well as detachments of the XX and II Legions, and daily awaited the arrival of the remainder of the II, who were then stationed at Isca Dumnonorium (Exeter) under the temporary command of Peonius Postumus, the camp prefect.

For some reason Poenius failed to answer the call to join the XIV and XX Legions – possibly because he was under attact from the Durotriges, who had also risen in revolt following Boadicea's dramatic victories.

When the conflict was finally over, this unfortunate officer fell on his sword rather than face the disgrace that would have resulted from his failure to follow a direct order – thus also incidentally robbing his own Legion of a share in the honour of defending the province against the terrible Iceni queen.

Reconstruction of a Roman villa of the kind which may well have been occupied by Codgidumnus, the staunchly pro-Roman King of the Atrabates. Many similiar unprotected farmsteads between Colchester, London and St Albans, fell victim to Boadicea's war-host.

The Last Battle
We really have no idea where the final confrontation between Boadicea and Suetonius took place. A site in what is now Leicestershire, near Mancetter, to the south-east of Atherstone and close to the line of Watling Street, has been suggested by Graham Webster, the leading authority on the revolt. Paulinus, he points out, would have chosen a position to give him the greatest tactical advantage, and going on the information included in Tacitus, he suggests that:

It was at the approach to a narrow defile which meant that the Britons were forced to advance into a front of diminishing width: the greater their force the more packed they would have become in their eagerness to reach the Romans

(*Boudica*: Webster)

Behind lay a thick forest, on rising ground that gave plenty of protection to

89

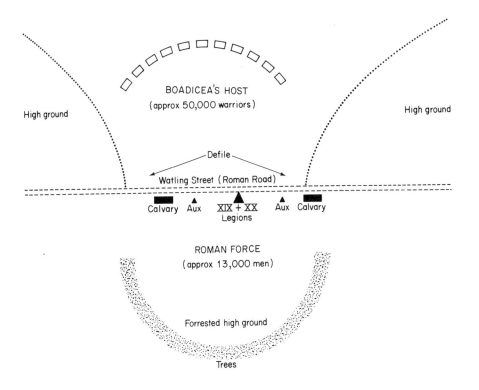

BOADICEA'S HOST
(approx 50,000 warriors)

High ground   High ground

Defile

Watling Street (Roman Road)

Calvary   Aux   XIX + XX   Aux   Calvary
                Legions

ROMAN FORCE
(approx 13,000 men)

Forrested high ground

Trees

Likely plan of the battle between Boadicea and Suetonius.

Paulinus' rear. Ahead the ground was open, affording no cover to the advancing Britons. It seems quite astounding in retrospect that Boadicea allowed herself to be drawn into giving battle in such terrain; but by this time her army – which has been estimated at anything between 100,000 and 230,000 – had gained a frightening momentum. The Britons believed that nothing could stop them – after Camulodunum and the IX Legion, after Londinium and Verulamium, they would simply roll over the Roman army and leave nothing but dead in their wake. So certain were they of victory that they had even brought their wives and families with them in huge wagons. These now formed a semi-circle behind the war-host, effectively enclosing them between two walls – the Romans in front and their own people behind. Tacitus says that women and children were even seated on top of the wagons to view the spectacle of Rome's defeat.

Against this imposing host of Celtic warriors were ranged an estimated 11–13,000 Roman soldiers, consisting of the XIV Legion, detachments of the II and XX at the centre, as well as cavalry and auxiliaries on the wings.

Both Dio and Tacitus record the speeches of the respective leaders before the battle – Dio's is lengthy, bombastic and wholly unlike anything a British leader would have uttered. Tacitus, whom we must remember was reporting events actually witnessed by his uncle, may get closer to the truth. At least we get a feeling of the kind of words that might well have resounded above the shouting, screaming, chanting warriors of the British side, or over the silent, waiting ranks of the legionaries:

Mounted in a chariot with her daughters before her, she rode up to clan after clan and delivered her protest: it was customary, she knew, with Britons to fight under female captaincy, but she was avenging, not, as a queen of glorious ancestry, her ravished realm and power, but, as a woman of the people, her liberty lost, her body tortured by the lash, the tarnished honour of her daughters.

(trans: J. Jackson)

The gods themselves were on their side, she continued, as witnessed by their just success. One Legion they had destroyed already, the rest were skulking in their camps and would never face so vast an army as their own. Let the men go home if they wanted, the women would finish this on their own! We may imagine Boadicea's harsh voice ringing out across the field, her red hair flaming, her strong arms raised, shaking a bloodied spear towards the Roman army.

Even Suetonius, according to Tacitus, broke his customary silence, commanding his men to 'ignore the noise and threats of these savages', pointing out that there were more women than men in their ranks and that they would soon give way before soldiers who had beaten them so often in the past. To this few, he claimed, lay the honour of the Legions and of Rome, so:

Keep close order, when you have thrown your javelins, push forward with the bosses of your shields and swords, let the dead pile up, forget all about plunder, win the victory and it's all yours.

(trans: Webster)

And so the Britons came on. There was little room for the usual wave of chariots, the shouted insults, thrown spears and swift withdrawals; the whole mass of the British host advanced together, and were met with a hail of Roman javelins, unyieldingly followed by a second. Many fell, and then the Legions began their advance. Supported by cavalry on both flanks to prevent any of the Britons escaping, they pressed forward with the inevitability of a steel ram. Three wedges were driven deep into the press of Celts who had no room to swing their long swords against the short *pila* of the legionaries.

They were cut down in swathes and began to retreat, only to find their backs hampered by their own wagons and families. In a few hours, it was over. Hundreds, perhaps thousands of Britons lay dead in great mounds; women and children and old men, even the oxen which had pulled the carts to the site were slain and blocked all retreat. In all, some 40,000 Britons probably fell that day, against less than a quarter of that number of the Romans. We cannot know the exact figures, and Tacitus and Dio undoubtedly exaggerate.

Dio Cassius tells us that Boadicea fell sick and died, although whether in captivity or not, he does not state. Tacitus inclines to her taking poison. In whatever manner her death took place, the revolt was over.

If Boadicea did indeed take poison, the reasons are not far to seek. She had probably been captured and had no wish to be packed off to Rome to form the central tableau of the Conquest of the Britons in the triumphal train of Suetonius. Like Cleopatra of recent memory, she preferred the honourable

A gladius, the Roman legionary's favourite weapon. Crouched behind his huge shield, he flicked the blade in and out, thrusting rather than hacking. An excellent weapon for close work, the grip is made of bone or wood, and the leather scabbard shown here decorated with medallions of victory or the god of war.

way out. It is also possible that she had other reasons for no longer clinging to life. History does not tell us of the fate of her daughters. Had the Romans captured them in battle they would doubtless have told the world. The girls would have been either summarily executed or perhaps married to men of no account. It is likely that they perished in battle, possibly the last affray.

Without her daughters to fight for and bereft of the protection of Andraste – whose nemetons she had liberally watered with the blood of Romans – Boadicea died.

No other woman after her has left such a mark upon British history. In terms of leadership, determination and ruthlessness not even Eleanor of Aquitaine nor Margaret of Anjou (the queens of Henry II and Henry VI respectively), nor Elizabeth I, possessed Boadicea's stature. She remains alone, a solitary pyre on which the hopes of Britain's independence smouldered fitfully and were consumed utterly.

It is impressive testimony that both Tacitus and Dio Cassius treat Boadicea's impossible plight with sympathy, while decrying her bloodthirsty slaughter of their fellow citizens. Barbarian and female she might have been, but her cause was a just one. To a Roman, honour and courage were virtues which cancelled many faults. These qualities Boadicea had in plenty. Both historians accord her the tribute of a worthy and noble adversary. Dio said:

Let us, I say, do our duty while we still remember what freedom is, that we may leave it to our children not only its appellation but also its reality. For, if we utterly forget the happy state in which we were born and bred, what, pray, will they do, reared in bondage?

Aftermath

Reinforced by 2,000 legionaries from Germany, as well as 1,000 cavalry and 4,000 auxiliaries, Suetonius now set about a systematic and terrible retaliation against the tribes of southern Britain. Calling upon the name of *Mars Ulator*, god of vengeance, he marched through Iceni and Trinovant territory, burning crops and farmsteads and slaughtering any Britons he found. He seems, indeed, to have become somewhat deranged, pursuing his trail of vengeance with a savage determination, almost as though some of Boadicea's blood-lust had communicated itself to him after her death. At any rate, he kept the army 'under canvas' for the remainder of the year – which must have made him extremely unpopular with the legionaries, who would normally have wintered in the comparative comfort of a stone fort.

Only the appearance of a new Procurator, Julius Classicanus, put an end to these events. Some kind of quarrel seems to have occurred between the two men, and we may suppose that it was over Classicanus' desire to take a more moderate line with the Britons.

In dispatches to Rome, he requested the recall of Suetonius, and finally got his way in the following year. A new Governor, Petronius Turpitilianus, duly arrived, whose policy was one of mediation rather than attrition, and by the end of the year the province had begun to settle back to a more peaceful existence.

Boadicea's failure after her initial triumph, remained in the minds of the Britons sufficiently to deter them from making another serious attempt at revolt. The northern tribes were either forced into submission or contained behind Hadrian's Wall and Britain became in every way a Roman province, though the shockwaves sent out by Boadicea's unparalleled success and the violence and wholesale slaughter caused by the revolt, continued to cause ripples in Rome's attitude to her provinces for some time thereafter.

It may be said that the rebellion finally helped to make the state of things in Britain better than they had been before – there seems to have been a genuine attempt to recognize the tribes as civilized people rather than as painted savages. Temples were raised to Celtic gods in the guise of their Roman equivalents – though the Druids, their power broken by Suetonius, were never again permitted to re-establish anything like a formal organization.

Not until the gradual break-up of the Empire some 500 years later caused the withdrawal of the Legions, was there any effort on the part of the Britons to reassert themselves. By which time they had a new adversary to contend with – the Saxons. But by then many of the tribes had been thoroughly romanized, and the face of Britain had changed forever.

Boadicea Remembered

Boadicea is best remembered for her courage and leadership which was, however, no match for the iron discipline of the Legions. As Caractacus had learned before her, it was virtually impossible to weld the fiery, independent tribes into anything like an army. Once the momentum of their early victories was spent, they collapsed, and were cut down. Rome triumphed as she had always done, though suffering a blow which she would never quite forget.

Boadicea assumed her place in history as one of the truly great heroines of Britain and is remembered as a champion of the people – though she has had a chequered career at the hands of writers through the ages. The irascible sixth century historian Gildas called her 'a treacherous lioness'; while at the other extreme the poet Tennyson apostrophized her as a great English heroine.

She was, first and foremost, a warrior queen: proud and unbending to the Roman yoke. Justice was certainly on her side in the beginning, and she could scarcely have been expected to appeal to Rome for redress of the wrongs done to herself, her family and her people. She took the only way, and blazed a trail of blood which has never been forgotten. The revolt of 60 A.D. is only a minor episode in the history of Rome, as indeed it is of Britain. Yet, in the end, one has nothing but respect for Boadicea and her wild tribespeople. As Lewis Spence memorably, if rather extravagantly, put it:

Vaster than any form in the early saga of this sea-fortress of the north looms the shade of Boadicea, triumphant even in name and memory, among the world's greatest examplars of womanly vigour, a goddess in armour descending to the succour of a folk enslaved.

The Notitia Dignitatum

The *Notitia Dignitatum* is a list, compiled in the third or fourth century A.D. of the principal officers and their areas of responsibility within the Empire. It was transcribed and copied successively up until the seventeenth century, when it was probably destroyed, and much of it is thereby corrupt. Within a larger whole, the *Notitia Orientis*, and the *Notitia Occidentis*, which deal respectively with the eastern and western halves of the Empire, are set the chapters dealing with the province of Britannia. It gives a fascinating glimpse of the division of Britain into areas with forts and officers responsible for units of the legions. Although the *Notitia* dates from after the period of the rebellion, it is unlikely to have changed much in the preceding years. Also, this organization itself may have been a result of the revolt, after which things became much tighter within the province.

The text is that of O. Seeck (1876) incorporating the amendations of A. L. F. Rivet and Colin Smith (1979), with translations from the Latin original by Caitlín Matthews. The inclusion of ? in place names indicates tentative identification.

Vicarius Britanniarum was the substitute for an absent or deceased provincial governor. He was responsible for the parts of Britain which, like the rest of the Roman Empire, was divided into provinces and dioceses for easier administration: *Maxima Caesariensis* was South East Britain; *Valentia* was north of the Wall; *Britannia Prima* was South-East Britain; *Britannia Secunda* was Britain north of the Humber; *Flavia Caesariensis* included the Midlands and Wales.

Comes litoris Saxonici per Britanniam Count of the Saxon Shore in Britain was directly responsible for the following officers and dispositions:

Praepositus numeri Fortensium, Othonae Military Officer of the Fortenses regiment at Bradwell

Praepositus militium Tungrecanorum, Dubris Military Officer of the Tungrecani regiment at Dover

Praepositus numero Turnacensium, Lemannis Military Officer of the Turnacensi regiment at Lympne

Praepositus equitum Salmatarum Branodunensium, Branoduno Military Officer of the Dalmatian cavalry, Brancaster

Praepositus equitum stablesianorum, Gariannonensium, Gariannonor Military Officer of the Stablesiani cavalry, Burgh Castle

Tribunus cohortis primai Baetasiorum, Regulbio Tribune of the First Baetasium Cohort, Reculver

Praefectus legionis secundae Augustae, Rutupis Prefect of the Second Augustinian Legion, Richborough

Praepositus numeri Abulcorum, Anderidos Military Officer of the Abulcorium regiment at Pevensey

Praepositus numeri exploratorum, Portum Adurni Military Officer of Scouting (Spying) regiment, Porchester.

The Dux Britanniarum Duke of Britain was responsible for the following officers:

Praefectus legionis sextae Prefect of the VI Legion at York

Praefectus equitum Dalmatarum, Praesidio Prefect of the Dalmatian cavalry at?

Praefectus equitorum Crispianorum, Dano Prefect of the Crispinian cavalry, Doncaster? Jarrow?

Praefectus equitum catafractariorum, Morbio Prefect of cataphracts?

Praepositus numeri barcariorum Tiridiensium, Arbeia Prefect of the Tiridatian regiment, South Shields

Praefectus numeri Nerviorum Dictensium, Dicti Prefect of Nervian regiment, at Wearmouth?

Praefectus numeri vigilum, Concangios Prefect of the Watch, Chester-le-Street

Praefectus numeri exploratorum, Lavatres Prefect of the Scouting regiment, Bowes

Praefectus numeri directorum, Verteris Prefect of the Pathfinding regiment, Brough

Praefectus numeri defenscrum, Braboniaco Prefect of the Defensive regiment, Kirkby Thornton

Praefectus numeri Solensium, Maglone Prefect of the Solensium troops, Old Carlisle

Praefectus numeri Pacensium, Magis Prefect of the Pacensian troops, Burrow Walls?

Praefectus numeri Longovicanorum, Longovicio Prefect of the Longovi troops, Lanchester

Praefectus numeri supervenientium Petrueriensium Derventione Prefect of the Superventores regiment, Malton

The Dux Britanniarum also had responsibility for 24 further Prefects and Tribunes posted along the Wall.

Chronology of the Rebellion

Much of Lewis Spence's information, on which the following is based, has been superceded by modern archaeological evidence. Nevertheless, there seems no reason to quarrel with his suggested time-scale of events.

60 A.D. Death of King Prasutagus.

61 A.D. Early March Suetonius departs for Anglesey. The outrages on the Icenian royal family take place.

Mid March–May Partition of Icenian territory proceeds. Annexation to Roman colony.

Mid March–May Suetonius makes preparations to attack Anglesey.

May–June Hosting of the Iceni and other tribes.

June Suetonius attacks Anglesey and proceeds to demolish native monuments, etc.

End of June Suetonius receives news of unrest among the tribes.

Early July Boadicea attacks Camulodunum.

61 A.D. Early July Suetonius arrives at Londinium. Londinium sacked. Suetonius retreats across the Thames in the direction of Regnum, conveying the fugitives from Londinium part of the way to that place.

Mid July Verulamium sacked.

Mid July–Mid August Suetonius takes up a position south of the Thames.

Mid August He recrosses the Thames and marches northward to Londinium.

End of August Meets Boadicea in battle.

September–October Suetonius gathers forces in Britain into one army 'to finish the war' and ravages the territories of the hostile tribes.

October–November Reinforcements sent from Germany. They go into winter quarters.

Further Reading

Brannigan, K. *Roman Britain* Readers Digest, 1980.

Caesar *The Conquest of Gaul* (trans. S. A. Handford) Penguin, 1951.

Clayton, P. *A Companion To Roman Britain* Phaidon, 1980.

Cunliffe, B. *The Celtic World* Bodley Head, 1979.

Dio Cassio *Roman History* (trans. E. Cary) Loeb Classics, 1925.

Durant, G. M. *Britain: Rome's Most Northerly Province* Bell, 1969.

Frere, S. *Brittania* RKP, 1967.

Gildas *The Ruin of Britain* (trans. M. Winterbottom) Phillimore, 1978.

Goodall, D. M. & A. A. Dent. *The Foals of Epona* Galley Press, 1962.

Lindsay, J. *Our Celtic Heritage* Weidenfeld, 1962.

Mellett, M. *Warrior Queen* Pan Books, 1978.

Merrifield, R. *The Roman City of London* Longman, 1965.

Newark, T. *Celtic Warriors* Blandford Press, 1986.

Norton-Taylor, D. *The Celts* Time Life International, 1976.

Piggott, S. *The Druids* Thames & Hudson, 1968.

Ritchie, W. E. & J. N. G. *Celtic Warriors* Shire Press, 1985.

Rivet, A. L. F. & C. Smith. *The Place-Names of Roman Britain* Batsford, 1979.

Robinson, H. R., *The Armour of Imperial Rome* Arms & Armour Press, 1976.

Ross, A. *The Pagan Celts* Batsford, 1986.

Scullard, H. H. *Roman Britain, Outpost of Empire* Thames & Hudson, 1979.

Smurthwaite, D. *Ordnance Survey Complete Guide to the Battlefields of Britain* Webb & Bower, 1984.

Spence, L. *Boadicea* Hale, 1937.

Tacitus *The Agricol & the Germania* (trans. H. Mattingly) Penguin, 1944.

Tacitus *The Annals* Books XIII–XVI (trans. J. Jackson) Loeb Classics.

Webster, G. *Boudica: The British Revolt against Rome AD 60* Batsford, 1978.

FIONN MAC CUMHAIL

CHAMPION OF IRELAND

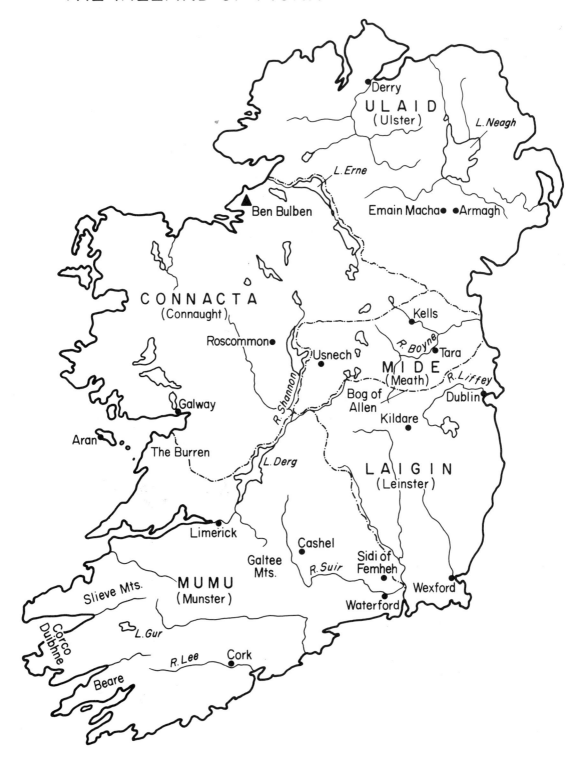

THE IRELAND OF FIONN

The Figure of Fionn

In Ireland, as well as in parts of Scotland today, people still speak of the hero Fionn mac Cumhail (Finn MacCool) as though his adventures had taken place only a few generations ago. Strange and wondrous tales are told of him: how, with his fearsome band of followers, the Fianna, he built the Giant's Causeway in a night; how he married a Faery Woman; and how he came to taste the flesh of the Salmon of Wisdom, from which he knew all things that were and had been and were yet to be. Others see him as a great and noble-hearted warrior of Ireland, whose deeds are recorded in the very substance of the land.

For the reality behind these tales, we have to turn to Ireland in the second and third centuries A.D., when the fierce and colourful Gaelic warriors lived, quarrelled and fought amid the hills and valleys and mountains. There Fionn, the warrior, chieftain, poet and seer saw his strange beginning; there gods and goddesses, the people of the *sidhe*, mingled with human men and women, and the border between the real world and the twilight realm of Faery was narrow and uncertain. In such times, you might meet an old woman on the road and only discover later that she was a goddess who held the sovereignty of the land as her lawful gift. Or the deer you were chasing might suddenly turn into a beautiful woman (as in the case of Fionn's wife Sadbh) only to vanish again, years later, as suddenly and unexpectedly as she had come.

In this world and in a time that was timeless, heroes like Fionn, or his son Oisin, or his grandson Oscar, or Cuchulainn, the 'Hound of Ulster', all moved in a twilight realm that was neither wholly real nor wholly imaginary. Questions of origin and historical status are still hotly debated. Yet beyond a certain point, an impenetrable wall is met with: history merges with myth and folk-lore, and the once bright figures become shadowy beings again.

Of Fionn himself, we have the following description, written down some 1,000 years after he may actually have lived, but still vibrant with the presence of a man who was as real to the writer as his own kith and kin.

And as to Finn himself, he was a king and a seer and a poet; a Druid and a knowledgeable man; and everything he said was sweet-sounding to his people. And a better fighting man than Finn never struck his hand into a king's hand, and whatever anyone ever said of him, he was three times better. And of his justice it used to be said, that if his enemy and his own son had come before him to be judged, it is a fair judgement he would have given between them.

And as to his generosity it used to be said, he never denied any man as long as he had mouth to eat with, and legs to bring away what he gave him; and he left no woman without her bride-price, and no man without his pay; and he never promised at night what he would not fulfil on the morrow, and he never promised in the day what he would not fulfil at night, and he never forsook his right-hand friend. And if he was quiet in peace he was angry in battle, and Oisin his son and Oscar his son's son followed him in that.

(trans: Lady Gregory)

History or Myth?

Contention still rages over the historicity of Fionn and the Fianna. Some hold them to be entirely mythical, a product of oral tradition and folk-lore; others say that Fionn was the historical captain of the warriors of King Cormac mac Art, High King of Ireland from 227–266 A.D.

According to the Annals of Ancient Ireland – written, it is true, long after the events they describe – Cumhail, Fionn's father, was the uncle of an earlier High King, Conn of the Hundred Battles. Conn's death is placed in the year 157, while Fionn's death is said to take place in 283 A.D., although the Battle of Gabhra, where he fell, is ascribed to a year later. These dates are close enough, and form a pattern sufficiently similar to establish a probable span for Fionn's life of the years 224–283 A.D., making him in his sixties at the time of his death and placing him firmly during the reign of Cormac.

The Fianna (Fionn's men), were a highly mobile, national militia, recruited from the war bands of the many local chieftains and Kings of Ireland – all serving, nominally, under the aegis of the High King at Tara. There seem to have been seven such bands, each consisting of some 3,000 men and a commander. Fionn, like his father Cumhail, began by commanding the men of Leinster and Meath – specifically the clan Bascna – but came in time to be captain of the whole Fianna, more than 20,000 men.

Their task was to protect Ireland's coastline from invasion, and to help keep the King's law or as the Annals of Clonmacnoise express it 'to uphold justice and to prevent injustice', as well as 'putting a stop to robbery, exacting the payment of tribute, putting down malefactors'. To do this successfully they were placed, in certain instances, outside the law, so that even their kin were unable to claim compensation in the event of the death of any one of the Fianna while on active service.

The setting up of this elite core of warriors is placed at the door of the King, Cormac mac Art, who is described as Ireland's first law-maker, and as conquerer of Alba (Scotland) and of most of Ireland itself. In the words of the unbiased chronicler of Clonmacnoise, he was:

Absolutely the best king that ever reigned in Ireland before himself . . . wise, learned, valiant and mild, not given causelessly to be bloody as many of his ancestors were; he reigned majestically and magnificently.

(trans: C. Mageoghagan)

None of this can be proved historically. Nevertheless, scholars have tended to accept it as probable, if not provable. Documents relating to the period are non-existent, and the later accounts, written down by monkish scribes hundreds of years later, are often inaccurate and contradictory.

The image which we derive from a reading of the cycles of stories relating to Fionn and Cormac may themselves be wide of the mark. That there was a High King in Tara may well have been recognised by all; but there were many who would not have acknowledged him or his right to command them, or to draw upon them to furnish men and arms for the Fianna.

A very similar situation existed in Britain some 300 years later, when fear of the invading Saxons caused the scattered and quarrelsome chieftains to band together under a leader who was neither a king nor owed allegiance to any one master. He too, like Fionn, commanded a band of dedicated soldiers, drawn from many areas of the country and also mobile by reason of their equestrian status.

The Giant's Causeway in Co. Antrim is said to have been built in one day by the 'giant' Fionn when he became tired of getting wet feet everytime he crossed to Scotland to steal cattle. This stems from a much later idea of the figure of Fionn.

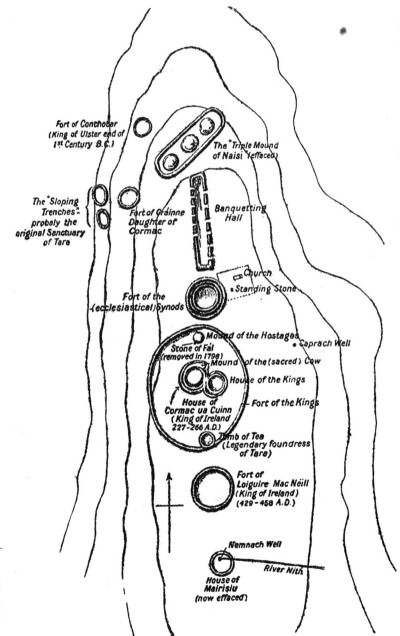

Fort of Conchobar
(King of Ulster end of
1st Century B.C.)

The "Triple Mound
of Naisi (effaced)

The "Sloping
Trenches"-
probaly the
original Sanctuary
of Tara

Fort of Gráinne
Daughter of
Cormac

Banquetting
Hall

Church

Standing Stone

Fort of the
(ecclesiastical) Synods

Mound of the Hostages

Caprach Well

Stone of Fál
(removed in 1798)

Mound of the (sacred) Cow

House of the Kings

House of
Cormac ua Cuinn
(King of Ireland
227-266 A.D.)

Fort of the Kings

Tomb of Tea
(Legendary foundress
of Tara)

Fort of
Loiguire Mac Néill
(King of Ireland)
(429-458 A.D.)

Nemnach Well

River Nith

House of
Mairişiu
(now effaced)

The principle sites of the Hill of Tara (after R.A.S. Macallister). Tara was the place of Kings for many generations before and after the Fianna, as the many archaeological remains still testify.

This man was Arthur, who like Fionn became mythologised into the towering figure of King Arthur, surrounded by his glittering Knights of the Round Table. With Arthur, it is clear that we are dealing with the memory of a remarkable man, whose legendary stature is a measure of his human qualities. Similarly, in the case of Fionn, there may well have been a real character, whose unique abilities enabled him to hold together a band of warriors from the many tribes, and then to command such loyalty from them that they became an unequalled force in the land.

Certainly, there is a roughness and humanity about the Fianna which make them far more believable than most heroes. Their stories take place in the open air, unlike the later Arthurian material which is more courtly in its setting. The Fianna's favourite pursuits were hunting, fighting and making love, and as we shall see in the stories retold later, they were not above placing personal safety above unnecessary heroics – despite their immense personal bravery. Fionn himself appeared so unwaveringly honest that he was often in trouble because of it: once he had given his word, we are told over and over again that 'he could not refuse' – not even if it meant, as it often did, putting himself and his men at great risk.

As with Arthur, we may never know the truth about Fionn. The best that can be said is that archaeological evidence points to a resurgence and consoli-

The King-mound at Tara. Here all of Ireland's high kings were installed, including Cormac mac Art, whom Fionn and the Fianna served.

103

dation in Ireland during the period of Cormac's reign. Also, we know that the attempts on the part of the Roman armies in Britain to infiltrate the Celtic kingdom across the narrow seas met with significant lack of success. Perhaps the numerous battles of Fionn against 'the King of the World' may recall his powerful repulsion of the most powerful fighting force then in existence.

Fionn's Ireland: third century A.D.

The Fionn cycle takes place in two worlds: that of the real Ireland and that of the otherworld, Tir-nan-Og or Tir-fa-Thon, the dwelling of the Lordly Ones. Between these two worlds, the free-ranging Fianna passed at will, their adventures taking them to and fro across the boundary of the unseen world at any time.

The reality of third century Ireland was a wild untamed land of forest, hill and marshland, teaming with game, birdlife and fish that stocked the rivers to bursting.

The people who lived there were farmers, Celts who had migrated from Europe almost a thousand years before. They kept cattle, pigs and goats, tilled the land and knew the arts of milling and weaving. They dressed in simple clothes dyed with bright colours, bathed frequently and cared about their appearance. They were a proud and warlike people, as their stories show, and they loved nothing better than to band together to raid their neighbours' lands for cattle and slaves. One of the most famous wars in their history began with such an event – the Cattle Raid of Cuailgne (Cooley) – in which Queen Medb (Maeve) of Connaught stole a famous bull from the lands of the Ulstermen and precipitated a conflict which involved Ireland's first great hero, Cuchulainn, and ended in his death.

The cow was, indeed, the basis of Ireland's economy until the eighth century, which finally saw the introduction of a coinage. By this standard, a cow was worth about an ounce of gold. Previously the measure was one cow to three slaves, usually female since these were believed to work harder and to be less likely to run away. The word for a female bondslave was *cumhal*, which caused at least one writer to assume that Fionn was the son of a slave! Burglary was virtually unknown, most local crime being based on the theft of cattle. After all, cattle could make a poor man rich overnight if he had the strength of arm to keep what he had acquired.

When they were not fighting, raiding or hunting, the people of Fionn's day lived in isolated farmsteads called forts – though these were not always intended for military use or defence. Circular, between 130 and 160 feet in diameter, they consisted of a flattened area surrounded by a bank and ditch set off with a wooden palisade. Within were several huts – depending on the size of the family – while the land outside the fence was cultivated, with the

livestock left to run free. Some 40,000 of these forts still exist in Ireland, where they are thought of as the dwelling places of the Faery people and are thus never ploughed or built over.

Chieftains and kings lived in larger versions of these forts, called *raths*. They were heavily defended and patrolled by warriors in constant readiness for attack. A system of roads connected these greater establishments and a law was enforced which said that they must be tended and kept open on three occasions; in winter, when the land became harsh and cruel; during time of war, when the movement of men was all important; and during the time of the horse-races – for then, as now, the Irish loved to hold races and to bet huge sums on their favourites.

There were something like 150 small kingdoms in Ireland at the time of Fionn and the Fianna. Each had its own ruler and, when allied, these formed a province under a greater king, who in turn owed allegiance to the High King – though this office was not really established until the beginning of the eighth century, some 500 years after the time of the Fianna.

Fionn's lord, Cormac mac Art (who was also, later, his father-in-law) was one of the first and greatest to claim the title. He established his capital at Tara and raised the Fianna from every province in the land, giving each lord a part in the defence of the realm while at the same time strengthening his own position.

The choice of Tara for the High King's seat was no accident. Ancient Ireland was divided into five provinces: Connaught (West), Ulster (North),

Staigue Fort, Co. Kerry, shown in a nineteenth century photograph. A circular rath of the kind once occupied by Irish chieftains during the period when the Fianna were active.

105

Leinster (East), Munster (South), Meath (Centre). Tara, traditionally the place of power where all true kings of Ireland were made, was in Meath. Geographically this is nowhere near the centre of the country, but mythologically it was correct.

By the same ancient system of division, the provinces were held responsible for the provision of certain skills among their inhabitants. Thus, Connaught was famed for its learning, Ulster for its warriors, Leinster for prosperity, Munster for music and Meath for kingship. Lists of the people and qualities expected to come out of these places – as though they grew there like cultivated crops – are still extant.

Tara itself, with its great hall, could offer hospitality to a hundred men in the style to which the Celts were accustomed: beer had to flow and meat had to be plentiful. Precise rules governed the seating arrangements of the guests, as they also governed the portions of meat they could be expected to receive. Thus, hunters received a pig's shoulder, as did harpists; while the King's fool, or his doorkeepers, got only chines. The seating plans from ancient manuscripts show both how complex were the rules, and how precise.

Despite his position as overlord of Tara, there were many who refused to accept Cormac's right to call himself High King. He had to establish his right through conquest initially, and even with the support of the Fianna, his tenure was never a strong one. Nonetheless, like all the High Kings then and after, he accepted the complex system of laws governing his occupations and duties. As an ancient manuscript puts it:

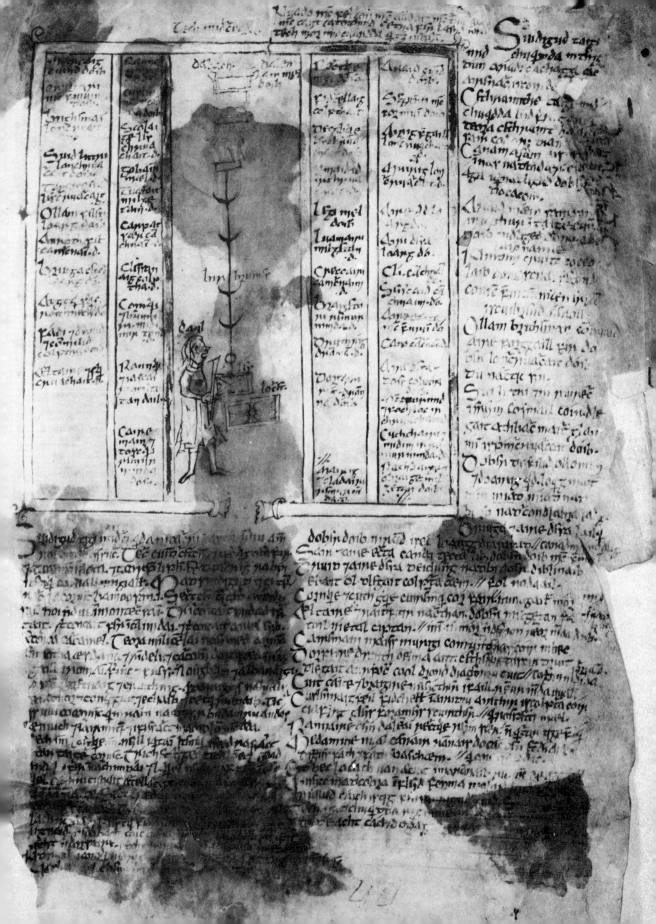

The fact that two out of the seven are given over to law-making and only one to lovemaking indicates the importance of the former to the Celtic people – indeed they were among the first Western cultures to develop an intricate system of laws governing daily life.

Warriors and Weapons

The Celtic warriors were amongst the fiercest and most terrifying of the ancient world. Their culture gave the warrior pride of place and expected him to perform bravely at all times. He often went into battle naked, both from bravado and as a magical act in which he expected to be protected by his gods. With his hair whitened with lime, combed into fantastic shapes, his body patterned with tattoos, he always attacked furiously, screaming his war shout or chanting extravagant boasts of his own past deeds of bravery.

The Celts were also headhunters, believing the head to be the seat of the soul, possession of which lent strength to oneself. Accounts of warriors with belts of skulls, severed heads decorating their chariots and horse harnesses abound. In earlier times, there had been a widespread use of the chariot in which the warriors would career up and down in front of their enemies, flinging spears or shouting insults until they were met by a champion from the opposing side. The Fianna, however, never seem to have used chariots. They were light-clad, mobile and ranged freely across the country on their swift horses, dismounting to give battle with swords and spears.

These weapons were of iron, long and heavy-bladed swords with bronze hilts made in three parts – guard, grip and pommel. They were an improvement over the earlier bronze-bladed weapons which tended to be more flexible. We hear of warriors straightening these beneath their feet during battle. The average sword was 3 feet in length with the hilt being some 6 inches of this. Blades tended to be about 2½ inches broad, tapering to $1\frac{7}{8}$ inches. They were used to cut and hack rather than to stab, and were carried in bronze sheaths with bronze chapes, which enabled their users to hold the scabbard behind one knee and draw the sword forth one-handed, whilst holding their shield with the other. Later, shorter swords became the fashion, worn slung across the upper part of the body. The Fianna would probably have used both kinds.

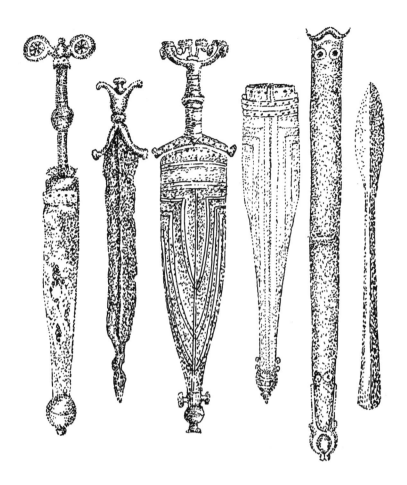

Knives, some with bone-hilts, others with bronze, were also carried, though not everyone would have used both knives and swords. Spears were long, slender-shafted with heavy warheads, some consisting of a central spike with several sharp phalanges opening out from the central blade. These went into the body easily but always tore on being drawn out. Slings would also have been used, though less frequently than sword and spear; and there are stories of balls made from the brains of enemies being used as sling-shots.

There was little armour of any kind, mail shirts being exceedingly rare and expensive. Leather shirts and breeches, some oversown with plates of metal or waxed linen, would have been worn by the wealthier warriors. However, to wear armour of any kind would have militated against the Celtic warrior's sense of honour.

Fionn is described as preparing for the Battle of Gabhra as follows:

Then rose the royal chief of the *fiana* of Ireland and Scotland and of the Saxons and Britons, of Lewis and Norway and of the hither islands, and put on his battle-dress of combat and contest, even a thin, silken shirt of wonderful, choice satin of the fair-cultivated Land of

(Opposite and above) *a selection of Celtic weapons coming from many different sites and periods. This array indicates the variety and artistic qualities instilled by the Celts into their tools of war.*

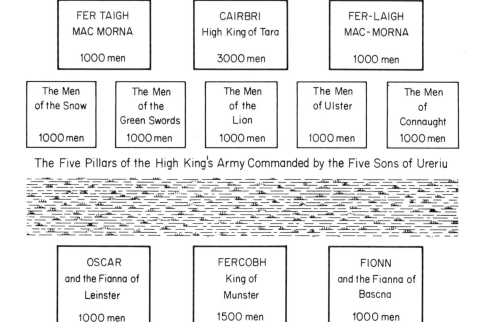

FER TAIGH MAC MORNA 1000 men		CAIRBRI High King of Tara 3000 men		FER-LAIGH MAC-MORNA 1000 men
The Men of the Snow 1000 men	The Men of the Green Swords 1000 men	The Men of the Lion 1000 men	The Men of Ulster 1000 men	The Men of Connaught 1000 men

The Five Pillars of the High King's Army Commanded by the Five Sons of Ureriu

OSCAR and the Fianna of Leinster 1000 men	FERCOBH King of Munster 1500 men	FIONN and the Fianna of Bascna 1000 men

Plan of the Battle of Gabhra, which took place in 297 A.D. on high moorland near the Hill of Gabhra in Co. Meath. This depiction is based on surviving manuscript sources and on records of the names of those who fought. Whether the battle actually took place at this site and in this manner can neither be proved nor disproved.

Promise over the face of his white skin; and outside over that he put his twenty-four waxed, stout shirts of cotton, firm as a board, about him, and on the top of those he put his beautiful, plaited, three-meshed coat of mail of cold refined iron, and around his neck his graven gold-bordered breastplate, and about his waist he put a stout corslet with a decorated, firm belt with gruesome images of dragons, so that it reached from the thick of his thighs to his arm-pit, whence spears and blades would rebound. And his stout-shafted martial five-edged spears were placed over against the king, and he put his gold-hafted sword in readiness on his left, and he grasped his broad-blue, well-ground Norse lance, and upon the arched expanse of his back he placed his emerald-tinted shield with flowery designs and with variegated, beautiful bosses of pale gold, and with delightful studs of bronze, and with twisted stout chains of old silver; and to protect the hero's head in battle he seized his crested, plated, four-edged helmet of beautiful, refined gold with bright, magnificent, crystal gems and with flashing, full-beautiful, precious stones which had been set in it by the hands of master-smiths and great artists.

(*Fianaigecht* trans: Kuno Meyer)

Helmets varied in form, but were at base a bronze cap with horns or peaks added. At the Battle of Mucrine (250 A.D.), some were described as 'crested' – perhaps in the likeness of Roman helmets which some well-travelled mercenaries would have seen. Shields, either oblong or round, were made from wicker work or hide. These were strengthened by strips of iron and bronze, and sometimes had a central boss which could be highly decorated.

Other weapons included battle-axes, used for throwing or hand-to-hand combat; and bronze or iron-tipped maces, often with elaborately carved hilts.

Weapons were sharpened on a ceremonial whetstone known as the 'Pillar of Combat' which was also struck in time of war or to announce single combat. It was set up outside the King's hall on the green.

Bronze helmet crest in the shape of a boar, showing the kind of beast often hunted by the Fianna. One such, the Boar of Ben Bulben, caused the death of Diarmuid O'Duibne, the greatest of Fionn's heroes.

War bands such as the Fianna all comprised three classes of men, who were bound by law to give a certain number of days' weapon-service to their king or overlord. These formed the main part of the war band, but were supplemented by the mercenaries which the king maintained at a fixed rate of pay. These were drawn from many places, including Britain and Scandinavia, and were much hated by the irregular soldiery, who, in most cases, did their stint of service and hurried home to wife and harvest. Men of uncertain allegiance would sometimes be paired with a 'safe' man in battle, often being yoked to him by the leg!

The King had an *aire-echta*, or champion, who avenged family insults or murders, and who was responsible, in time of war, for guarding the most vulnerable passes into the King's domain. He had five men to serve under him, while the King himself had a personal guard (*lucht-tighe*) of personal warriors.

Female warriors were not unknown among the Celts, though they seem to have primarily served in the capacity of trainers. Many of the greatest heroes were taught by women: Cuchulainn by Scathach, who ran a kind of warrior-school; Fionn by Liath, whose training methods included throwing him into deep water, to teach him how to swim, and racing with him until whoever was the faster would strike the loser with a peeled wand. Women also seem to have cared for the sick and those too old or severely wounded to fight. Hostels for the sick were administered at public expense.

As part of their task was the defence of Ireland's coast, the Fianna had an intricate system of look-outs and signals posted at clifftop, ford and passes of strategic importance. Signals were passed by relays of runners (often women) or by beacon-fires at night. The Fianna could thus be at the site of an attack in record time. Battles were often very organised affairs, joined by mutual agreement on certain days and at specified times.

Although this decorated Iron Age scabbard dates from a period several hundred years before Fionn, the stylized images of mounted warriors give a good idea of how the Fianna may well have looked.

III

Camps must have resembled impromptu fairgrounds, such as the Irish erected at certain festival times, everything ordered in streets of booths or tents with the King's tent set on an eminence and trenches with palisades thrown up round the whole.

Before battle, each warrior took a stone and these were piled in cairns. Afterwards, those stones not claimed enabled the number of the dead to be calculated.

Thus, the Fianna kept Ireland safe and law-abiding throughout their existence. Despite our lack of detailed historical knowledge, we can say without doubt that they must have been one of the finest bands of fighting men ever to have existed.

This short sword is a product of the Celtic Hallstatt culture. It would have been carried by a nobleman of the kind who served with the Fianna.

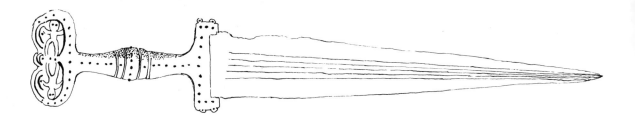

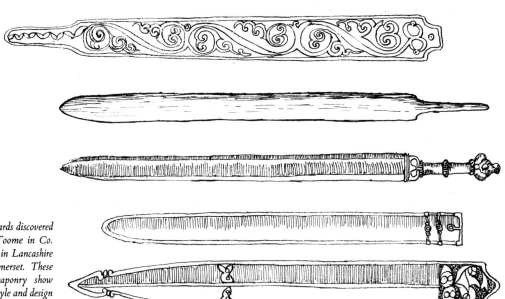

Swords and scabbards discovered as far apart as Toome in Co. Antrim, Worton in Lancashire and Mere in Somerset. These examples of weaponry show how defined the style and design became during the Celtic era.

The Fianna were the greatest hunters in Ireland, famed for their horsemanship and courage in the chase. The greatest of all the hunters was Fionn himself, here in the act of spearing his quarry, his favourite hounds by his side.

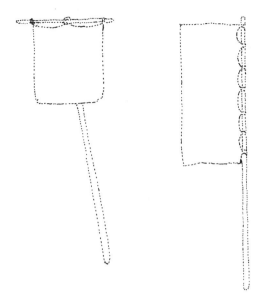

The Heroes of the Fianna

Nothing quite like the Fianna has existed before or since. Unlike other war bands of the time they were drawn from every province and part of Ireland. The owed allegiance only to Fionn (though they must in fact have existed before, since Fionn's father Cumhail was their commander before him) and through him to the High King. But they did not spend all the year fighting; from Beltain to Samhain (April to October) they hunted and lived off the land, seldom remaining in one place more than a few nights. The rest of the year, they were liable to be billeted on noble or freeborn people without charge – part of their wages for the protection of the land. What their regular wages were is not recorded, though Fionn once speaks of giving one man 'three times fifty ounces of gold and silver in one day'.

Certainly they were well clothed:

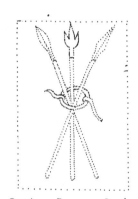

Oscar's Banner Squab Ghabhaidh *Terrible Sheaf.*

And there were fifty of the best sewing-women in Ireland brought together in a rath on Magh Feman, under the charge of a daughter of the king of Britain, and they used to be making clothing for the Fianna through the whole of the year. And three of them, that were king's daughters, used to be making music for the rest on a little silver harp; and there was a very great candle-stick of stone in the middle of the rath, for they were not willing to kindle a fire more than three times a year for fear the smoke and the ashes might harm the needlework.

(*Gods and Fighting Men*: Gregory)

Goll Mac Morna's Banner Fulang Doghra *Prop of Lamentation.*

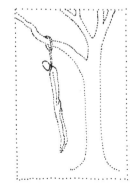

Though they were thus well cared for, the Fianna lived a wandering life, rarely staying in one place more than a few days. For this reason, there are many places in Ireland and Scotland which are associated with the Fianna – yet few large fortresses or sites carry their name. Fionn himself had his headquarters at the Hill of Almu (or Allan) in Kildare, though there are no signs today of the fortified Dunn from which the Fianna once rode to hunt and battle. From there, riding in small bands, the whole of Ireland and much

Diarmuid, Fotla and Conan Maol held the Ford of the Quicken Trees against hundreds of Fionn's enemies, whilst he and the rest of the Fianna were kept in enchanted imprisonment in the Hostel of the Quicken Trees.

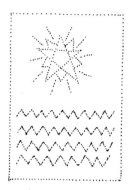

Diarmuid O'Duibne's Banner Loch Luinneach *The Lively Light.*

Oisin's Banner Dun Naomhtha *Sacred Citadel.*

Fionn's Banner Dealbh Ghreine *Image of the Sun.*

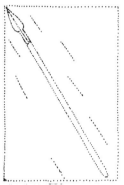

The Raighne Clan's Banner Aoincheannach Oir *The Single-headed Golden One.*

of Scotland was their province – though they remained always ready to answer the *Diord Fionn*, the Call of Fionn.

Many of the Fianna were of otherworldy origin – strange folk who came to take service with Fionn mac Cumhail for a year, and who at the end of that time vanished again into the mists of Tir-nan-Og. People like Dubh, Agh, and Ilar (Black, Battle and Eagle) who undertook as Gregory says to 'do the watching for all the Fianna of Ireland and of Alban' or to 'take the weight of every fight and every battle that will come their way'. While the third offered to 'meet every troublesome thing that might come to my master . . . And I have a pipe with me . . . and all the men of the world would sleep at the sound of it, and they in their sickness.'

Among the most famous of the Fianna were Caoilte mac Ronan, Fionn's nephew, who was famed for his swiftness of foot – at full speed he appeared like three men and could overtake the March wind. There was also Diarmuid ui Duibhne who 'never knew weariness of foot, nor shortness of breath, nor, whether in going out or coming in, ever flagged.' He also possessed a beauty spot which made him irresistible to women. Another, Conan Maol, began as an enemy of the Fianna and had to pay a fine for his part in the death of Fionn's father. Later he joined the Fianna but continued to mock them with his 'foul-mouthed tongue'. Goll mac Morna was also Fionn's enemy at the start, but he relinquished the leadership of the Fianna in Fionn's favour and became his faithful follower. His huge and cheerful humour was famed among all the company of the Fianna.

These and many more made up the great company, whose motto was:

> Truth in our hearts.
> Strength in our hands.
> Consistency in our tongues.

Requirements for admission to the Fianna were rigorous and demanding. Among other tests the would-be applicant had to be able to leap over a pole held at head high and knee high without breaking stride, pull a thorn from his heel while running across rough country, and to dodge spears hurled at him by a ring of warriors while he was half buried in the earth. Small wonder

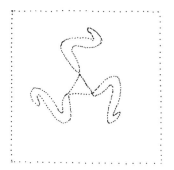

Mac Ronan's Banner Lamh Dhearg
Red Hand.

Caoilte's Banner Tri Chosa
Three Legs.

Faolan's Banner Coinneal
Chatha *Torch of Battle.*

that the Fianna were the finest body of fighting men in Ireland and Scotland, who were never defeated until their enemies banded together to overthrow them at the battle of Gabhra in the year 284.

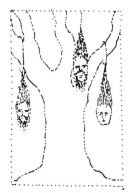

The Heritage of Story

The stories of Fionn and his heroes are as old as the hills of Ireland, though they were not in fact written down until the early Middle Ages. Before that they circulated orally. When the Irish Gaels (called *Scotti*) infiltrated into the West of Scotland (then the dwelling-place of the Picts) in the first century A.D. they took with them the tales of Fionn mac Cumhail. So, in time these stories came to be as much a part of Scottish Highland folklore as that of Ireland.

The Mac Lugach Clan's Banner Graobh Fhuileach *The Bloody Tree.*

By the tenth century, when the great hero-cycle of Cuchulainn and the Red Branch Knights was first being recorded, tales of Fionn were being told by the common people by the fireside all over Ireland. These stories were to them what the tales and songs of Robin Hood were to the Saxon peasants in England a hundred years later. They have continued to be told and retold right into the present – with new stories still being added in Scotland and Ireland as late as the nineteenth century.

Literary references began to appear around the eleventh century, and in the twelfth this blossomed into a fully fledged series of ballads about Fionn and his warrior band. This shows parallels between the Robin Hood ballads already mentioned, the Arthurian cycle, and the Homeric ballads upon which the Greek poet based his great works the *Illiad* and the *Odyssey*.

By the sixteenth century, new stories were being written, and Fionn's fame had outstripped that of other, once more famous heroes. But Fionn's greatest moment came in the eighteenth century, when the Scottish poet James Macpherson (1736–1796) wrote a series of epic poems based on the stories of Oisin (Fionn's son) and the hero he called Fingal. Had he chosen simply to publish these under his own name they might have vanished without trace. Instead, however, he elected to pass them off as translations from the ancient Scots and Irish Gaelic. This so excited the antiquary-mad populace of the time that these books became best sellers and placed the name of Fionn and Oisin in the minds of a vast number of readers. Both Napoleon and Goethe loved to read these stirring tales, believing them to be real. Indeed, they caused such a revival of interest in ancient Celtic stories that they inadvertently touched off what was to become known as the Celtic Twilight, a literary movement which attracted writers as varied as Matthew Arnold, W. B. Yeats, Fiona Macleod and Lady Augusta Gregory, to whom we owe our own present day knowledge of the Fionn cycle.

Macpherson's forgeries, for such they were in time recognized to be, touched off such a furore in literary circles that people almost came to blows as they alternately attacked or defended the poet's scholarship. In fact, Macpherson had used some original sources for his work, adapting and altering them to suit the taste of the time – just as all the many story-tellers had done since the time of the Fianna.

Today, the Fionn cycle is possibly the least well known of the great mythical cycles. Yet its range is as wide as any of the tales of Arthur, Cuchulainn, Charlemagne or Sigurd. There are stories of heroism to be sure, but there are stories which contain elements of high comedy, high tragedy, magic and love. The story of Diarmuid and Grainne and their flight across Ireland from the wrath of Fionn is one of the great love stories of all time, and certainly influenced the composition of its more famous sibling story of Tristan and Isolt in the Arthurian saga. The magic, rich and otherworldly, is of a high quality – we may think of the intervention of Angus Og in the Diarmuid saga, or the coming of Niamh of the Golden Hair – or indeed of Oisin's sojourn in the Land of Youth and his strange meeting with the monk Patrick. There are tales of honour and treachery, truth and falsehood, strength and weakness; subtle stories and stories written out of the passionate soul of the Gaels.

The early stories of the Fianna written in christian times show an easy-going fellowship and understanding between pagan and christian, with Oisin and St Patrick swapping stories and the latter having the deeds of Fionn recorded in his monastery. Later, this decayed into ill-feeling and almost buffoonish characteristics in which Oisin can say that if he saw his son Oscar fighting with God and saw Oscar fall then he would have to admit that God was the stronger of the two! In this way the stories of Fionn parallel the changes which took place in Ireland over the centuries. Yet they remained a guide to the earliest times and enshrined within them the memory of the people, without which no land is called living. In a text called *Acallam na Senorach* (the Colloquy of the Ancients) composed around 1200 A.D., many of the stories of Fionn are combined into a rich tapestry. Oisin and Caoilte, supposedly still living in the fifth century, travel about Ireland with the Saint,

These two Gaulish images of Celtic hair styles give an excellent idea of the care and attention lavished by the Celtic warrior class on their appearance. Beards were neatly trimmed and hair dressed to the best effect.

and at every place they visit recall another story of the Fianna. In this way, the stories and associations with places are enshrined in a form that ensures they will be remembered for at least as long as the stories are read and retold.

In another text, this is taken a step further. Caoilte, who was famed for his swiftness of foot, has to rescue Fionn from the clutches of a king, and he is given the seemingly impossible task of finding two of every animal and bird in Ireland and bringing them to the king's court. He does so – not without some difficulty even for a hero of Caoilte's stature, and in the text we find a list of the creatures and the places where he found them. The ancient names become like a song, chanted by a bard before the kings of ancient Ireland, and the land itself rises before our eyes as we listen to the great catalogue of names:

It is with the flocks of birds he began, though they were scattered in every part, and from them he went on to the beasts. And he gathered together two of every sort, two ravens from Fiodh da Bheann; two wild ducks from Loch na Seillein; two foxes from Slieve Cuilinn; two wild oxen from Burren; two swans from blue Dobhran; two owls from the wood of Faradhruim; two polecats from the branchy wood on the side of Druim da Raoin, the Ridge of the Victories; two gulls from the strand of Loch Leith; four woodpeckers from white Brosna; two plovers from Carraigh Dhain; two thrushes from Leith Lomard; two wrens from Dun Aoibh; two herons from Corrain Cleibh; two eagles from Carraig of the stones; two hawks from Fiodh Chonnach; two sows from Loch Meilghe; two water-hens from Loch Erne; two moorhens from Monadh Maith; two sparrow-hawks from Dubhloch; two stonechats from Magh Cuillean; two tomtits from Magh Tuaillainn, two swallows from Sean Abhla; two cormorants from Aith Cliath; two wolves from Broit Cliathach; two blackbirds from the Strand of the Two Women; two roebucks from Luachair Ire; two pigeons from Ceas Chuir; two nightingales from Leiter Ruadh; two starlings from green-sided Teamhair; two rabbits from Sith Dubh Donn; two wild pigs from Cluaidh Chuir; two cuckoos from Drom Daibh; two lapwings from Leanain na Furraich; two woodcocks from Craobh Ruadh; two hawks from the Bright Mountain; two grey mice from Luimneach; two otters from the Boinn; two larks from the Great Bog; two bats from the Cave of the Nuts; two badgers from the province of Ulster; two landrail from the banks of the Sionnan; two wagtails from Port Lairrge; two curlews from the harbour of Gallimh; two hares from Muirthemne; two deer from Sith Buidhe; two peacocks from Magh Mell; two cormorants from Ath Cliath; two eels from Duth Dur; two goldfinches from Slieve na-n Eun; two birds of slaughter from Magh Bhuilg; two bright swallows from Granard; two redbreasts from the Great Wood; two rock-cod from Cala Chairge; two sea-pigs from the great sea; two wrens from Mios an Chuil; two salmon from Eas Mhic Muirne; two clean deer from Gleann na Smoil; two cows from Magh Mor; two cats from the Cave of Cruachan; two sheep from bright Sidhe Diobhlain; two pigs of the pigs of the son of Lir; a ram and a crimson sheep from Innis.

Such is the power of the Fionn saga to move and transport us to other times

A bronze cult chariot from Spain depicting a mounted huntsman with hound in pursuit of a boar. The Fianna were great hunters and spent much of their time in the chase.

117

and other places, where the old magic of the Celts still lives on and where we find ourselves entering another kind of world – one where the old values and strengths of the heroes may be ours for a while, and perhaps enable us to view our own world with new eyes.

Fionn's Magic

It used to be said that Fionn had wisdom and knowledge far beyond that of ordinary mortals, and there are three tales which tell how he came by it. In the first of these a man of the *sidhe*, the Faery People, stole food from the Fianna, for which insult and nuisance Fionn gave chase. But while he was in pursuit of the man, he saw a woman of the *sidhe*, who had come out of the mound to fetch water. When she saw Fionn she too fled, so that he gave chase to her also. But she was too quick for Fionn and reached the safety of the mound. But Fionn was so close behind her that as the gates of the Faery Hill closed shut, he caught his thumb in the crack of the door. So great was the pain and so sudden, that Fionn pulled his thumb back and put it into his mouth. But because his thumb had been in the Otherworld, even if only for a moment, from this came all his knowledge.

On another occasion Fionn was hunting near the Well of the Moon, that was watched over by three women of Faery, the daughters of Beag son of Buan. The well supposedly had the power to grant knowledge which was not for ordinary men. Thus as Fionn came closer and closer, the three women ran out to distract him and prevent him coming near the well. One of the women happened to be carrying a jar of water, and she threw this at Fionn to stop him coming any further. Some of the water went into his mouth in that moment, and it is supposed that all knowledge came to him.

The third story is told later elsewhere in this book but again the outcome is the same: Fionn acquires wisdom by supernatural means, and has thereafter only to put his thumb or two fingers into his mouth to receive instant illumination.

The story is an ancient one – a similar account is given of the Welsh poet Taliesin, who happened to receive three drops of the Brew of Inspiration from the cauldron of the Sow-Goddess Ceridwen. Taliesin became the greatest poet of the age and was famed for his wisdom. Fionn's knowledge however is more gnomic, more homely, as in this example, where he gives advice to a would-be champion of the Fianna:

If you have a mind to be a good champion, be quiet in a great man's house; . . . do not beat your hound without a cause; do not bring a charge against your wife without having knowledge of her guilt; do not hurt a fool in fighting, for he is without his wits. Do not find fault with high-up persons; do not stand up to take part in a quarrel; have no dealings with a bad man or a foolish man. Let two-thirds of your gentleness be showed to women and to little children that are creeping on the floor, and to men of learning that make the poems, and do not be rough with the common people . . . Do not threaten or speak big words, for it is a shameful thing to speak stiffly unless you carry it out afterwards'. . . Do not be a bearer of lying stories, or a tale-bearer of lying stories, or a tale-bearer that is always chattering . . .

(trans: Lady Gregory)

Perhaps nowhere in ancient literature has more sound advice than this been given. It is unique to Fionn and is part of the enduring fascination of the cycle.

Among the Celts there were said to be three kinds of wisdom or poetic utterance, and with their love of codifying things they classed them under specific headings. There was *Teinm Laida* (illumination of song); *Imbas Farosna* (knowledge which illumines); and *Dichetual Dichennaib* (extemporary incantation or incantation from the ends of the fingers). Much speculation has been lavished on the exact meaning of these terms. *Teinm Laida* seems to relate to inspired utterance, possibly in trance, of the kind practised by poets. *Imbas Farosna* may be devination by way of the poet's wand, whereas *Dichetual Dichennaib* seems to refer to the insertion of two or more fingers in the mouth, clearly the same action as that performed by Fionn when he wishes to know something. Another method was the placing of the hands in a certain fashion on the poet's staff, which performs much the same function as that of the wizard or magician – poetry and magic being still indistinguishable at this time.

One explanation may lead us to ogham, an ancient form of writing consisting of groups of marks placed at intervals along a straight edge. They are found carved on stones all over Ireland and Scotland. There were many kinds of ogham, which was also associated with magic and poetry. Finger ogham was a kind of sign language which enabled poets to talk to each other without being detected. Ogham carved on wooden sticks seems reminiscent of *Imbas Farosna* and may be the origin of this mysterious method of acquiring knowledge.

Newgrange is one of the finest ancient sites in Ireland. Although it dates from a period many hundreds of years before Fionn, it was still in use as a sacred site. This was how the Fianna envisaged the dwelling places of the Tuatha de Danaan – the Sidhs or Hollow Hills of legend. Newgrange of Brugh na Boyne was the home of Aengus mac Og, the Otherworldly patron of Diarmuid.

Fionn seems always to have used his own skills wisely and well, and his wisdom becomes a bright thread running through the tapestry of the deeds of the Fianna.

*　　*　　*

It is time now to tell some of those stories, for in no other way can we come to know and understand the magic they wield, which has kept their memory green in the lives of story-tellers from their own time to this. In retelling these stories of the Fianna there is a deliberate attempt, as far as possible, to preserve the feel and spirit of the originals, occasionally quoting from earlier translations. However, in keeping with all storytelling, individual touches are added, and much has had to be omitted, since to tell all the stories would require a book several times the length of this one.

Oisin and St Patrick

One day the monk Patrick came to the Hostel of the Red Ridge to say Mass, and while he was chanting the orisons some people came to him and said: 'There is a wonder that you should see.' They took Patrick to a little smoky bothy nearby and showed him the man that lay sleeping within. A great warrior he seemed, larger in limb than any man there, for all that his hair and beard were white and his body heavy with age. At his side lay a great sword with a broad iron blade and a hilt of bronze, and leaning against the wall of the bothy was a long straight-shafted spear with a heavy head and a shield of the finest hide with bosses of iron. By the side of that lay his great war-cap of leather strengthened with bronze.

'Whence came this man?' asked Patrick, and the people told him that he had come riding out of the mists one morning on a great tall horse and had offered to move a great stone that lay in the middle of a field, that not ten of their own number could move. And in so doing he broke the girth of his horse and fell to the earth, at which the people witnessed a great change, for until that moment he had seemed to them a hero in the finest flower of his days, but when he arose from the earth he was as he now seemed, a hoary old man, still stronger than most of them, but deep in years. Since that moment he had not spoken a word, but had lain in the hut with his face turned to the wall.

It seemed to Patrick that he had heard tell of warriors such as this, and that they had lived in pagan times, so he decided to question the man, and entering the hut he awoke him.

'I am Patrick, and I serve the Christ. By what name are you known?'

'I am Oisin, son of Fionn, whom I serve. I am one of the Fianna of Ireland.'

Patrick looked at the old warrior in amazement. 'I have heard of the Fianna' he said, 'but it is more than three centuries since they were in Ireland.'

'Then it is true,' said the warrior. 'They are all dead and I am the last of the Fianna' and he wept for a long while.

At length he raised his head and asked: 'I would know of this time in which I find myself, for it seems unlike the days when I was young.'

'I shall be happy to tell you,' answered Patrick. 'But first I would have you tell me how you have lived these past three hundred years, when all of your kin lie dead?'

'That is soon told,' said Oisin sadly, and he spoke at length of the days of the Fianna and how he had come to love Niamh, a woman of the *sidhe*, the Lordly Ones who live in the land of Tir-nan-Og. And on a time she had come for him, to take him to her own land and people, taking him up on the back of a steed as white as milk.

'And fast as were the horses of the Fianna, the mount of Niamh was faster, and in truth it seemed that the earth fell away beneath its hooves, and that when we reached the sea it did not pause but galloped over the tops of the waves as though they were a hard roadway. Many were the wonders we saw,' said Oisin. 'Cities and courts and palaces of silver and gold that seemed to float above the sea: and deer running hard with a red-eared, white-bodied hound following on. At another time, coming towards us, we saw a woman on a black horse who had a golden apple in her right hand. And following after her a youth on a white horse who wore a crimson cloak and carried a sword of gold. And they passed us on the right hand. But in time we came to the land of youth itself, and of that I must speak either no words at all, or continue talking for all the days that are left to me. So I will but say that it is always green spring and golden summer there, and no sickness is there, nor

The Kells High Cross in Co. Meath shows the crucifixion and the wounding of Christ by the spear of Longinus, the centurion. Christianity overlaid many aspects of pagan Ireland; whatever was loved and respected of the old order was assimilated into the new ways. The stories of Fionn and his Fianna were no exception. Oisin's return from the Other-world of pagan Ireland into the newly Christian land of Patrick's conversion enabled these stories to be widely transcribed.

death, and the folk who dwell there are perilously fair, and garbed in finest silk and with gold upon them, heavy at neck and wrist.

'There I stayed, and it seemed to me that only a year passed, which I spent with Niamh of the golden hair. Then upon a time I took thought of Fionn my father and of my companions, and the need arose in me to see them again. And Niamh looked upon me sadly and bade her women prepare her steed. ''For'' she said, ''I see that I cannot keep you here. But only remember this, that when you are come again into the land of Ireland, do not dismount or let your foot so much as touch the earth, lest you see me no more nor return to Tir-nan-Og.''

'So I mounted upon the milk white steed and returned as I had come, riding the tops of the waves as though they were a road; and I saw again the woman with the golden apple, followed by the youth with the scarlet cloak, but this time they were coming towards the Land of Youth, and passed me upon the left hand.

'So at last I came to the shore of Ireland and it seemed changed. I rode everywhere in search of the Fianna, until I came to this place and chanced to set foot on the earth. Until that moment I had been in the brightness of my youth; but from that moment I have been as you see me now. And the white steed of Tir-nan-Og turned and galloped away from me, back, as I believe, to the place where Niamh of the golden hair awaited him.

'So you have my story, Talkend' said Oisin, calling Patrick by the name which means 'shaven one'.

Patrick sat in silence a long while, thinking of all that he had heard, and then he said: 'Come with me, Oisin son of Fionn, and when you are in my house we shall talk more of these things.'

And so Oisin accompanied Patrick upon the road back to his monastery, and as they walked the two men by turn talked and were silent, and in that time they found the beginning of a friendship between them, and when the two angels that were Patrick's guardians visited him at night, they told him there was no evil in the ancient warrior. So that when they came at last to Ard Macha, Patrick gave over a wattled cell to Oisin, and spent many days and some nights in talk with him.

He found the warrior willing enough to listen to stories of the Christ and his Disciples, though there was no inclining in him towards following the new faith. And if at times they spoke harshly together because of this, at others they talked as friends.

In time Patrick ordered one of his scribes to leave off his work transcribing the Gospels into the Irish tongue and instead to write down the stories of the Fianna: 'For there is a great wisdom in this Fionn, even though he was a pagan, and such things should not be forgotten in Ireland, less it should become a lesser place.'

And of the stories that Oisin told, that the monk of Ard Macha wrote down, these are some that are told again in this time and this place, lest we also become smaller people, and forget what once was.

The Boyhood Deeds of Fionn

Fionn's father, Cumhail, was the first captain of the Fianna, but he was slain in battle by the sons of Morna. Muirne, Fionn's mother, took her small son, that was but a few months old, to the woods of Sleive Bladhma to be cared for by two women, Bodhmall the Druidess and the Liath Luachra, who was both a warrior and a teacher of warriors.

And Fionn saw his mother only once again, when he was six years old, but otherwise he saw no people at all save his two guardians, and they taught him wisdom and strength, which are the two attributes of all heroes. And when he was come to his youngmanhood they taught him to run and found him fleet of foot and sure in his going. And they taught him to swim, and found him at home there in the water as a fish; and on another time they took him into a field where there were hares and instructed him to let none escape from there. And none did, so that they declared him a worthy champion, though he had as yet fought no battle except in trial against Liath Luachra.

At last his guardians said that he must go away: 'For the Sons of Morna are seeking abroad to kill you.' And Fionn learned all the truth of his parentage and went into Connacht in search of Crimhall, his father's brother, that was believed to live there.

On the way he fell in with some youths who were swimming in a lake, and he outswam them all in contest, for which they were displeased. But one among them saw how fair he seemed in his body and called him *fionn* which means 'fair', and thus he came by that name, for until that time he had none.

Then Fionn went into Carraighe and took service with a king who all unknown to him had married his mother. And one night he played chess with the king and won seven games together. Then the king looked at him narrowly and said: 'You are the son of Cumhail, that was lord of the Fianna. I bid you depart, for I wish not to have it said that you were killed while under my protection.'

So Fionn travelled on, still searching for Crimhall, and it chanced that he met a woman who wept tears of blood for the death of her son at the hands of a great warrior who dwelled nearby. So Fionn went up against this champion and slew him, thus fighting his first fight, and the man he slew had been the first to strike a blow at his father Cumhail, and had carried off his treasure bag.

Now this bag was made of crane skin and contained many magical items and much wisdom besides. When he had it Fionn knew by its aid how to find Crimhall, who was living with the last of the old Fianna who had refused to serve under the Sons of Morna. They knew him at once when they saw him, for he had the look of Cumhail about him, and bore the crane-bag. Very glad they were to see him and swore that they would follow him only.

But Fionn had a thirst now for the knowledge he had tasted through the magic of the crane-bag, so he went to take service with a poet and seer named Finegas, who lived by the side of the Boinne river. But Fionn did not use his own name; he took that of Deimne, and for seven years he remained with Finegas, learning all that he had to teach.

Now Finegas had stayed there by the side of the Boinne, watching for the day when he would catch the Salmon of Wisdom, for there was a prophecy that said he would eat of it. And at last, when Fionn had been with him just five years, he caught it and gave it to his young apprentice to cook. 'But see that you eat none of the flesh,' he said.

After a time, Fionn came with the cooked fish and the old poet looked at him and said: 'Have you eaten any of the fish?'

Fionn shook his head. 'No – but as I was cooking it I burned my thumb and put it into my mouth to ease the pain.'

Then Finegas gave him the whole fish and said, 'Your name is not Deimne, it is Fionn, and it was of you that the prophecy spoke.'

So Fionn ate all of the fish and had of it all the knowledge of the nine hazels of wisdom from beside the Well of Wonder that is beneath the sea. And thereafter he had only to put his thumb into his mouth to know whatever thing he wished, because of which he became known throughout Ireland – not only for his strength, but also for his wisdom.

Now that he was come into the fulness of his manhood, Fionn went straight to the High King, Cormac mac Art, at his hall in Tara and announced that he was the son of Cumhail, come to claim his place in the Fianna and to serve Cormac. And though the Sons of Morna murmured amongst themselves – especially Goll, the eldest, who was now the captain of the Fianna, Cormac smiled upon the young hero and took him into his service.

*   *   *

Now this was near the time of Samhain, and every year for the past nine years at this time had come a warrior of the Tuatha de Danaan, from *Sidhe Finnachaidh*, and he had burned the roof of Tara with his magic. None might withstand him because of the Faery music he played that caused all the warriors to fall into a deep sleep.

When he heard of this, Fionn came before the King and said that he would rid Tara of this trouble forever, providing that in return his inheritance be recognised. And this the King swore to do upon the surety of all the tributary kings of Ireland and of his royal Druids.

That night, before the warrior of the *sidhe* was destined to appear, one of the High King's men, Fiacha son of Conga, who had served with Cumhail and had a fondness for his son, came to Fionn and offered him help: 'For it is Aillen, son of Midhna that comes this night, and none may resist him without help. But I have a spear which can kill him, in the hands of the right man.'

So Fiacha brought the spear to Fionn, and the property of it was this: that when the cover was taken off the blade, it made a sound of warfare, and if it was laid against the forehead of the warrior who bore it, he would be afflicted by no evil magic. So Fionn took the spear and went out against Aillen mac Midhna, and slew him. He struck off his head and took it back to Tara and fastened it upon a pole for all to see.

When day came, and the High King and his men woke from the sleep of enchantment which Aillen had caused to fall upon them, Cormac called Fionn before him and solemnly invested him with the captaincy of the Fianna. And to Goll mac Morna, who had held that post since the death of Cumhail, he made this offer: 'Will you stay and serve under Fionn mac Cumhail, or will you suffer banishment from Ireland for ever?'

And Goll, who had but one eye, looked with his good one at the young warrior and bowed his head. 'I will stay and serve with Fionn, son of Cumhail. And if I betray him, let me be straightway killed for it.'

Nor did Goll ever betray his captain, but became one of his foremost warriors in time to come.

Thus Fionn became captain of the Fianna, and never in its history or in the history of Ireland has there been such a company of warriors.

How Fionn Got His Grey Hair

Now all the Fianna were great hunters, and none more than Fionn himself, who had two great hounds, Bran and Sgeolan, who came to him from the enchanted realms. And one day they were hunting near Allmu of the White Walls where Fionn had his chief place in Ireland, and they set up a hind that ran so swiftly before them so that no dog, not even Bran and Sgeolan, could catch her. And it seemed to Fionn, who outpaced all the rest of the Fianna, that the hind was making for Allmu as though in search of sanctuary. Sure enough, when they were close to the walls of the dun, Bran and Sgeolan, who had kept close upon the heels of the hind all the while, gave tongue that they had cornered their quarry. But when Fionn came upon them he saw a strange sight, for instead of falling upon the hind and rending her in twain, the two great hounds were licking it and fawning upon it as though it were a long lost sister. Then Fionn knew that there was magic afoot and commanded the rest of the Fianna to call off their dogs. And he took the hind into Allmu, with her trotting before him, and Bran and Sgeolan bounding at either hand.

That night the hind sat always near Fionn's feet and when he went to his sleeping place, she came and lay by him. And in the night he awoke and saw lying by his side the most beautiful woman he had ever seen and she had the eyes of the hind that had followed him at the end of the chase.

The story she told was this: that she was of the Faery people, the Lordly Ones of Tir-nan-Og, and that one of her kind had desired her, though she had always refused him. So at last he had struck her with his hazel wand and turned her into a hind.

'But now I am with Fionn mac Cumhail I know that I am safe, and I would ask that you allow me to stay,' she said. Fionn looked at the woman and asked her name.

'You may call me Sabha,' said she.

Fionn said, 'Sabha, you may stay here for as long as you will, save only that you agree to be my wife.'

And Sabha looked at Fionn in her turn and said that she would.

So Fionn and Sabha drank the bride-cup together and they were happy for a year, in which time Fionn almost gave up hunting or going afoot from Allmu. But at the end of that time, enemies of Ireland were sighted off the coastline and the Fianna had to ride forth, for it was their task to keep the shores and hills free of wrong-doers or of invasion. And though Sabha begged Fionn not to go, yet go he must, but he bade her remain within Allmu until he returned and to speak with no one not of the court.

So the Fianna rode forth and gave battle to their enemies. They were victorious and came home eagerly – none more so than Fionn, who as Allmu of the White Walls came in view, was already searching the ramparts for a sight of Sabha.

When he could not see her, Fionn's heart gave a great lurch and turned over in his breast, and he rode swiftly into the court demanding to know what had occurred. His steward came forward and told him that not two days after he had ridden out of Allmu, there had come a man that seemed in every way like him, and who had two hounds the like of Bran and Sgeolan with him. And Sabha, on seeing this, gave a cry of joy and fled on swift feet to meet the man. But when she came up to him he suddenly struck her with a hazel wand and she became a hind again and, in that moment, the two hounds vanished away and the man that had the appearance of Fionn changed into a strange dark figure who led the hind away.

Then Fionn was broken hearted, for he knew it was the Faery lord who loved Sabha who had taken her away and he believed that he would never see her again. But for all that he began to search, and many long days he spent combing the hills where he had first had a sight of her. Until at last he began to realize that his quest was in vain, and so turned again to the leadership of the Fianna, which he had allowed to lapse while he searched.

Thus seven years passed and once again Fionn rode to the hunting, and this time the quarry that Bran and Sgeolan discovered was even stranger – a little naked boy wandering in the bracken on the hill of Benbulben. And though Fionn spoke to him, he knew no words of human speech, so Fionn took him back to Allmu and had him cared for and taught to speak, until the day came when he could tell his story.

And this was the way of it: for as long as he could remember he had lived in a cave in the hills with a hind for company. Then one day a dark man had come who seemed to want the hind to go with him, and when she would not, the man struck her with a hazel wand and after that she went, though always looking back to where the little boy stood watching. And though he wished to go also he might not move so much as a foot until he heard the cry of Fionn's hounds and was discovered by Bran and Sgeolan.

Then Fionn knew that the boy was his own son and the child of Sabha, and that now he would never see her again. Yet he still could not give up entirely and leaving the boy with the Fianna, he went alone to the mound on Slieve Gallion, near Armagh, where he knew the Smith of the *sidhe* dwelt beneath the hill.

Now, unknown to him, Cuillen the Smith had two daughters, Aine and Milucra. Aine had seen Fionn and had evinced a great love for him. But Fionn had eyes only for Sabha and failed even to notice Aine, so that when by her magic she knew Fionn was in that part of Ireland, she determined upon a plan to be avenged upon him.

Thus, when Fionn was nearing Slieve Gallion, he came upon a little dark lough in the shelter of the hills and there beside it was sitting a most beautiful woman, weeping full sore.

'Why do you weep, woman of the white arms?' asked Fionn.

'I have lost a red-gold ring that was the gift of my sweetheart,' answered she. 'And I put a *geise* upon you in the name of all the Fianna of Ireland to find it again for me.'

So Fionn stripped off his clothes and dived into the lake, and three times he swam its length and breadth before he found the ring. But when he swam to the bank and stretched forth an arm to give it to her, the woman snatched it from him and with a high, queer laugh, herself leapt into the water and was gone.

When Fionn tried to climb out of the lough, the moment his foot touched the earth, the strength and youth went from him and he lay upon the ground like a feeble old man. Then great terror fell upon him, and he put his thumb into his mouth in fear that the gift of knowledge was also lost to him. But it was not, and at once he knew who was responsible for his state and he knew also that he could nothing to undo matters.

Thus he remained a long while, scarcely able to care for himself until, at last, the Fianna came seeking him, and seeing the ancient man by the lough, demanded whether he had seen a fair strong man come that way of late.

Fionn answered, 'I have indeed and I was that man,' and he told them all the story of what had happened to him.

Then Caoilte mac Ronan, who was one of his chief warriors, spoke up: 'I say that we should call upon the master of this Faery mound and make him aware of our presence.'

There were cries of agreement from the men of the Fianna, and they went straightway to the Sidhe of Cuillen and began to dig and root at the hill. This they did for three nights and three days, and at the end of that time, Cuillen the Smith himself appeared, bearing a golden cup in his hands, and coldly he bade Fionn drink from it. When he did so, immediately he sprang up hale and strong as ever he had been, save that his once golden hair was now grey as ash. But of Cuillen there was no sign, and then Fionn knew at last that there was no seeking Sabha further. Therefore he let his hair remain grey and sought no further recompense of Cuillen. . . .

'And that,' said Oisin, 'is how I came to be born, for my father named me Oisin, which means "Little Deer". But my mother he never saw again in this life, and I returned too late from Tir-nan-Og to tell him of her.'

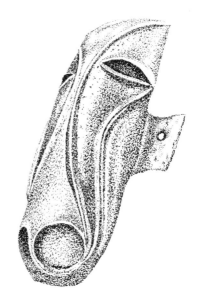

How the Fianna Won Their Horses

This magnificent bronze face-plate horse fitting probably came from a chariot rather than an individual mount; but decorations of this kind could well have been used by the Fianna.

The Fianna were famous horsemen, and used their fine mounts to travel from place to place. Thus they were ever able to be at the site of a battle, or at a pass to be kept against invasion, before any enemy could prepare against them. Yet it was not always so, for in the beginning the Fianna hunted on foot and used to ride small hill ponies, or themselves run all day to arrive where they were needed.

At one time Fionn had with him the son of the King of Britain, that had come to take service with twenty-seven men of his, and they all went hunting together. Fionn sat on the hill of Cnoc Fianna and cheered on his hounds, for he loved nothing so much as to listen to the music of the hunt. The son of the King of Britain, who was named Arthyr, had been set with his men at the head of a valley to watch for the coming of the quarry. When they saw Fionn's two great hounds, Bran and Sgeolan, racing ahead of all the rest, they decided among themselves that they must have these dogs and take them back to Britain. So when the two hounds reached the place where they were, Arthyr and his men called them, put chains upon them and carried them to their ship, sailing swiftly away so that none might know where they had gone.

The Hill of Almu was Fionn's fortress home. Its white walls were to be seen shining from afar as the Fianna returned from their campaigns, to be welcomed by their companions and families.

Now when Fionn realised what had occurred he at once set his thumb of knowledge between his teeth and thus he knew who had taken his dogs and where they had gone. Gathering eight men of the Fianna, including Goll mac Morna, Caoilte mac Ronan and his own son, Oisin, he went to the shore and called upon the god Manannan, Lord of the Sea, to send him a ship. For there was a fellowship between Fionn and Manannan that was of old standing. So the boat came, and though there were none on board, yet her sails filled and she crossed the waves like a bird, so that in no time at all the nine men of the Fianna were in Britain. They went to where Arthyr and his men were hunting the lands of Lodan son of Llyr, and there they found the King's son and his men, and with them the two hounds who were most glad to see their master again.

Arthyr feigned friendship to Fionn, suggesting that the theft of the hounds had been but a jest, and inviting the Fianna to dine with him. But soon enough fighting broke out between the two groups and things might have gone ill for the Fianna, who were greatly outnumbered, had not Oisin seized Arthyr round the neck and held him as a shield before him while he slew a dozen of his men. Then Arthyr sued for peace and said that Fionn should have the dogs back and also a gift of two horses – a magnificent grey and a fine chestnut mare that were themselves a gift of his father the King. These Fionn accepted and took them back with him to Ireland; and from their stock came all the mounts of the Fianna thereafter. And it is also said that from them another king of Britain, also named Arthur, took the notion of using horses in battle, which helped him to defeat his enemies just as it had helped Fionn to defeat his. And Patrick held this to be true, for he knew of that other Arthur in his own day.

This flexible bridle bit found in London is an excellent example of the kind of equipment used by Celtic horseman.

The Hostel of the Quicken Trees

Most would agree that of all the warriors who served with Fionn mac Cumhail in the Fianna, Diarmuid O'Duibne was the greatest. No task for him was too great, no feat of arms or course of hunting too hard that he would not try it. And he had besides a face and form that women loved, which caused great sorrow among the Fianna in time to come. But while Diarmuid rode with them, they were the most unbeatable men in all of Ireland.

The coming of Diarmuid was this wise: as a boy he went with other boys to be trained by the great warrior-woman, Mongfinn, but in time he came to leave there, and, with his youthful companions, made for Allmu of the White Walls to take service with Fionn.

On the way they came to a ford in the river and by its banks was an old woman who begged them to carry her across. All of the boys refused, fearing

Fionn met his death at the Battle of Gabhra. Having slain all his other adversaries, Fionn finally encountered the five sons of Urgriu, on whose spear points he died.

to dirty their immaculate clothes with the mud of the river. Only Diarmuid took pity on the old woman, and waded across the river with her in his arms. As he reached the other side, however, his companions having gone ahead without him, he found the old woman had become a great shining figure that he knew for one of the Lordly Ones out of Tir-nan-Og.

She smiled at him and said, 'Diarmuid O'Duibhne, you are a good son and will do many great deeds; and for the goodness you had to myself today I promise that no woman shall ever refuse you, nor be able to resist your look. And I tell you also that you have not seen the last of this place, for here shall be another feat attempted, that shall be remembered.'

And with these words there was suddenly no one there at all.

So Diarmuid went on to Allmu of the White Walls, and there Fionn saw him, and with his thumb of wisdom he knew what had occurred and that the old woman had been the Battle Goddess Morrighan, herself. But for her gift he felt troubled – doubts which were to prove well founded later on.

As to the prophecy that Diarmuid would come to that ford again, this is the way that it came about. Many years later, Fionn fought a battle against the King of Lochlan, and slew him and all his sons save one only – Midac, whom he took into his own house and afterwards gave lands on the coast of Ireland. But in all that time never a word of thanks was had from Midac, who continued in secret to plot against Fionn.

One day, it chanced that the Fianna were hunting in the hills to the west of Allmu, and as sometimes happened, Fionn and some of his men became separated from their fellows who were following the track of a boar towards Cnoc Fianna. As they went they saw a tall and handsome warrior coming towards them, and Fionn greeted him cheerfully enough when he saw that it was Midac. And the King of Lochlan's son smiled smoothly enough (though there were some among the Fianna who knew his true colour) and invited them to sup with him at the Hostel of the Quicken Trees, which was nearby.

To this Fionn agreed readily, and commanded that certain of the band, Oisin and Diarmuid, Fodla and Caoilte mac Ronan, and his own youngest son, Fiachna with his foster-brother Innsa, should remain behind until the remainder of the hunt came up with them. Then Fionn and Goll mac Morna, and Conan Maol and the rest, rode after Midac to the Hostel of the Quicken Trees.

It was a fair and beautiful building, with bright intricate carvings on the wood of its uprights, and a fresh thatch that shone in the sunlight like gold. And all around it grew quicken trees, with berries full and red upon them.

Fionn and his men followed Midac within and were amazed at the richness they beheld: fine hangings on every wall, soft couches to rest on, and a bright roaring fire in the hearth to warm them.

'Certainly you have done well by yourself,' said Fionn to Midac, but when he looked around their host was nowhere to be seen. 'Is this not a strange thing? And no servants to be seen either?' he asked.

'There is something stranger than that,' said Goll, 'For but a moment since the walls were hung with fine stuffs and now they seem but rough planks through which the wind blows.'

'And there is something else strange,' said Fiachna, 'When we came in there were seven doors but now there is only one, and that closed tight.'

'What is more,' added Conan, 'these soft couches we were sitting upon seem to have become as hard as the earth – perhaps because they are!'

Seeing treachery and magic thus revealed, the Fianna made to rise and break out of the hall – only to find that they could not move, but were anchored fast to the floor as though with bands of iron.

Then Fionn put his thumb of wisdom between his teeth and groaned aloud: 'Now is the treachery of Midac mac Lochlan revealed,' he said, 'for I see a great host coming against us, led by Sinsar of the Battles, and his son Borba the Haughty, and coming with them are the three sons of the King of Torrent. It is the last named whose spells hold us here and only the scattering of their blood on the floor will set us free. But of that there is little chance.'

Then the men of the Fianna sent up the war-cry, the Diord Fionn, and so loud was their cry that Fiachna and Innsa heard it and hurried down to the Hostel of the Quicken Trees to discover what was amiss. When they heard what had come to pass the two young warriors felt their battle-rage come upon them and they at once said they would defend the hostel at whatever cost – for there was a ford nearby that the enemy host must cross before they came where Fionn and his men were imprisoned.

. Meanwhile, the host that was coming to destroy Fionn had made camp at a few miles' distance. It occured to one of Midac's chieftains that if he went with his own men and slew Fionn and brought the head back to his master, great fortune would be his. So he set off and came to the ford where Innsa and Fiachna waited. There ensued a great combat in which Innsa fell to Midac's chieftain, and Fiachna in turn slew him, along with so many of his warriors that only a handful returned to Midac.

Fiachna buried Innsa in a shallow grave and bore the news of his death and the slaughter of their enemies to Fionn, who wept for the death of his foster-son. But still he and the Fianna were held fast, nor would Fiachna abandon them and go for the rest of the warband.

Meanwhile, another chieftain of Midac's, named Ciaran, fell to wondering why his brother and their men had not returned, and set forth in search of them. When they came to the ford, they found it choked with the bodies of the slain, and Fiachna waiting to meet them.

Then there followed one of those combats that live in the memory of men long after. Fiachna held the ford alone against many dozens of attackers, and at the end of it only one man escaped to take the news to Midac.

He became so enraged that he gathered a part of his own men and made for the ford, where he found Fiachna still, leaning on his sword and bleeding from many wounds. When Midac saw all the bodies of his men where they made a wall of dead in the stream, he flung himself forwards and engaged the young hero in single combat.

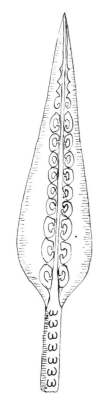

Spearheads (above and opposite) *discovered at Hiedersingen, near Stuttgart in West Germany. These magnificent examples of Celtic design are typical of the kind of weapons carried by the Fianna. The curvilinear designs are of bronze, cast into the blade.*

Meanwhile, Oisin, Fodla and Diarmuid had been waiting for word from Fiachna. When none came, Diarmuid and Fodla decided to go down to the Hostel of the Quicken Trees to find out what was amiss, while Oisin went after the rest of the warband. As they were nearing the place, they heard the sounds of battle and began to run, emerging at the place in time to see Fiachna, hard-pressed, give way before the fury of Midac's attack. Without pausing in his stride, Diarmuid flung his spear – a great throw which took Midac in the breast and laid him on his back – though not before he had struck once more a fatal blow that gave Fiachna his death.

Then, as Fodla gave battle to the rest of Midac's men, Diarmuid struck off the head of Fionn's enemy and carried it to the door of the Hostel. And when he found what had occurred there he groaned aloud, but said that he and Fodla would hold the ford against all comers until Oisin returned with the rest of the Fianna: 'And if the sons of the King of Torrent come hither while we wait, you may be sure you shall be set free the sooner.'

Diarmuid returned to the ford and found that Fodla had driven off the few remaining men of Midac's warband, and he was so exhausted with fighting that once he saw Diarmuid, he fell into a deep sleep there on the bank amid all the dead, and Diarmuid covered him with a cloak and left him to rest undisturbed.

Now, at last, the main body of the host that Midac had gathered, namely that of the three sons of the King of Torrent, came to the ford, and there for long hours Diarmuid held them at bay, single-handed, not liking to wake the sleeping Fodla. But in time the noise of the battle *did* awaken him and little pleased he was that he had missed so much of the fight.

The two warriors together drove back the enemy with dreadful slaughter, and in the end Diarmuid himself slew all three of the King's sons, and took their heads. Then while Fodla chased off the rest, Diarmuid went again to the Hostel of the Quicken Trees and sprinkled the blood on the doorstep and the earth within. But though Fionn and his men were able to move, they still had no strength, and Fionn told Diarmuid that they would not be able to fight before morning, when their strength would return.

So once again Diarmuid returned alone to the ford, and there he and Fodla awaited the last of their enemies: Sinsar of the Battles and his son Borba, with all their men.

This was the fourth combat of the Ford of the Quicken Trees, and it was a hard fight that continued all day and did not stop at sunset. But Diarmuid and Fodla, in a momentary lull in the fighting, spoke to each other and Diarmuid advised that they should hold off from attacking with equal ferocity to that of their enemies and save their strength until help arrived, or until Fionn could join with them.

In the early light of dawn came not only Sinsar and Borba, but also the King of the World with all his men; and then things might have gone ill indeed with Diarmuid and Fodla, but that with the first ray of the sun, Fionn and Goll and the rest received back all their old strength. Chanting their battle cry, they joined in the fray. Things might still have gone ill for them, but before the morning was passed, Oisin and the rest of the Fianna came upon the scene. With all his warriors at his side, Fionn rose up in his battle fury and inflicted such slaughter that few men lived to speak of their defeat. Among the slain were both Sinsar and Borba, the sons of the King of the World. After that, it was a long time before any man of Ireland stood again against the Fianna. But it was only afterwards, when they rode away from the Hostel of the Quicken Trees, which they left in flames, that Diarmuid remembered the words of the Goddess he had carried on his shoulders long since, and then he knew that this was the same ford.

'And may it be a long while,' said Oisin to Patrick, 'before that fight is forgotten, nor the deeds of Diarmuid that day eclipsed by what came after.'

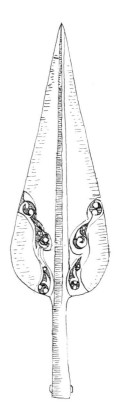

Diarmuid and Grainne

Now although Fionn served as chieftain of the Fianna at the behest of Cormac, the High King of Ireland, there came to be disquiet between the two of them, for in his heart Cormac feared the power of the Fianna, that they might some day look towards his throne and his kingship.

This grieved Fionn greatly, for he was a loyal man and hated there to be enmity between himself and the King. And it came to him that he should take a new wife, for he still thought of Sabha, Oisin's mother; and his second wife, Maighneis, had been dead for several years. So that Fionn grew lonely and when it was suggested that he ask for the hand of Cormac's daughter, Grainne, he was more than eager. He deemed that this was a way to heal the breach between himself and the High King, while at the same time gaining for himself a wife who was, by all accounts, the most beautiful in all of Ireland.

He duly sent messages to Cormac to ask for his daughter, and Cormac was not loath to give her up, for he too saw the chance to make a potential enemy a son-in-law. But as for Grainne herself, she was less willing. 'For,' she said, 'Fionn is no longer young, and there may yet come one whom I can truly love.'

But her father would not listen and commanded her to do as she was bidden, and to Fionn he sent back messages of friendship and acceptance of his offer.

So a great feast was prepared at Tara of the Kings, and folk came from all the five provinces of Ireland to grace the wedding of Fionn to Grainne. But on the night of the feast, Grainne sat silent and pale beside her new lord until she saw Diarmuid amongst the guests; and a blush of colour stole into her cheeks and she asked his name.

Then, taking the guest cup in her hands, Grainne moved among the

133

throng speaking gently to one or laughing merrily with another, until she came to where Diarmuid sat and said softly, 'Diarmuid O'Duibhne, my heart is filled with love-longing for you.'

Diarmuid looked at the woman who had just become his lord's wife and for a moment his look answered her own, then he said that no man of Fionn's would ever betray him.

But Grainne said, simply, 'I lay this *geise* upon you, Diarmuid O'Duibhne, that you take me from this place tonight or leave this land as a man dishonoured.'

Then Diarmuid grew pale, for no warrior might refuse such a *geise*, yet he knew that once he left Tara with Grainne there would be no place for either of them beyond the reach of Fionn. But nonetheless he could not do otherwise, and as Fionn and all the Fianna, and the warriors of Cormac slept, Diarmuid O'Duibhne and Grainne, the daughter of the King, slipped out of Tara and fled away into the night.

Next day and for many days after they ran, for there would be no rest or respite from the pursuit of Fionn. Many times they heard the call of hounds, and more than once Diarmuid recognised either Bran or Sgeolan, but each time he managed to throw the scent.

So the days grew into weeks, and the weeks into months, and still the pair fled from the wrath of Fionn. Nowhere might they rest for more than a night, and to this day, right across Ireland are places known as the 'beds' of Diarmuid and Grainne, where they were believed to have slept. And if Diarmuid began with no heart for the venture, as day followed day in the company of Grainne, slowly the barrier melted and he began to love her in truth.

But Grainne grew very thin and brown and her once carefully dressed hair was wild as a cloud from which her face looked out great-eyed at the world. But she never flinched from the steepest path or the hardest road, and followed unhesitatingly wherever Diarmuid led.

Several times Aengus Og, who was the foster father of Diarmuid, rescued them when the Fianna were close upon their heels, so that never once in all that time did Fionn set eyes upon either one of them, though he followed for more than a year and a half. Until at last, Aengus Og himself went to Fionn and asked whether he would not give up the chase and let Diarmuid and Grainne live in peace. Fionn, who was growing old, shrugged and said that he would, so long as Diarmuid stayed away from Allmu. Then Aengus went in turn to Cormac and asked him the same thing. Though Cormac was in no way pleased that a man had taken his daughter when she had just become betrothed to a man of Fionn's standing, yet he agreed.

His son, Cairpre, was less willing, and became the greatest enemy of the Fianna from that time.

So Diarmuid and Grainne were allowed to settle down together on land that belonged to the O'Duibhne's, and Diarmuid had besides a gift of land from Fionn, as befitted a hero who had served him well. Thus, all went well

with them for a number of years, until Diarmuid had four sons to his name and had begun to lose some of his youthful beauty.

Then, one day, Grainne said to him: 'Is it not a shame that in all these years Fionn has never once visited us here, or that you have never ridden hunting with the Fianna on these lands?' Diarmuid, who in truth had missed his old comrades, roused himself to send word to Fionn that if he saw fit they should forget the enmity that had been between them and ride once more together.

So it was that in the spring of that year, Fionn and a small band of the Fianna came to Diarmuid's house and there was feasting and much talk of old battles and sport. And when Fionn proposed to hunt the lands around Ben Bulben, that lay within Diarmuid's lands, there was a gladness between them.

Now there was one beast that Diarmuid might never hunt because of a *geise* laid upon him long ago in his youth – and that was the boar, for it was said that in this way would he come by his death. Yet several times in the night, he awoke to the voice of hound, and, it seemed, the noise of a great pig. He would have risen from his bed had not Grainne held him fast in her arms and bade him await the dawn. But when the day came at last, he would wait no longer. He set out alone with only a single hound for company, in search of that voice he had heard in the night. And so he came to a place near the top of Ben Bulben, and there was Fionn, alone, awaiting him. The two men looked at each other a long while.

'Have you come to try and kill me, Fionn mac Cumhail?' said Diarmuid.

But Fionn only looked at him strangely and said, 'One of the hounds of the Fianna escaped into the night and we have been trying to catch him again, but there is a great boar at large on this mountain and it has already killed several

Though it comes from France, this bronze figurine of a stag illustrates ideally the image of the beast hunted by the Fianna as part of thier legal quarry.

135

of our hounds. You should not be here, Diarmuid O'Duibhne, knowing of the prohibition upon you.'

Diarmuid shook his head, 'I shall not run away from any pig,' he said. 'I will wait here to see what comes.'

So Fionn went in search of his men while Diarmuid remained sitting in the early morning sun on Ben Bulben. Thus he was when he heard a great crashing in the bushes below him and there came in sight the largest and fiercest looking boar he had ever seen.

'Now here is my death,' said Diarmuid, looking at the beast's red eye. 'I shall see if I can overcome it.'

He drew his sword and went forward against the beast with only his hound at his side. She, poor beast, died in the boar's first rush, and in the second Diarmuid received his own death wound, though he slew the boar also. And so was another prophecy of himself fulfilled, that if ever he hunted a boar thus would he find his death.

Thus Fionn and the Fianna found him later that day, with still some life left in him, and Fionn stood over him and said, 'I am not sorry to find you thus, for you have done ill by me.'

'In the name of the friendship that was once between us and for the deeds I have done in your name,' gasped Diarmuid, 'I ask you to give me water from your hands.' For he knew that Fionn had a special power: if he gave succour to any man in this way, that man would be healed.

Fionn hesitated for a moment, and others of the Fianna who were at hand murmured that he should help Diarmuid, for the sake of the good he had done in past times. So Fionn went to a place where water bubbled up from the earth and gathered some in his cupped hands. But as he made to take it to Diarmuid, he remembered Grainne and the hurt he had been done, and allowed it to trickle out between his fingers. Then he took thought of the Hostel of the Quicken Trees and of other deeds of Diarmuid, and grew ashamed, so that he went for more water. But he was too late, for the life had gone from the hero before he could reach him.

Thus was the death of Diarmuid, and many of the Fianna mourned for him, as did Grainne, who dwelled alone for many years and taught her sons to hate Fionn. But in time her sorrow faded and with it her anger, and when Fionn called upon her to come back to Allmu of the White Walls as his wife, she did not refuse, but made peace between herself and his sons and the men of the Fianna.

The Death of Fionn

On a day in the summer of the year when Oisin came to stay at the monastery of Ard Macha, one of the monks came in haste to fetch Patrick with the news that 'Another devil is come, just like the other, but blacker.'

When he hastened to the bothy which was Oisin's, he found a great white horse, larger than any he had seen, tied up before it. Within he found Oisin deep in conversation with a great black-browed warrior who carried a sword big enough to need two ordinary men to lift it.

Oisin rose to his feet, his eyes shining as they had rarely done since his first meeting with the monks.

'There is a new story I would have you hear, Talkend,' he said, 'One that you may not hear from my lips, but which concerns the death of Fionn mac Cumhail and the ending of the Fianna. Will you hear it?' So Patrick sent for his scribe and sat down to listen to the black-browed stranger. This is the tale he told. . . .

The time came when Cormac mac Art died and his son, Cairpre, became High King of Ireland in his place. But Cairpre hated the Fianna just as Cormac had loved them, and he plotted daily to find ways to destroy Fionn and his companions.

Now Cairpre had a daughter named Sgeimh Solais, who had many suitors. When at length one was found who was deemed suitable, a great banquet was planned to celebrate the forthcoming nuptials.

It was customary at such times for the High King to award the Fianna twenty ingots of gold as an extra fee for keeping guard over Ireland, and for them to send their youngest member to collect this tribute. On this occasion, it fell to the lot of a youth named Ferdia to collect the gold. Though Fionn and his men waited all day outside the walls of Tara of the Kings, it was late before Ferdia returned. When he did, it was not as a living man but as a corpse, flung over the walls of Tara with these mocking words of Cairpre:

'Too often have the Fianna made demands of the High Kings of Tara. This is the only answer they will get from now on.'

Fionn strode out to the front of the Fianna and shouted up at the walls of Tara, 'Cairpre mac Cormac, you have earned your death by this action. When next we meet, look to yourself.'

Then he and all of the Fianna that were with him, turned away from Tara and returned to Allmu of the White Walls to prepare for war.

But there were those of the Fianna who would not fight against the High King, preferring either to remain neutral or to join the opposing army. Thus, in the end, Fionn had only the men of his own clan Bascna, and those of Leinster under the captaincy of Oscar son of Oisin, and the army of King Feircobh of Munster, who had married into Fionn's family and was a firm comrade besides. This was in all but 3,500 men.

But Cairpre had 3,000 warriors of Tara on his side, as well as the clan of Morna – for though Goll mac Morna remained true to Fionn, there were many among his own clan that remembered the old feud and who hated Fionn for ousting Goll from the captaincy of the Fianna. These were 2,000 men, led by Fear-Taigh and Fear-Ligh mac Morna, Goll's younger brothers. As well as these, Cairpre had 1,000 men each from the tribes of Ulster and Connacht. From the Men of the Snows, the Men of the Green Swords and the Men of the Lion, he also had 1,000, each company led by one of the five sons of Urgriu. In all, it was an army of 10,000 men that Fionn had to meet with his own small force. The place of meeting was at Gaohra which lay to the West of Tara.

It was a very hard battle, with terrible losses on either side. None there were who fought more bravely than Oscar, son of Oisin, so that men said it was his day. Five score of the Men of the Green Swords and seven score of the Men of the Lion alone he slew. And at the last he came face to face with the High King himself.

He cast his spear at Cairpre, which passed through his body and stuck out beyond. But Cairpre with his last breath struck Oscar a terrible blow which let out most of the life from him. Yet when he saw that Cairpre's men had set his helm upon a pillar so that it might seem that he lived yet, Oscar drew upon the last of his strength to fling a thin slab of stone which struck the helm and broke it in pieces. But his own heart broke at that moment and he fell dead.

Then Caoilte mac Ronan and Conan Maol lamented the death of the great Fenian, and together they lifted and carried him to where Fionn stood. There, amid the press of battle, Fionn gave a great cry of anguish and raised the Diord Fionn, the Cry of the Fianna. He spoke words above the body of Oscar, before he plunged again into the thick of the fighting, and men say that never in all the history of the Fianna were such deeds done as were done by Fionn mac Cumhail that day. A mighty man he was still, though his hair and beard were white as flax, and in his shining war-coat and helmet of gold he was a figure terrible to all his enemies.

Fear-Taigh and Fear-Ligh mac Morna he slew and many dozens of warriors from the men of Connacht and the men of Ulster and none might stand before him. But at the last he stood alone, with most of his fellows dead or sore wounded, and then there came around him the five sons of Urgriu, who had commanded the pillars of the High King's army. When Fionn saw them he let fall his shield, which was all hacked and hewn, and grasping his great sword in both hands he went to meet them. . . .

'Thus perished that day Fionn mac Cumhail, captain of the Fianna of Ireland, and with him fell the most of his captains and many of his men. The might of the Fianna was smashed in that battle, and never again rode to hunt upon Cnoc Fianna, or Ben Bulben, Slieve Cua or Slieve Crot.'

The stranger fell silent while Oisin wept for the death of Fionn and for his own son, Oscar. Even Patrick was not wholly dry-eyed, though his sternness forbade that he should weep for a pagan. And Oisin, seeing or sensing this, rose to his feet and made this lay:

I used to serve an army on a hill, Patrick of the closed-up mind; it is a pity you to be faulting me; there was never shame put on me till now.

I have heard music that was sweeter than your music, however much you are praising your clerks; the song of the blackbird of Leiter Laoi, and the sound of the Diord Fionn; the very sweet thrush of the Valley of the Shadow, or the sound of the boats striking the strand. The cry of the hounds was better to me than the noise of your schools, Patrick.

The twelve hounds that belonged to Fionn, the time they would be let loose facing out from the *Siuir*, their cry was sweeter than harps and than pipes.

I have a little story about Fionn; we were but fifteen men; we took the King of the Saxons of the feats, and we won a battle against the King of Greece.

We fought nine battles in Spain, and nine times twenty battles in Ireland: from Lochlann and from the eastern world there was a share of gold coming to Fionn.

My grief! I to be stopping after him, and without delight in games or in music; to be withering away after my comrades; my grief is to be living. I and the clerks of the Mass books are two that can never agree.

If Fionn and the Fianna were living, I would leave the clerks and the bells; I would followed the deer through the valleys, I would like to be close to his track.

When he was done he said: 'I will not stay here longer, Talkend; though you have been kind this is not my home. One has come for me who will take me back to where Niamh awaits me yet, and mayhap her magic can make me young again.'

Patrick looked at the strange warrior, who nodded. 'It is Caoilte mac Ronan who is under your roof. I have come for my old comrade to take him where the Fianna await his return.'

Then Patrick arose and blessed them both and bade them speed well. Nor was it without sorrow that he watched them ride away together on the back of the great white steed, for he had grown fond of the old warrior in the months that he had remained at Ard Macha. But as to the stories of the Fianna, those Patrick kept; and it is said that he collected others from men who still remembered the ancient times, so that the memory of the Fianna and their heroes should not die out in the world.

Hero List of the Fianna

'This is the enumeration [and description] of Finn's people: their strength was seven score and ten officers, each man of these having thrice nine warriors, every one bound (as was the way with Cuchullin in the time when he was there) to certain conditions of service, which were: that in satisfaction of their guarantee violated they must not accept material compensation; in the matter of valuables or of meat must not deny any; no single individual of them to fly before nine warriors.

Of such not a man was taken into the Fianna; nor admitted whether to the great Gathering of Usnach, to the Convention of *Taillte*, or to Tara's Feast; until both his paternal and his maternal correlatives, his *tuatha* and kindreds, had given securities for them to the effect that, though at the present instant they were slain, yet should no claim be urged in lieu of them: and this in order that to none other but to themselves alone they should look to avenge them. On the other hand: in case it were they that inflicted great mischiefs upon others, reprisals not to be made upon their several people.

Of all these again not a man was taken until he were a prime poet versed in the twelve books of poesy. No man was taken till in the ground a large hole had been made (such as to reach the fold of his belt) and he put into it with his shield and a forearm's length of a hazel stick. Then must nine warriors, having nine spears, with a ten furrows' width betwixt them and him, assail him and in concert let fly at him. If past that guard of his he were hurt then, he was not received into Fianship.

Not a man of them was taken till his hair had been interwoven into braids on him and he started at a run through Ireland's woods; while they, seeking to wound him, followed in his wake, there having been between him and them but one forest bough by way of interval at first. Should he be overtaken, he was wounded and not received into the Fianna after. If his weapons had quivered in his hand, he was not taken. Should a branch in the wood have disturbed anything of his hair out of its braiding, neither was he taken. If he had cracked a dry stick under his foot [as he ran] he was not accepted. Unless that [at his full speed] he had both jumped a stick level with his brown, and stooped to pass under one even with his knee, he was not taken. Also, unless without slackening his pace he could with his nail extract a thorn from his foot, he was not taken into Fianship: but if he performed all this he was of Finn's people.

A good man verily was he that had those Fianna, for he was the seventh king ruling Ireland: that is to say there were five kings of the provinces, and the king of Ireland; he being himself the seventh, conjointly with the king of all Ireland.

Finn's two poll-wards were Noenalach, and Raer grandson of Garb; the two stewards of his hounds: Crimthann and Connla Cas; his dispenser: Cathluan son of Crimthann; his master of the banquet: Corc son of Suan; his three cupbearers: Dermot grandson of Duibhne, and Faillin, and Colla son of Caeilte; the two overseers of his hearth; Caeilte and Glanna; his two makers of the bed; Admoll and mac Neri; his twelve musicians: Fergus True-mouth, Fianu, Bran, two Reidhes, Nuada, and Aithirne Aghmar, and. . . . Flann and Aedh, Cobthach of the high strains, and Cethern; his physician: Lerthuile; his two keepers of the vessels: Braen and Cellach Mael; his barber: Scannal; his comber: Daelgus; his charioteer: Rinnchu; his two masters of the horse: Aena and Becan; his strong man: Urchraide grandson of Bregaide; his six door-keepers: Cuchaire and Bresal Borr, Fianchad and *Mac-dá-fer*, Imchad and Aithech son of Aithech-bal; his carpenter: Donngus; his smith: Collan; his worker in metal: Congaran; his horn-players: Culaing and Cuchuailgne; his two soothsayers: Dirinn and Mac-reith; his carver: Cuinnscleo; his candle-holder: Cudam; his two spear-bearers: . . . and Uadgarb; his shield-bearer: Railbhe, and so on.

(The Enumeration of Finn's People
trans: Standish O'Grady)

Fionn's Battles

This list of some of Fionn's greatest battles comes from an ancient Irish poem describing his shield, the history of which is then given, including details of the great battles in which it was carried:

What of battles were fought by thee under Cumhall's son of the bright hands, thou brightest shield that hast not been defamed, 'twere hard to number them.

By thee was given the battle of Ceann Cluig, when Dubhthach, son of Dubh, was slain: the battle of Móin Mafaidh without woe, when Déidgheal hard-mouth was slain.

The battle of Luachair, the battle of Ceann Aise, and the battle of Inbhear Dubhghlaise, the battle of Teathbha, stiff was its entanglement, the battle of Cluain Meann of Muirisg.

The battle of Lusga, the battle of Ceann Cláire, and the battle of Dún Maighe, the battle of Sliabh Fuaid, whose heat was tense, the rout in which fell rough grey-eyed Garbhán.

The battle of Fionntráigh, whereby the warsprite was sated, where blood and booty were left behind, two bloody battles round Ath Móna, and eke the battle of Cronnmhóin.

The battle of Bolgraighe of great deeds, in which fell Cormac the exact, the battle of Achad Abhla that was not slack, the battle of Gabhair, the battle of the Sheaves.

The battle of Ollarbha, where the strife was fierce, wherein generous Fathadh was slain, the battle of Eise, great were its deeds, and the battle of Ceis Corainn.

The battle of Carraig, the battle of Srubh Brain, and the battle of Beann Eadair, the battle of Sliabh Uighe that was not slack, and the battle of Magh Málann.

The battle of the brave Colamhnaigh, and the battle of

Inbhear Bádhna, the battle of Ath Modhairn, clear to us, and the battle of Beirge above Boyne.

The battle of Magh Adhair not belittled, and the battle of Dún Fraochán, the battle of Meilge of the mighty struggle, that caused loud cries and wails of woe.

The battle of Beirbhe, great was its deed, the after-battle with the King of Lochlainn of the ships, the battle of Uighe, undoubtful were its tidings, and the battle of the Isle of Gaibiel.

The battle of Móin, the battle of Ceann Tíre, and the fortunate battle of Islay; the battle of the Saxons, great was its glory, and the battle of sturdy Dún Binne.

The battle where tall Aichil was slain, the ready-handed high-king of Denmark, the battle of Inbhear Buille in truth, and the battle of fierce firm Buinne.

Twenty battles and twelve outside of Ireland in full sooth as far as Tír na n-Dionn of fame not small, Fionn fought of battles with thee.

Eight battles in Leinster of the blades thou and thy side-slender lord fought: in thy space of grace, no falsehood is this, sixteen battles in Ulster.

Thirty battles without reproach thou gavest in Munster of MacCon – it is no lie but sooth – and twelve battles in Connacht.

Twenty-five victorious battles were fought by thee, thou hardy door, eighteen battles, a rout that was not slack, thou didst gain over the Tuatha De Danann.

Not reckoning thy fierce indoor fights and thy duels of hard swords, these while thy success lasted strong were thy share of the battles of Ireland.

(trans: Eoin MacNeill)

Further Reading

Bruford, A. *Gaelic Folk Tales and Medieval Romance* Dublin, Folklore of Ireland Soc., 1969

Campbell, J. G. *The Fians*, D. Nutt, 1891

Cross, T. P. and Slover, C. H. *Ancient Irish Tales* Figgis, 1936

Cunliffe, B. *The Celtic World*, Bodley Head, 1985

De Breffny, B. (ed) *The Irish World*, Thames & Hudson, 1977

Delaney, F. *The Celts*, Hodder & Stoughton, 1986

Dillon, M. & Chadwick, N. *The Celtic Realms*, Weidenfeld, 1967

Dillon, M. *Cycles of the Kings*, Oxford Univ. Press, 1946

Gregory, Lady A. *Gods and Fighting Men*, Colin Smythe, 1970

Joyce, P. W. *A Social History of Ancient Ireland* (2 vols.), Longman, 1903

Kruta, V. *The Celts of the West*, Orbis, 1985

Laing, L. *The Archaeology of Late Celtic Britain and Ireland* Methuen, 1975

Lindsay, J. *Our Celtic Heritage*, Weidenfeld, 1971

Macalister, R. A. S. *The Archaeology of Ireland* Blom Inc., 1972

Maccana, P. *Celtic Mythology*, Hamlyn, 1970

McCone, K. R. 'Werewolves, Cyclops, Diberga and Fianna: Juvenile Delinquency in Early Ireland' in *Cambridge Medieval Celtic Studies* No. 12, pp 1–22, 1987

McMahon, A. (ed) *The Celtic Way of Life* O'Brien Press, 1976

MacNeill, E. & Murphy, G. *Duanaire Finn (The Book of the Lays of Fionn)* Dublin, Irish Texts Soc. (3 vols) 1908–53

Macpherson, J. *The Poems of Ossian* Patrick Gedds, 1846

Mageoghagan, C. *Annals of Clonmacnoise* London, 1627

Meek, D. R. 'The Banners of the Fian in Gaelic Ballad Tradition' in *Cambridge Medieval Celtic Studies* No. 11, pp 29–69, 1986

Meyer, K. (ed. & trans) *Fianaigecht* Hodges, Figgis, 1910

Morris, J. *The Age of Arthur*, Weidenfeld, 1973

Murphy, G. *Ossianic Lore*, Mercier Press, 1955

Newark, T. *Celtic Warriors*, Blandford Press, 1986

Nutt, A. *Ossian and the Ossianic Literature*, D. Nutt, 1899

O'Grady, S. H. *Fionn and his Companions*, Talbot Press, 1970

O'Grady, S. H. (ed. & trans.) *Silva Gadelica* (2 vols), Williams and Norgate, 1892

O'Rahilly, T. *Early Irish History and Mythology*, Dublin Institute for Advanced Studies, 1946

O'Riordan, S. P. *Antiquities of the Irish Countryside*, Methuen, 1965

Rolleston, T. W. *The High Deeds of Finn*, Harrap, 1910

Ross, A. *The Pagan Celts*, Batsford, 1986

Russel, V. *Heroes of the Dawn*, Maunsel, 1913

Scott, R. D. *The Thumb of Knowledge*, Institute of French Studies, 1930

Sutcliff, R. *The High Deeds of Finn mac Cool*, Bodley Head, 1967

MACBETH

SCOTLAND'S WARRIOR KING

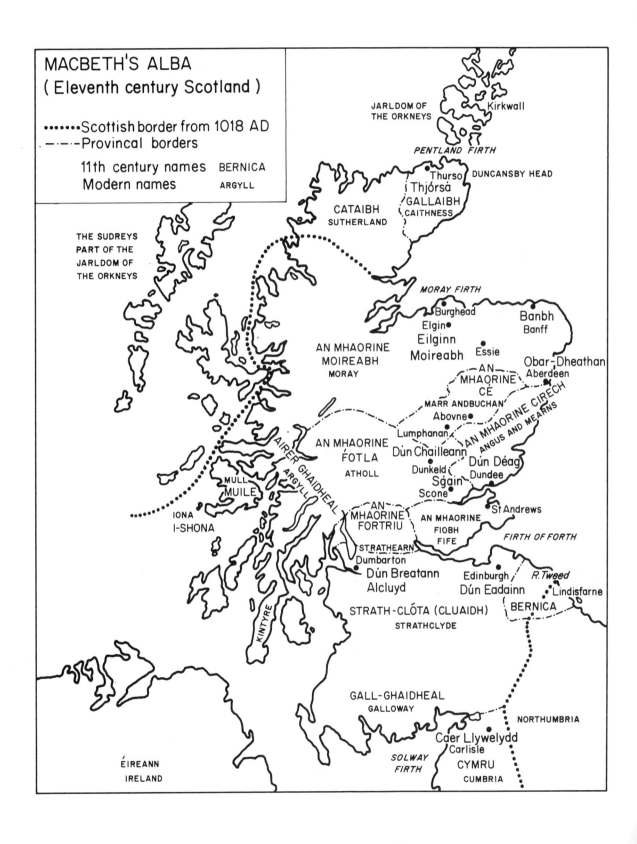

MACBETH'S ALBA
(Eleventh century Scotland)

••••••Scottish border from 1018 AD
–·–·–Provincal borders

11th century names   BERNICA
Modern names   ARGYLL

JARLDOM OF
THE ORKNEYS   Kirkwall

PENTLAND FIRTH

DUNCANSBY HEAD
Thurso
Thjórsá
GALLAIBH
CAITHNESS

CATAIBH
SUTHERLAND

THE SUDREYS
PART OF THE
JARLDOM OF
THE ORKNEYS

MORAY FIRTH

Burghead
Elgin   Banbh
Eilginn   Banff
Moireabh   Essie

AN MHAORINE
MOIREABH   AN-   Obar-Dheathan
MORAY   MHAORINE   Aberdeen
                               CÉ
                    MARR ANDBUCHAN
                    Abovne   AN MHAORINE CIRECH
                    Lumphanan   ANGUS AND MEARNS
AN MHAORINE
FÓTLA   Dún Chailleann
ATHOLL   Dún Déag
            Dunkeld   Dundee
MULL   Sgain
MUILE   Scone
AIRER GHAIDHEAL
ARGYLL
            AN
            MHAORINE   St Andrews
IONA   FORTRIU   AN MHAORINE
I-SHONA   FIOBH
                        FIFE   FIRTH OF FORTH

STRATHEARN
Dumbarton
Dún Breatann   Edinburgh   R.Tweed
Alcluyd   Dún Eadainn   Lindisfarne
KINTYRE   BERNICA
STRATH-CLÓTA (CLUAIDH)
STRATHCLYDE

GALL-GHAIDHEAL
GALLOWAY   NORTHUMBRIA

ÉIREANN   Caer Llywelydd
IRELAND   Carlisle
            SOLWAY   CYMRU
            FIRTH   CUMBRIA

The Real Macbeth

Macbeth was High King of Scotland from 1040–1057. His life, as misrepresented by chronicles written as much as three centuries after his death, was the foundation for a major character in a Shakespeare play which in turn generated many other works of creative fiction. There is a version by Guiseppe Verdi as a full opera composed in 1847. A further musical work was composed by Richard Strauss in 1887 and of course many film and stage variants now exist on the basic theme as created by Shakespeare. The most recent and perhaps the best film version to date is that directed by Roman Polanski, though it must be said that no film has yet been made telling the historical and true story of Macbeth. A number of books, mainly fiction, have been inspired by the tale of Macbeth. Perhaps the most comprehensive and historical of these is Dorothy Dunnet's epic novel *King Hereafter*.

The period in which Macbeth rose to power, the eleventh century, was extremely complex. Kings rose and fell across Europe, often with very short disputed reigns; popes and archbishops were made and unmade; savage Norse raiders carved out territories for themselves by the sword, while in the south their distant cousins the Normans were gradually becoming the great new military power of the century.

An enormous book would be needed to cover fully such a vast tapestry of politics, social change and religion, all woven inextricably together. Indeed, many detailed and lengthy historical sources and reference works are necessary to even begin to approach the true Macbeth. And it may well come as a surprise to the modern reader to discover that this man was almost the exact opposite of the character so powerfully drawn by William Shakespeare.

Much of the history of Macbeth can only be understood in the broad complex context of English and European history, as this context had profound effects upon Alba (Scotland). So, in concentrating upon the central hero, his culture, his battles – and his final end – a great mass of European history is inevitably omitted. But wherever immediate politics or cultural background help us to understand Macbeth, these are included.

It is not possible to write about Macbeth without considering, at least by comparison, the remarkable work of literature created by William

Shakespeare six centuries after the true historical period. Some of the major comparisons, such as the characters of Duncan and Macbeth, are included when the kingship and the succession by election are discussed. The simple fact that Scottish High Kings were elected is central to a proper understanding of the period; this concept was quite alien to later writers, and probably incomprehensible to Shakespeare. The world famous play is a study of evil and corruption: the fact that it revolves around an entirely fabricated and non-historical Macbeth is almost irrelevent – until we decide to examine the true Macbeth.

There is no intention here of debunking or discrediting Shakespeare; any such attempt would be absurd and unsuccessful. Yet the play *Macbeth* has so strongly, coloured our general image of that Scottish king, the first to try and unify Scotland, that we must regard the historical Macbeth as a quite different from the fictional one. The two are only superficially related; one is a character profoundly drawn in one of the greatest dramas ever written; the other is a Scottish king whose reign marked a turning point in history. They share a name and some general background, but otherwise there is little in common between them.

Although the actual facts of Macbeth's reign agree in some respects with those dramatised by Shakespeare, history offers us a very different picture of the true Macbeth. He is normally regarded as a usurper, a tyrant, and an intolerable oppressor of his subjects. In reality, whilst he was indeed the murderer of his predecessor, this was in circumstances which made the crime nothing unusual for the historical period.

On seizing the throne, Macbeth used his power well, and was an effective and competent king; certainly not the crazed tyrant suggested in the world famous play. The difference between the true Macbeth and the fictitious figure of drama can be understood by looking further at his background. Also we have to delve into the changes of attitude and the political influence which eventually generated the Shakespearean picture.

During the reign of his predecessor Duncan, Macbeth was the Mormaer of Ross and Moray; he ruled over a large area of Scotland, consisting of all the land to the north of the Moray Firth and Loch Ness, in addition to territories in the Orkneys.

Duncan set out to subdue the independent chiefs of the north, and while engaged in this campaign was killed, either by Macbeth or on his orders. His death occurred in a place known as Bothgowan, which has been interpreted as meaning 'in a smith's hut'. This killing, eventually to be immortalised by Shakespeare in his retelling of historical chronicles, is likely to have taken place near Elgin, in the year 1039.

But the detailed history of this murder is more complex. Macbeth is said to have been encouraged by his wife Gruach (pronounced 'Gro-ah'), who was a granddaughter of the earlier King Kenneth III. Kenneth had been murdered and succeeded by Duncan's grandfather, Malcom II. The pattern of death and succession was not merely limited to Macbeth and Duncan; it had an immedi-

ate family background of revenge and politics. Furthermore, it echoed the ancient Celtic custom by which kingship was not hereditary, but elective. In very primal Celtic cultures, kings were established through magical or pagan religious processes; one of these was through combat between chosen individuals. Such combats had been transformed into political warfare by the time of Macbeth in the eleventh century, but originated in a purely magical tradition, within which the people would follow the elected or chosen king regardless. In fact, it was this misunderstanding of the ancient system of kingship that led later English chroniclers to treat Macbeth as a usurping tyrant, a theme to be taken up centuries later by Shakespeare. England had already moved towards a hereditary monarchy by the eleventh century, relying on political patterns rather different from those still prevailing in Scotland.

Macbeth reigned for seventeen years after the death of Duncan, and as has been said, ruled well. He is the first king of Scotland who is mentioned as benefactor of the church (as religion had been decentralised previously under the non-political Celtic church). Macbeth, however, favoured the growing Roman Church and for obvious political reasons offered his services to the Pope, being the first Scottish king to do so.

Macbeth's dominions were more extensive than those of any previous Scottish king, embracing the whole of what is now called Scotland, other than Orkney, Caithness and Sutherland, and parts of the Hebrides. These regions were ruled by Earl Thorfinn, a Norse jarl, who we shall return to repeatedly in our examination of the life of Macbeth. Scotland extended further south during Macbeth's reign than it does today, though this extension was to be lost by Malcolm III, who took the throne by force from Macbeth and his stepson Lulach.

Horse gear from Viking boat
burial at Balladoole in the Isle
of Man. Viking culture was
absorbed into the existing Celtic
backgrounds of Orkney, the Isle
of Man and parts of Ireland,
including Dublin.

Shakespeare took his version of the history from the Chronicles of
Holinshed, or perhaps from those of Hector Boece. These sources were
familiar only with the concept of hereditary monarchy; if we trace the lineage
of the kings of Scotland *backwards* Macbeth might be termed a 'usurper' for
after him the throne definitely became a hereditary property. It is this significant role as a figure at the crossroads of Scottish history that should be rightly
accorded to the historical Macbeth.

Macbeth the Man

Macbeth is described by chroniclers in complimentary terms, very different
from the literary image of a mad, despotic murderer. Contemporary writers
such as Marianus Scotus, Tighernach, and Duan Albanach variously call
Macbeth 'ruddy of countenance, tall with yellow hair'; 'a liberal king . . .
fair and tall'; 'the red king . . .'. St Berchan called him a handsome youth, so
there can be little doubt that his appearance was comely.

Doada, Macbeth's mother, was second daughter of Malcom II, High King
of Scotland before Duncan. She married the Mormaer of Moray, Findlaech
MacRuaridh and Macbeth, whose name means 'Son of Life' was their only
child, born in 1005.

During his early life, Macbeth would have been fostered out for his
education, as was the ancient Celtic custom. Youths in powerful families
learned a wide range of skills, covering traditional law, poetry, music, and of
course warfare and individual skills in battle. Scotland did not maintain a
regular army in the modern sense, but each great family had to provide bands
of warriors, who in turn were individually responsible for their efforts to
protect areas, or if needed, the entire realm.

Macbeth was elected to the High Kingship in August 1040 at Scone, the
traditional king-making centre or sacred place of Scotland. Duncan, the
previous ruler, had reigned for five years as High King. He had suffered five
defeats in war, and his policy of aggression and expansion had proved
disastrous for Scotland. When elected to the High Kingship, Macbeth was
thirty-five years of age, mature and at the prime of life.

Macbeth grew up in a land that was partly Celtic and partly Norse. The
large Norse territories in the far north and the islands of Orkney played an
important role in the development of what was to later become Scotland. In
the case of Macbeth and his eventual rulership, the Norse balance of power
was crucial to success.

Generally, what we now know as Scotland was called Alba in the eleventh
century, though the name Scotland (from *Scotti* or Irish skirmishers) was
beginning to appear. Scotland and Ireland shared a common language, cultural heritage, and frequently employed each other's mercenaries for cam-

paigns or sea defences. The overall picture is of a diffuse, constantly feuding collective of chieftains and rulers in both Scotland and Ireland, with a powerful Norse element ruling the far north and posing a constant threat to southern territories during the summer, sailing and raiding seasons.

While Alba, or Scotland, spoke a Celtic language, the Orkneys and Sutherland and Caithness primarily spoke Norse or a mixture of Norse/Celtic dialects due to intermarriage. The northern border of Alba was south of Sutherland and Caithness, but the southern border extended far into what is nowadays England . . . including Cumbria, and stretching approximately to the present border of Lancashire.

The six ancient provinces of Alba were established around the ninth century by union of the Picts and Scots – the Picts being the earliest inhabitants of the land, while the Scots were later incomers from Ireland. Over these territories, the *Ard Righ* or High King was elected to rule. It is significant, particularly in the context of the later vilification of Macbeth in literature, that this kingship was elective and not hereditary. This important difference of ruling system led to many later misunderstandings of the early politics of Scotland.

Before his election to the crown, Macbeth was involved in the hereditary power struggle between two of the largest provinces, Moray and Atholl. Macbeth's father ruled Moray, which was a large territory (larger than the modern Scottish county) stretching from the east coast of what is now Aberdeenshire to the west coast. This province was so powerful that chroniclers sometimes referred to the mormaers of Moray as 'Kings of Scotland', implying that its size and importance favoured the election of kings from among the mormaers.

The second largest province was Atholl in the west. The feuds between Atholl and Moray were often of a violent and bloody nature. Atholl included Scone, the king-making centre of Alba (in what is now Perthshire), and stretched westwards to the Western Isles, including Mull, Islay, Jura, Arran, and to the holy island of Iona. On Iona, kings were buried, and from Iona Christianity had spread to pagan Scotland by the efforts of the missionary saints under the guidance of St. Columba. It was from the mormaers of Atholl that High Kings of Alba were usually elected, because of their descent from earlier Irish (Dalriadic) rulers who had unified the west of the land.

Macbeth's Scotland: Eleventh Century

To understand the culture, the feuds, and the final fusion into a united kingdom for the first time under Macbeth, we need to examine briefly the way of life in tenth and eleventh century Scotland. Firstly, there were no large cities or towns: life was essentially rural and decentralised. The cultural basis was that of the family or clan, with much isolation and wilderness leading to

Silver jewellery from a Viking hoard buried in Skaill, Orkney. In Macbeth's time, Viking raids on the British coast were extensive.

149

fiercely independent people and territories. It was this independent strongly tribal background that developed into a system of elective leadership, and which did not favour hereditary kingship as it eventually developed in England and other parts of Europe. Cattle were the major source of wealth, livelihood, trade – and, of course, of theft and dispute. This style of life derived from the primal Celtic culture, represented best in the Irish epic of the *Cattle Raid of Cooley* and the adventures of Cuchulainn. But the people of the tenth and eleventh centuries were not tribal nomads; they had developed agriculture in the fertile regions, and had a strong reliance upon the sea, its trade routes, and upon fishing. It is clear that trade with mainland Europe was conducted by sea, and that many Irish and Scottish missionaries carried the word of the old Celtic Church to the east by such sea routes. In the period of Macbeth, however, there was a constant threat to sea travel and trade by the Norse or Viking marauders, particularly during the summer season which was the traditional (and essentially practical) period for raiding, sailing, and all forms of warfare on land or sea.

Settlements with any significance were centred upon two types of location; the ancient fortresses or *duns*, and the monastic centres. Although the original Celtic Church, predating the Roman Church, was not political or highly organised in the modern sense, monasteries had become centres of trade and industry by the eleventh century; this held true in some regions of Scotland, though not to as great an extent as in Europe.

Warriors – Scottish and Norman

In Macbeth's youth, there were constant threats from the North and South, with raiding Norsemen and Anglo-Saxons at either border region.

Scottish warriors of this period tended not to use body armour, or bows. This preference reminds us of the earliest records of the fighting Celts, who are described as charging naked into battle, inspired by a terrible frenzy. By the tenth and eleventh centuries, Scots were fighting with swords and small *targets* or round shields, covered with stiff leather. Chieftains' shields carried rich decorations, often used as means of identifying a leader during the confusion of a battle. The swords used by the Scots tended to be the long swords of enduring Celtic preference, with additional broad bladed daggers and spears.

Recreation was found through horse racing and hunting, particularly the deer hunt which originally held a sacred significance as well as the secular one of sport or food.

We might safely assume that the use of the fighting axe was common at least in the northern territories and western isles, where Norse settlers had mixed with the native Celtic population. The concept of the mailed and mounted warrior, soon to appear with the powerful Norman warriors, would not have been found in Scotland at the time of Macbeth's youth; but it almost certainly began to register in the south of Scotland during his reign, with the increasing Norman presence and interest in English territories.

The St. Ninian treasure from
the Shetland Isles, including
communion implements, an
engraved bowl with animal
motifs, an ornate sword pommel,
a sword scabbard tip, a silver
hanging bowl with a close detail
showing the dog motif.

Viking warrior, from a tenth century carving.

Towards the close of his reign, Macbeth gave refuge to Norman warriors fleeing from retribution in England. These men were employed as mercenary troops to help defend the southern border; this action was possibly due to Macbeth's alliance with Thorfinn of Orkney and the potential balance of power both in England and Europe, though it is difficult to find evidence. The presence of Normans in Scotland, however, would have been seen as an ongoing threat to the English supremacy, and perhaps the beginning of an increased interest by Duke William of Normandy in the Scottish border territories as an access area into England. The Scottish and Celtic systems of government and elected kingship, together with the role of religion, were vital factors in Macbeth's rise to power.

Scottish Kingship

The old Scottish system of law, by which High Kings were elected and not drawn from hereditary lines as a matter of course, was a direct descendant of the oral traditions of law found in all early Celtic cultures. Late variants of these laws survived in Ireland, Wales and Brittany. They were the cause of much confusion to chroniclers and historians who failed to understand their foundation, assuming that the Scots were barbarians who flouted the general (English) laws of civilised existence. It was this system of elective kingship which made Macbeth into the first king of a progressive and increasingly united Scotland. Paradoxically, it also led to his unjustified vilification in later literature as an unscrupulous man of evil and so it is a system well worth examining.

Scotland was ruled by a complex of chieftains, ranging from small heads of

families, through to the mormaers or stewards, and culminating in lesser or petty kings directly under the High King. Significantly, all of these offices were well defined by ancient sets of laws, and all were maintained through election rather than inheritance. Candidates for power were nominated by their chieftain when death seemed imminent; such nominees were known as *tanists* (seconds). This system, so curious to the modern mind, seems to date back to a sacro-magical role of kingship common to primal western cultures. Elements of this pagan quality to kingship remained in eleventh century Scotland, which had a curious mixture of Christian and pre-Christian beliefs and practices.

The *tanist* or nominee needed tribal or clan approval to take his place as ruler. The greater leaders such as the mormaers or the High Kings were elected by a national assembly of chieftains and leaders of religion. There was a tendency for the great families to be elected to great roles; their experience in ruling and power led to a general pattern in which kingship was kept within certain family lines. But this was not identical to the English or European law of primogeniture, and there was no guaranteed succession.

It is this elective system that was so hard for later chroniclers to understand, and which led to the great drama of Shakespeare, which had little to do with the historical Macbeth. The principle behind elected kings was that they should be drawn from among those best suited and most worthy of the office . . . not merely from a family that sought to hold power. Petty chieftains and High Kings alike could be deposed by their people, and this acted as a guard against corruption or abuse of power.

Great families, such as Moray and Atholl, tended to be elected to the High

Modern Scone, originally the sacred centre of Scotland where the Celtic kings were installed after their election.

Kingship or other high office. In effect, this was a hereditary element within the elective system. The tendency for such families to feud with one another often led to attempts at deposing a High King through the ambition or vengeance of another chieftain or mormaer. In short, the system, which may have had its roots in a religious or magically-orientated society, had become politicised. With an ambitious series of invading kings ruling over nearby England, which developed an increasingly hereditary system, there were further options to abuse the Scottish system, by making alliances over the border. Such alliances were also made with Norway and Sweden.

Celtic Government

Despite the possibilities of abuse, the Celtic electoral system of rulership, from High King to local leader, worked well within the tolerances of its society and regions. It was supported and unified within a broader communal base of land tenure, from which the elected leadership system was derived. All land was held in common, there was no concept of private ownership or royal rights over tracts of land. The laws and restrictions of land and property administration were held in an ancient originally oral tradition. This began to become corrupted through the influence of the Roman Church, which was based upon a political system of ownership and manipulative legality, rather than tradition and consensus. Regional traditions of common ownership, labour and assistance remained in the remote parts of Scotland until the nineteenth century, so deep rooted were patterns of collective living.

Perhaps the most interesting aspect of Celtic traditional law, from the modern viewpoint, is the role of women. Unlike the legal situation which developed in England, and which persists in many aspects even today, marriage did not deprive a woman of her rights or her potential. Women were entitled to take elective office equally with men, and retained their personal powers, possessions and authority. This emphasis upon feminine equality and power derives from an earlier culture, best represented to us in the Irish sagas, in which women were direct representatives of the power or sovereignty of the goddess of the land. In this context, it is interesting to note that royal power (in England as well as Scotland) often depended upon the King marrying a certain woman. In the case of Macbeth, his marriage to Gruach, originally wife of his rival, confirmed his role of leadership. We should not take these primal magical aspects of early history too literally; they worked more in the manner of long established but vaguely defined sub-traditions. They occurred because they had always occurred, and because such processes as the relationship between a queen, the king, and land, were part of the deepest foundation of Celtic culture.

The Celtic Church

Religion played a crucial role at the time of Macbeth's life and his ascent to the throne of Alba or Scotland. The Celtic Church, one of the primal Christian churches predating the political Roman Church, came to Scotland

Celtic crozier found in Scandinavia and probably Viking loot from Scotland.

as early as 563 A.D. St Columba, banished from his native Ireland, established the first monastery on Iona, already a holy island with druidic pagan sanctity. Missionaries soon set to work to convert the Picts and Scots, and the Celtic Church was, loosely speaking, the state church of Scotland until at least the eleventh century. Even after the introduction of Roman monastic order through the reformation of the Saxon Queen Margaret (wife of Malcolm Canmore), there were still pockets of the Celtic or *culdee* orders surviving as late as the fourteenth century. Many Celtic church practices, fused with pagan tradition, survived well into the nineteenth and twentieth centuries in remote regions of the Highlands and islands, as communal prayers, rituals, and folklore.

The Celtic Church placed an emphasis upon communal living, non-ownership of land (in keeping with the traditional law of Celtic culture) and a diffusion of the Gospels in the common tongue (Gaelic or whatever happened to be the native language of a region). Great artists and scholars of Latin, Greek and Hebrew were found among the Celtic monks. It seems very likely that the education of the young Macbeth, son of a great mormaer, would have been at least partly under the guidance of the Celtic Church.

One of the important matters at the time of Macbeth's reign was the difference between the political land- and property-owning Roman Church, and the simpler more traditional Celtic Church. As an increasing tendency for

Scottish Christian relics: the Dunvegin Cup and the Kilmichael–Classrie Bell Shrine. The still active Celtic church in Scotland was supported by Macbeth.

155

the churches to own land developed, so did abbeys, settlements, crafts and trade centres become potential fortresses, targets for attack, and political weapons of bribery or corruption. Crinan, the father of Duncan, was both a warrior and an abbot. From his apparently ecclesiastical position at the Abbey of Dunkeld, Crinan was also Mormaer of Atholl and led an unsuccessful armed insurrection against Macbeth. This type of worldly exercise of power through a centre of religious authority was by no means typical of the Celtic Church, though many of its primates and saints were, of necessity, also warriors. Generally, the traditions and background of the Roman and Celtic Churches are very different. We may see the conflict between the older form of Christianity and its Roman political version as crucial to the emergence of a new and increasingly European Scotland. Similar conflicts were occuring all over Europe, where religion was used as an excuse to preserve or seize power.

The Rise to Power

Macbeth's rise to power and his final election to the High Kingship of Scotland thus took place against a complex political background. It also was closely interwoven with the fortunes and fates of other significant figures of the time.

Thorfinn of Orkney

Closely involved with Macbeth's rise to power was another important figure of the period. It would be no exaggeration to say that Thorfinn of Orkney was crucial to Macbeth's ascendance. Thorfinn descended from Malcolm II, who supported Thorfinn's claim to part of Orkney, and to the mainland territories of Caithness and Sutherland. To do this, Malcolm worked a vague dividing line between Celtic and Norse law, solely to obtain his own ends.

When Thorfinn's father, Sigurd Hlodversson, was slain at the great battle of Clontarf (1014) in Ireland, Orkney and the northern territories lay open to disputed claims. The defeat of the Norse invaders at the hand of the Irish was devastating; Norse expansion into Celtic regions was halted. Thus Malcolm's support of the young Thorfinn was designed to gradually claim back those territories taken from the Celts by force of arms. Thorfinn was sent to be fostered in the Norse–Celtic region of Caithness, ready to lay claim to a share of Orkney as soon as he was old enough.

Thus, to the north of Alba as ruled by Malcolm II, lay a large territory of both mainland and islands. Ultimately, these came under the rule of Thorfinn, who was sponsored by the Scottish king. It would not have been possible for Macbeth to come to the throne and develop Alba into a united kingdom, without some agreement with the powerful Thorfinn. Although we have no formal record of such an agreement, this is undoubtedly what must have occurred.

However, Malcolm II did not rest with his inroads into the Norse territories through diplomacy and patronage. To the south, invading Danes and Saxons were battling for the rule of England, which fell to the great King Canute in 1016. Malcolm used the conflict to expand his own territories, invading the territory once known as Bernica on the east coast well into Northumbria. The Scots defeated the Northumbrians at Carham in 1018. Thus, the dispute for this territory between English and Danish overlords was turned to a decisive Scots advantage, and the rule of the High King was extended to its furthest point south.

Death of Macbeth's father
In the year 1020, when Macbeth was about fifteen years of age, his father Finlaech MacRuaridh was slain by his nephews Gillecomgain and Malcolm. The killing probably took place because of Finlaech's increasing connections with the rival House of Atholl. He had married King Malcolm II's daughter Doada, and given support to the High King by placing his clans under royal command during Danish raids. Thus, whilst no definite reason is known, we may presume that the ongoing feud between Moray and Atholl led to the killing. The nephew Malcolm was elected as Mormaer, and died after nine years of rule; Gillecomgain was immediately elected to rule after his brother.

Unlike his uncle Gillecomgain stood firmly against the Atholl High King. He sought to improve the Moray claim to High Kingship by marrying Gruach, who was later to become the wife of Macbeth. Gruach was the granddaughter of Kenneth III, who had been killed by Malcolm II in 1005.

This pattern of dispute, election, and symbolic defiance through marriage, is crucial to the eventual kingship of Macbeth.

Death of Gillecomgain
History tells us little of what happened to Macbeth after the death of his father. Presumably he was under the protection of Malcolm II, and grew into adulthood in some safe place, receiving his training in arms and skill as befitted a member of a noble family who had supported the High King. In 1032, according to the *Annals of Ulster*, the Mormaer of Moray and fifty of his men were burned to death. Gillecomgain, cousin to Macbeth and killer of Macbeth's father, had finally fallen victim in turn to the Moray and Atholl feud. During Malcolm's old age, pressure had been building over the High Kingship and his nominated successor; a number of battles and killings were a direct result of this tension, as the election of a new High King was imminent. Thus, Malcolm II, at the age of almost eighty, sought to eliminate as many possible candidates for the High Kingship as he could in the limited time left to him. Gillecomgain's marriage to Gruach, his powerful Moray position, and his obvious hostility to Atholl, brought about his death. His son Lulach and Gruach, however, escaped the slaughter, though in 1033 her brother (another Malcolm) was killed in the ruthless process of eliminating opposition to the Atholl claim and to the nominee of the aged king.

Glamis Castle, despite its legendary claims, has little real historical association with Macbeth.

Mormaer of Moray

In 1033, Macbeth was elected as Mormaer of Moray. There is much debate over the part he may or may not have played in the killing of Gillecomgain, the slayer of his father. Certainly, the deaths of Gillecomgain and Malcolm Mac Bodhe (brother of Gruach) were part of the Atholl plan to retain power by wiping out all potential candidates for High King from the Moray faction. But there is no contemporary evidence to suggest that Macbeth was directly involved.

It seems unlikely that Macbeth was a direct puppet of Malcolm II, otherwise he would not have been elected as Mormaer. Whatever the reasons for his election, he soon married Gruach (the widow of Gillecomgain and granddaughter of a Scottish king) and adopted her son Lulach. Thus, on coming into his territorial power, he took on the traditional stance of opposition to the House of Atholl. Suddenly, Macbeth had become one of the most powerful men in Alba, with a strong claim as potential candidate for the High Kingship. Curiously, the ageing Malcolm II had not removed Macbeth from the scene, though we have no evidence to support or deny any such attempts.

Duncan becomes High King

Malcolm finally died at Glamis, on November 25th in 1034. His nominated successor was Duncan Mac Crinan, his eldest grandson, who was elected as High King at Scone in December 1034. Thus does one of the most bitter conflicts for power related in dramatic literature make its *true* historical appearance.

Duncan was thirty three years old, and had some experience of rule as petty king of Cumbria. His election seemed to place the House of Atholl firmly in the highest role of power in Alba.

After the death of King Canute in 1035, and the subsequent struggles of the English and Norwegian crowns, Thorfinn became ruler of the entire Orkneys, Hebrides, and the mainland regions of Caithness and Sutherland. The rise of Thorfinn is only of interest in as much as it affected the career of Macbeth, but by 1039–40, two grandsons of Malcolm II ruled Scotland from north to south: Thorfinn, the old king's Norse protegé, and Duncan his elected heir to the High Kingship of Alba. This two-fold division of power finally brought Macbeth to the throne, but not without the catalysing effect of Duncan's inability to rule adequately.

Macbeth was, of course, another grandson of Malcolm II through his mother Doada. Thus, the cautious policy of marrying a daughter, Doada, into the opposing Moray faction to gain support would soon turn against the House of Atholl.

Duncan Overthrown

MACDUFF   O horror, horror, horror! Tongue nor heart Cannot conceive or name thee.

MACBETH & LENNOX   What's the matter?

MACDUFF   Confusion now hath made his masterpiece. Most sacrilegious murder hath broke ope The Lord's anointed temple, and stole thence the life o' th' building

MACBETH   What is't you say – the life?

LENNOX   Mean you his majesty?

MACDUFF   Approach the chamber and destroy your sight With a new Gorgon. Do not bid me speak; see and then speak yourselves. Awake! Awake! Ring the alarum bell. Murder and treason! . . .

In Shakespeare's drama, Duncan is described as a gracious king, slain by a foul usurper. The historical truth, well attested, is rather the opposite. When Duncan was deposed, no complaint was raised, and Macbeth was *elected*. This matter of election is not entirely proof of universal approval, but goes a long way towards proving that Macbeth was a better choice for the people of Alba than was the late Duncan.

In *The Orygynale Cronykil of Scotland*, Andrew Wyntoun describes Duncan as a vicious tyrant; certainly his record as a ruler and military leader is poor. The fictional warping of history, by which the roles of Macbeth and Duncan were gradually reversed, did not begin until some centuries after the original events; by which point time and cultural changes had obscured the reality of the situation.

Perhaps Duncan's most unpopular and dangerous move was to force campaigns on northern and southern fronts almost simultaneously. Duncan

Ornamental sword hilts (above and opposite) by the Frankish swordsmiths who produced the best weapons of the period, and which were widely used throughout Europe and Northern Scotland.

attempted to expand into the territories of Caithness and Sutherland, ruled by the powerful earl Thorfinn of Orkney as part of the Norse territories. He also tried to take advantage of the disputes over English succession, by invading Northumbria. Thus, forces moved both north and south, to Caithness under the command of Duncan's nephew Moddan, and to Durham under the command of Duncan himself. Both attempts failed miserably.

Duncan, showing himself not only to be heartless but totally incapable of basic military strategy, sent repeated cavalry charges against the massive walls of Durham; once the cavalry were defeated, the city troops counter-attacked and killed thousands of the Scottish infantry. The heads of these men, killed through the incompetence of the king that they had helped to elect, were impaled around the city walls.

While in retreat, Duncan met with his nephew Moddan, who had been forced to withdraw from Caithness and Sutherland in the face of a large opposing force assembled by Thorfinn and his foster father Thorkell. Duncan then resolved to throw all his remaining combined forces against Thorfinn, with a land army commanded by Moddan, and Duncan heading a fleet of eleven ships to attempt to trap the Norse warriors in between two attacking armies.

Defeat at Sea

Earl Thorfinn met Duncan's fleet off Deerness, where after a prolonged sea battle, the Scottish ships were routed. Much of the history of this period is recorded in the *Orkneyinga Saga* which describes the battle between the Orkney and Scottish fleets in detail:

> The Scots bunched together on the High King's ship just before the mast. Then Jarl Thorfinn leaped from the poop of his ship forward into that of the High King, laying about him boldly. When he saw that the numbers were thinning upon the High King's ship, he called on his men to come aboard. And when King Duncan saw this, he gave orders to cut the lashing and stand off to sea . . .

Duncan escaped from his doomed flagship to another vessel, and headed south. Thorfinn combined his forces with another fleet led by his foster father Thorkell, and pursed the High King into the Moray Firth. Duncan made his way ashore, and the two Orkney fleets attacked the coastal settlements of the region.

Meanwhile Moddan and his force of Atholl clansmen had reached Caithness, where they awaited reinforcements of Irish mercenaries. Thorkell and his men, however, surprised Moddan's unfortunate troop while they slept. As Moddan leaped from a burning building, Thorkell beheaded him with a single blow. Duncan now assembled as large an army as possible and confronted Thorfinn on 14 August 1040, only to be defeated.

It is at this point in the tale that Macbeth again appears. The *Orkneyinga Saga* tells us that Duncan fled the battle 'and some say he was slain'.

Marianus Scotus, however, says that 'Duncan High King of Scotland was slain on 14 August by his general Macbeth, son of Finlay' (*Chronicon Univer-*

Known as the 'ruddy' or 'red-haired' king, Macbeth leads a raid upon rebels. In eleventh century Scotland, it was not unusual for a king to fight in person, taking the same risks as his warriors and thus ensuring his relationship as leader of his men.

sal). This seems unlikely, given the circumstances of the feud between Atholl and Moray, unless some unchronicled duplicity was practised by Macbeth. No further evidence of this curious incident is now available, and we might assume from subsequent events that Macbeth was on good terms with Thorfinn of Orkney, without whose support he could not have remained as High King for fifteen years.

It seems more likely that we are dealing here with a clerical or copying error, and that Macbeth and his Moray forces helped to dispose of Duncan after the High King's failure against the Orkney men. One possible interpretation of this statement is that the Celtic title mormaer or something similar has been translated to mean 'general' by Marianus Scotus.

After the defeat and death of Duncan, who had become widely unpopular as a result of his expansionism and inability to rule or command adequately, events suggest an alliance between Thorfinn of Orkney and Macbeth Mormaer of Moray. The result was that Thorfinn was firmly established without any opposition or Scottish claims upon Orkney or Caithness and Sutherland, while Macbeth was elected to the High Kingship.

Duncan was actually killed at Bothgowan which means 'the blacksmith's house'; today the name has become Pitgaveny, near Elgin.

Contemporary reports vary slightly, for John of Fordun says that Duncan was wounded and carried to Elgin where he died; the *Register of St. Andrews* states that he died at Bothgowan. The Orkney forces ravaged far south into Fife, burning, killing, and destroying. We may presume that it was during this period that some arrangement was made between Thorfinn and Macbeth, for the Orkney forces eventually withdrew northwards. Macbeth made his way to Scone, the hallowed place of king making, to claim support and election as High King. He was crowned in the summer of 1040.

Macbeth as King

During his rule, Macbeth gave much to Scotland. Contemporary chronicles described him as liberal, and his reign as productive, plentiful, generous. St. Berchan, referring to the aftermath of the conflict between Duncan and Thorfinn wrote:

After the slaughter of the Scots, after the slaughter of foreigners, the liberal king will possess Scotland. This strong one was fair, yellow haired, tall. Very pleasant was that handsome youth to me. Brimful of food was Scotland, east and west, during the reign of the brave ruddy king.

How different is this account from that given by Shakespeare, hundreds of years later and as spoken by Macduff:

Fit to govern! No, not to live! O nation miserable with an untitled tyrant bloody-sceptred, when shalt thou see thy wholesome days again. . .

The fearsome Earl Siward, leader of the English expedition against Scotland and Macbeth, prepares to leap to his death from the walls of York. Stricken by camp fever or dysentry, he demanded to be dressed in full armour and carried outdoors, rather than die inside like an animal on straw.

The Early Reign

From 1040 to 1045, the Kingdom of Alba was relatively peaceful, with the newly elected High King rebuilding after the ravages of Duncan's unsuccessful campaigns. Contemporary and later chroniclers generally confirm that Macbeth and his wife were good rulers. The tyrannical despotic element simply does not appear in the early sources of his history, those very sources which by their nature of closeness to the man and his rule are probably the most accurate.

Hector Boece, writing much later, in the early part of the sixteenth century, suggests that Macbeth became cruel and oppressive after 1050. Prior to that, Boece admits that the King initiated certain legal reforms (*History of Scotland*, 1527).

These reforms are interesting for they include statutory support of orphans and women, inheritance for daughters, and control over itinerant and non-productive members of the population for the benefit of the community. Laws of this sort are typical to the ancient oral traditions of law preserved in Celtic countries. They certainly would not have been novel or unusual in eleventh century Scotland which already upheld an exceedingly complex set of laws providing for women, common welfare, state support for the less fortunate, and as described earlier an archaic but operative system of common ownership and election of leaders, be they male or female.

Boece, much like Shakespeare copying from the histories without fully understanding their background, would not necessarily have grasped the cultural foundation for those laws which he ascribed generously to Macbeth. It is likely, though, that in the period of reform following his election, the new King declared formally that he would uphold certain essential laws deriving from ancient tradition – particularly if they were those that had fallen into disuse during the reign of the previous King.

We may also consider sources more contemporary for evidence of Macbeth's government of Alba in those early years; both the king and his wife Gruach were benefactors of the Celtic Church. They are recorded (in the *Register of St. Andrews*) as giving land to the Culdees of Loch Leven. Andrew Wyntoun also records, some centuries later, that Macbeth 'did many pleasant acts in the beginning of his reign . . .'

Thorfinn Invades the South

But the early years of the reign were not totally peaceful, and two invasions or series of raids occurred into England which shed some further light on the relationship between Macbeth and Earl Thorfinn of Orkney.

In 1041, Thorfinn established a base camp as far south as Strathclyde, from which he indulged in raids over the border into Northumbria. Earl Siward rooted out these invaders, and forced them to retreat. Thorfinn returned to Orkney, but raised a large army for the following spring of 1042.

The *Orkneyinga Saga* tells us that for this retaliatory expedition troops were drawn not only from Orkney and Caithness, but from Ireland and

Viking swords and axe head (above and opposite); typical weapons of the Macbeth period.

162

Scotland. The presence of Scottish troops indicates that Macbeth was somehow in allegiance with Thorfinn, even if it was only to the extent of allowing warriors to hire as mercenaries to the Norse Earl. Yet there was no official or formal declaration of war between Scotland and Northumbria, nor was Macbeth on record as a defined or formal ally of Thorfinn. This nebulous situation must have suited Macbeth well; he could keep the general support of the powerful Earl who had allowed him to stand for the Scottish throne, yet avoid a total declaration of hostilities that might spill over into war with England.

Thorfinn's fleet struck at Cumbria on the north western coast of England, and defeated the Mercians there in two battles before the onset of winter. (We must remember that the campaigning season was fairly short, and that all wars were punctuated by the need to return homewards before winter; this was a vital feature of all medieval warfare and seasonal and weather factors were often decisive in the outcome of campaigns.) The conflict was nobly recorded by Arnor, the *skald* or bard to Earl Thorfinn as the following extract shows:

> Upon England's shores
> The Jarl bore his banner
> Ever and again.
> Reddening the Eagle's tongue,
> The Prince bade them carry
> The Standard steadfastly.
> Flame flared,
> Roofs fell, smoke curled,
> To heaven rose the fiery gleam
> While the armed band pursued.
>
> Many horn blast
> Was heard 'mid the fortresses
> Where high wind waved the banner
> Of the stout hearted Prince.
> He of the open hand,
> Rushed into battle.
> Now fear fell
> On the Wolf Lord's host.
> In the battle at dawn
> Swords were washed
> And wolves tore the slain. . . .

The Revolt of Crinan

Contemporary chronicles record that in 1045, Crinan, father of Duncan and Abbot of Dunkeld, was killed with 180 of his Atholl men. This was the only internal revolt of any significance that occurred during Macbeth's reign. The campaigns that eventually destroyed him were backed by troops from Northumbria, England, or Denmark. Obviously, Crinan judged that after five years of Moray-sponsored rule, the time was ripe for an Atholl revolt. His forces met with those of Macbeth at Dunkeld, north of Perth. Both the Mormaer of Atholl and his men were killed, and no further Atholl insurrec-

tion occurred for some years until the invasions in support of Malcolm, by then exiled at the English court.

After Crinan's revolt and death, nine years of increasing stability occurred in Scotland. Macbeth made the traditional monarch's pilgrimage to Rome to obtain absolution from the Pope – and of course to confirm and connect his political sources of support within Europe and the Church of Rome which claimed a general overlordship of all kings, states, and variant Churches.

Peace and Prosperity

It seems that Macbeth's years of peace and prosperity were due in a great measure to the strength of Earl Thorfinn. Shortly after the Atholl revolt and the death of Crinan, Thorfinn came into conflict with his nephew Rognvald Brussisson, who disputed the division of Orkney. As this dispute matured, Rognvald had the support of King Magnus of Norway, and for a while the prospects looked hard indeed for Thorfinn, and were thus threatening to Macbeth. If Rognvald defeated Thorfinn with the aid of Magnus, then a renewed powerful Norwegian claim upon Orkney, Caithness and Sutherland would soon follow.

Despite warships supplied by Norway to aid his cause, Rognvald was defeated in a terrible sea battle in the Pentland Firth. He fled to the court of

King Magnus, but almost immediately returned to make a desperate assassination attempt upon the unsuspecting Thorfinn. The *Orkneyinga Saga* relates how Rognvald and his men set fire to the hall in which Thorfinn sat drinking, and how it was assumed that Thorfinn and his wife Ingibjorg had died in the conflagration. But Thorfinn had carried his wife to safety, breaking through the back wall of the hall, and had rowed to Caithness.

In secrecy, Thorfinn took reports of Rognvald's movements, and finally trapped him upon the island of Stronsay. Rognvald's attempt to escape was foiled by his own lapdog, which barked and gave away his position. The usurping nephew was killed by Thorkell, foster father to Thorfinn.

If Magnus of Norway had been able at this stage to invade in force, using the death of his man Rognvald as an excuse, Orkney might have fallen. But Magnus was soon embroiled in conflict over the rulership of Denmark. This was claimed both by Magnus and by the regent Sweyn after the death of Hardecanute, who had been king of both England and, at one remove, of Denmark. Thus, Thorfinn was able to assert his independence from Norway, and provide alliance and protection for Alba from his position of strength in the far north.

Edward the Confessor, crowned in 1043, now ruled England. The crown and its connection to Europe was the subject of complex feuds and disputes. This situation enabled Alba and its king Macbeth to remain in comparative isolation and freedom from invasion. Paradoxically, it was this same complex political situation that nurtured Malcolm Canmore, son of Duncan. He absorbed the concept, hitherto hardly recognised in Alba, that there was a hereditary right of kingship passing from father to eldest son. This is where the deepest roots of the concept of Macbeth as a usurper may be tentatively traced; roots which were to sprout in chronicles and histories several centuries after the death of Macbeth, and to flower in Shakespearian drama and derivative works of art.

Invasion, Downfall and Death

The turning point in Macbeth's period of generous and unifying rule was 1054. Malcolm, son of Duncan, gained support from the English king Edward for his claim the High Kingship of Alba. Such a claim was inadmissible under Celtic law; but it was certainly admissible in England, where primogeniture carried considerable weight. Overall command for an invasion force was given to Earl Siward of Northumbria.

Siward was a truly heroic character, large in size and nature, to whom many exploits were traditionally attributed. His significant service to Edward the Confessor was to cut off the head of a rebellious earl (Jarl Tosti) and deliver it to the King. In July of 1054, Siward Dirga (Valiant) led a large army of his own Northumbrians, plus Danes and Anglo-Saxons, over the border into Scotland. The *Anglo Saxon Chronicle* records that he slaughtered many

Scots, and that Macbeth was put to flight. Siward lost his own son in this conflict, and so the war became not only a matter of political expansionism, but one of personal revenge. Malcolm accompanied the invading forces, raising Atholl supporters to his cause.

The primary objective of the invading army was Scone, centre of king-making. Presumably Malcolm hoped to accumulate enough support to be elected or declared king as soon as Macbeth had been disposed of. The battle listed in the chronicles is of course the famous scene in Shakespeare's play in which 'Birnam wood do come to Dunsinane'.

Despite the curious tradition found in Shakespeare, we can also trace this motif to the thirteenth century prophecies of Thomas the Rhymer, who predicted that 'Fedderate Castle shall ne'er be ta'en/till Fyvie wood to the war is gaen . . .'

This utterance was dramatically fulfilled in the eighteenth century, when invading English troops used trees from Fyvie wood as battering rams to breach the previously unconquered castle of Feddarate. It is impossible to tell where Shakespeare drew his tradition from; did the wood motif come from an actual tradition relating to the eleventh century and Macbeth, later adapted by Thomas the Rhymer into a coincidentally accurate prophetic verse? Or did Shakespeare – as seems more likely – draw the theme from his own reading of the popular verses and *Romance* of Thomas the Rhymer?

The siting of the battle at Dunsinane seems likely, but is not confirmed by contemporary chroniclers. Dunsinane lies between Scone and Perth, so it is certainly in the correct region. William of Malmesbury, writing in the twelfth century, suggests that the conflict took place at Dundee. Once again, there is no body of supporting evidence from the period.

The battle was not decisive with losses of 3,000 Scots, and 1,500 English and Danes. Siward lost his son, Oshern, and was forced to withdraw without placing Malcolm upon the throne, and without killing Macbeth. He also lost his nephew, another Siward; the price he paid for his invasion was high.

Malcolm was officially recognised as King of Cumbria, confirmed by Edward the Confessor, and thus described in a letter from the English court to Pope Boniface. But he was not yet King of Scotland. As an added setback to his ambitions, Earl Siward died in York the following year – not in battle, but of some type of illness, possibly dysentry. Before his death, he ordered that he should be attired in full battle array with armour, shield and axe: 'I will not die like a cow on straw . . . ' Tradition preserves the tale of his dramatic death leap from the city walls rather than die on his sick bed.

The Earldom of Northumbria was now taken over by Edward's favourite Tostig Godwinson. Two years elapsed in which Tostig, a firm comrade of Malcolm, supported plans for renewed invasion of Scotland.

Viking swords from the ninth and tenth century: single edged (above); double-edged and five-lobed pommelled, double-edged (opposite).

The Death of Macbeth
Ultimately, Macbeth's end was inexorably linked with the subsequent history of Duncan's family.

166

The immediate relatives of Duncan had not been wiped out by Macbeth, nor had any immediate plan of revenge been exacted upon them. Duncan's father Crinan, the Abbot of Dunkeld, had been a renowned warrior in his day. He made arrangements for his three grandsons to be fostered outside the immediate circle of the court of Alba, not only for their immediate protection, but to train them as potential candidates for the High Kingship.

The eldest of these boys was Malcolm, aged nine. His mother was cousin to Siward, who became Earl of Northumbria in 1041. This relationship was to prove crucial to Macbeth. Both son and mother were sent to the English court, where they lived through the short violent reign of Hardecanute, into that of Edward the Confessor.

The young Malcolm thus learned English ways rather than Celtic, speaking the various languages of the different factions. These included Norman French, which was already spoken at court before the Norman Conquest as a result of Edward's own exile in Normandy before he became king. Malcolm's period in England can be viewed as the beginning of the end for the old style elected High Kingship, for when he took the throne from Macbeth some years later, he brought many European ways into Celtic Scotland, accelerating changes already begun.

The second son of Duncan MacCrinan was Donald Ban, aged seven at the time of his exile. He was fostered either in the Hebrides or in Ireland, thus retaining Celtic customs of education and culture. This native upbringing was to show when he, in turn, became High King after his brother Malcolm.

The third son, Maelmuir, was sent to the court of his relative Siward of Northumbria; he eventually succeeded his grandfather as Mormaer of Atholl.

Thus, three potential claimants to the throne were fostered in three diverse areas, and at least two were in camps directly hostile to Macbeth: Malcolm in England, and Maelmuir in Northumbria. We may presume that Donald Ban was hidden right in the midst of staunch Atholl supporters in the west of Scotland or in Ireland, to be trained for the enduring conflict between his House and that of Moray represented by Macbeth. On confirmation as king of Cumbria, supported by the English crown, Malcolm continued to work towards his goal; the High Kingship of Scotland, and of course the death of Macbeth. Traditionally, Malcolm would have had support from the Atholl clans, but it is not clear who succeeded Crinan as mormaer after his death in 1045. After the invasion of 1054, Macbeth retained control of much of Scotland, including Scone, the traditional seat of power.

The lengthy process of destroying Macbeth, over a period of at least three years, suggests that his good qualities of rule, as recorded by early chronicles, had gained him widespread support. He was by no means easy to dispose of, but history and the tides of change in Europe now worked against him. His visit to Rome for absolution by Leo IX was now rendered valueless as a political connection; Leo died in 1054 as a prisoner in the ongoing feud with the invading Normans in Italy. The firm support for Malcolm from Edward, and from his vassal Tostig, could not be countered with appeals to papal

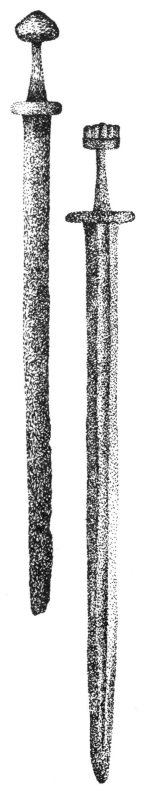

authority. Furthermore, Macbeth had given refuge to a number of Normans banished from England during the struggles for power; these warriors were almost all killed during the great battle of 1054. The sheltering and use of Norman mercenaries, however, was seen as a direct threat to English power, as Scotland might become a base from which the ambitious Duke William of Normandy might eventually press his claims or attacks upon England.

In 1057, on 15th August, Malcolm killed Macbeth. Traditionally, this occurred in or near an ancient circle of stones called Peel Ring, at Lumphanan in Mar. Malcolm and his troops had pursued Macbeth northwards from Scone. Little is known of the reasons for this movement other than the presumed fact that the invading Anglo–Danish army had gradually weakened the southernmost defences and gained support from the Atholl faction – to such an extent that it became imperative for Macbeth to move his court and take a fresh stand in safer territory.

Macbeth was buried on the island of Iona, the sacred place where so many Scottish kings were traditionally interred. This honourable and venerable custom reveals once again that he was regarded as a just and rightful king. In contrast, Malcolm was buried in Dunfermline upon his death. This must reflect that he was not considered as worthy as his predecessors of the ancient burial right upon Iona, an island shrouded in mystery and traditions of sanctity.

The curious aspect of Macbeth's death in the stone circle may be worth further consideration. Just as we have the relics of an early culture in the theme of certain women remarrying the kings, mormaers or clan leaders in succession (as did Gruach, Macbeth's wife), so we may have a similar confused echo in the story of Macbeth's death. So many traditions are attached to kingship and ritual death in Celtic culture that it is hard not to find an overtone of such traditions in the fact that Malcolm imposed a 'cruel death' upon the High King in a stone circle.

The Short Reign of Lulach

Scotland did not pass into the rulership of Malcolm immediately upon his killing of Macbeth. The invading troops presumably retired or were forced to retire southwards again, for Macbeth was carried with ceremony to Iona. His stepson Lulach, appointed as his *tanist* or potential successor, was elected as High King.

Lulach was elected at Scone in the manner of Celtic law, which clearly indicates that Malcolm was by no means popular or powerful enough at this stage, even after the death of Macbeth. But sheer weight of numbers, English support, and the weakening of Scotland through a long series of campaigns and destruction, were beginning to have their inevitable effect. Lulach resisted Malcolm's forces for seven months. A contemporary chronicle records that he was slain on 17th March, 1058, by treachery. Lulach was, in turn, to follow Macbeth for burial upon Iona, as was his mother Gruach. Their graves were to remain in the tiny burial ground next to the abbey for at least eight hundred years; today the burial stones have been moved for preservation.

King Malcolm

Thus on 25th April, 1058, Malcolm was finally crowned as High King by Bishop Tuthald, in Scone. It is interesting to realise that during this long campaign and the gradual suppression of the Moray House (which was to persist during Malcolm's reign with his oppression and eventual banishment of Lulach's son Mael Snechta) that no aid was forthcoming from Thorfinn of Orkney.

By 1059, or thereabouts, Thorfinn had died. In 1059, Malcolm married his widow, Ingibjorg – yet another example of a male ruler's power being confirmed through his marriage to the right woman. It seems likely that Thorfinn died of an illness, and was thus unable to lead direct support for Macbeth. He was one of the greatest of all Orkney rulers and widely lamented by Norse saga makers or chroniclers. The ruins of his great hall and his abbey on Birsay may still be found today.

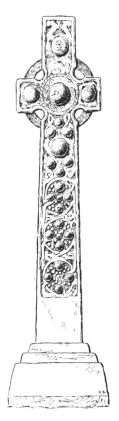

St. Martins Cross on the island of Iona.

The Kings of Scotland, including Macbeth, in the nineteenth century frieze in the Natural Portrait Gallery of Scotland, Edinburgh.

Thorfinn was the greatest warrior. He took the earldom when he was five winters old [ie supported in his claim by Malcom II] and he ruled for more than sixty winters; he died of disease in the latter days of Harald Sigurd's son.   *The Heimskringla of St. Olaf's Saga.*

The coincidence of dates of death between Macbeth and Thorfinn has caused some writers to suggest that Thorfinn died while campaigning in support of his Scottish ally; but there is no contemporary evidence to support this. Indeed, Norse sources state that he died of disease. The curious fact that Malcom Mac Duncan, now King Malcolm III, married Thorfinn's widow has added to the puzzle of this complex situation. Dorothy Dunnet, in her epic novel *King Hereafter* has gone so far as to suggest that Thorfinn and Macbeth were one and the same person, also conflating Gruach and Ingibjorg. The physical descriptions of the two men, however, would alone counter such a theory; Thorfinn described as tall grim and dark, while Macbeth was ruddy or golden in colouring.

Historical Legacy

During the seventeen years of Macbeth's reign, there were the first indications of a unified Scotland. This must not be taken in a literal sense, and much of the concept and process of unification may only be seen with hindsight. What is certain is that his murder and the eventual acquisition of the crown by Malcolm marked a turning point in the decline of ancient Scotland. It led to the gradual but almost total anglicising of the country and its methods of government. Once again, this hinges upon the matter of primogeniture, in which an eldest son has a firm right to his father's property or crown. Once this concept was introduced by force into the foundation of the Scottish Celtic system, it was inevitable that profound changes would follow.

This sequence of changes brought Scotland into step with the rapidly altering political consciousness of Europe. There would have been no likelihood of an idealised Alba or Scotland preserving Celtic communal traditions while all countries around were falling to the swords of the mighty and devising complex systems of preserving selected superior groups in power. Macbeth's reign was a lull in the storm of change, created by the balance of power between himself and Thorfinn of Orkney, and coincidentally assisted by the rapidly changing power struggles in England and Europe.

With Malcolm Canmore's claiming of the Scottish crown, feudalism came into the land, and there it remained. He gave large areas of land to his supporters, particularly in the Moray regions which would otherwise have opposed him. This granting of land as a possession to overlords was in itself essentially alien to the Scottish or Celtic system. It was much more than a move to weaken opposition, for it struck directly at the cultural roots of the people.

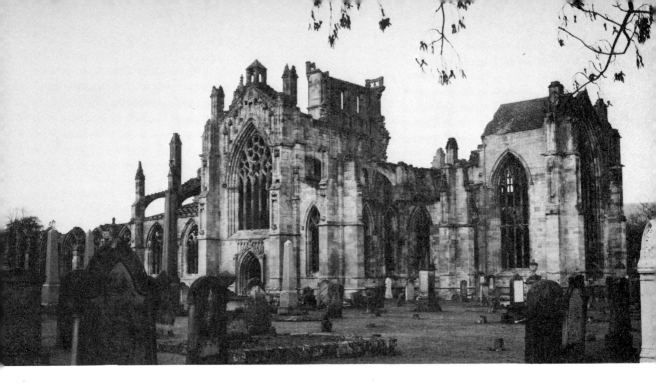

Melrose Abbey, one of the great border abbeys of Scotland. Such centres represented the 'new style' monarchy in Scotland after the death of Macbeth, when election of kings ceased.

The dramatic events of the year 1066, by which William of Normandy forced his way upon the English throne, drove Edgar Aetheling, the English heir and only survivor of his family, into Scotland. As he had grown up in Hungary, Edgar could not speak English, and was not held in any esteem by the English nobles. Of course, the succession became irrelevant after the battles of 1066, but Edgar was given refuge by Malcolm. After the death of Ingibjorg during childbirth, Malcolm married Edgar's sister Margaret.

This marriage helped to hasten the decline of Scotland as a culture separate from Europe. Margaret was a supporter of the Roman Church, and made considerable efforts to Romanise the older primal Celtic Church, which had always kept itself separate from its younger and much more politically conscious relative in Rome. The most effective of her reforms was to place her Saxon confessor, Turgot, in the position of primate of Scotland. Although various *culdee* or Celtic practices were to remain for long periods of time, the formal status of the Celtic Church as the national spiritual organisation for the Scots was effectively destroyed by Margaret. She was, of course, canonized for her services, and Turgot wrote her biography.

But Margaret's formidable influence was not confined to religion; she controlled Malcolm. This control, leading to four invasions of England in support of her brother Edgar's claim to the English throne, also helped to weaken Scottish independance. After much bloodshed along the borders and in Northumbria, William the Conqueror finally invaded Scotland in retaliation. Malcolm submitted to William in 1072, at Abernethy, and swore to accept him as overlord.

However, the conflict between England and Scotland was not settled. By 1079 Malcolm was engaged in further hostilities over the border. After the death of William in 1087, his son William Rufus invaded Cumbria, which he took as part of England, and which it has remained to the present day. Malcolm failed to come to terms with William Rufus, and was finally killed during another invasion of Northumbria in 1093.

Upon the death of Malcolm (and that of his wife Margaret which followed shortly afterwards), his brother Donald Ban, now aged sixty, was elected High King at Scone. His brief reversion to Celtic style rule was soon wiped out by an invading army sponsored by England. This invasion was designed to set Duncan, son of Malcolm and previously hostage at the English court, upon the throne of Scotland. Duncan declared himself King by hereditary right, a declaration impossible under Scottish law.

Duncan was to rule for only a few months, and was killed by a supporter of Donald Ban, who returned to rule (as elected High King) for a further three years, until 1097. His reign was cruelly terminated by Edgar, yet another son of Malcolm and Margaret, supported once again by William Rufus and an invading army. Donald Ban was taken prisoner and blinded. Although he was buried at Dunkeld, his body was later taken to Iona as a sign of respect for a High King. Significantly, both Malcolm and Margaret remained buried in Dunfermline and were not accorded this honour.

Edgar, son of Malcolm, again declared a hereditary right to the crown, and the course was set for an Anglo–Norman ruling class in Scotland. From feuding between the Moray and Atholl factions, the struggle for the Scottish crown had finally become a matter of international politics, with a foreign power supporting rival claimants within one ruling faction. It seems ironic that this bitter true story of blood relatives fighting and killing one another should have been passed over, while the true history of Macbeth as a good king who benefitted his realm has been forgotten.

Shakespeare's Characters – and History

A comparison of the characters as portrayed by Shakespeare and their historical likelihood is illuminating. Not only do the historical persons bear very little relationship to those assembled by Shakespeare (who drew entirely upon relatively late chronicles), but we find that some of the major figures are the opposite of their fictional namesakes. This is most apparent in Macbeth himself, and in his opposite, Duncan.

While the historical Macbeth was a king of good character, Duncan was a tyrant. Lady Macbeth, Gruach, seems also to have been a person of good character and a beneficial queen; many of the ruthless qualities exhibited by the Shakespearian lady are more noticeable in Margaret, English wife of Malcolm III who invaded Scotland and killed Macbeth.

We need, however, to exercise a certain amount of caution when making such brief comparisons, particularly at such a long historical remove and through the filters of many literary sources. While it is easy to compare persons through such diffuse hindsight, the opposites and similarities are really little more than the natural rhythmn that arises in any historical period.

Sir Laurence Olivier plays Macbeth in Shakespeare's play.

In other words, when we examine the chronicles of kings, queens and people of power, some few are of good character, while many more are ruthless and devious. Furthermore, the standard of judgement is coloured by time and cultural change. Macbeth was a relatively good kind by any standard, less bloodthirsty and destructive by far than his immediate predecessor Duncan; yet he undoubtedly killed and manipulated his supporters, as did any leader of the period. Within a few years Malcolm, son of Duncan, was already colouring Macbeth as a usurper, a theme that was to be developed so readily in centuries to come. Thus, from the viewpoint of the hereditary monarch, Macbeth and the system which he upheld of elected leadership, were evils that threatened the hard won status quo of armed power and primogeniture. Some of the people in the list which follows *do* appear on the surface to be inversions or confusions of one another. Yet there is no evidence whatsoever that this is anything other than coincidence and the organic change of characters that runs through history. Shakespeare and his chronicle sources did *not* confuse these characters with one another.

MACBETH   Presented by Shakespeare as a usurper, tyrant, and murderer. But history shows that he was an elected king with seventeen years of general support and beneficial rule to his credit.

LADY MACBETH   Portrayed as a powerful influence upon the corrupt acts of the tyrant Macbeth; a ruthless woman bent upon revenge. History reveals that Gruach, Macbeth's real wife, was from an honoured bloodline, and apparently aided in his rule and civil and religious reforms.

DUNCAN   Described by Shakespeare as the rightful king, wrongly murdered. The actual Duncan was tyrannical and a destructive leader who foolishly sacrificed large numbers of his men in fruitless campaigns of expansion. He was not poisoned as in Hector Boece's chronicle or murdered as in Shakespeare, but slain in battle during his disastrous campaign against Thorfinn of Orkney. As there was no hereditary kingship, subsequent efforts to 'restore' Duncan's line to the throne were alien to Scottish law and culture.

MACDUFF   A Scottish noble according to Shakespeare, who carries revenge and justice to the evil Macbeth who killed his wife and children. In history, Macduff simply does not appear in any early account of the reign of Macbeth, but suddenly springs up in texts from the fourteenth century onwards. He is an entirely fictitious character, who once having entered into a chronicle (the first being John of Fordun in 1384 in which Macduff is merely exiled for his political beliefs) is developed and amplified into the avenger who eventually emerges in Shakespeare's play.

BANQUO   A late invention, with no true historical context. First brought into the embellishments of Macbeth's tale by Hector Boece, he was later developed by Shakespeare. The invention of Banquo is political, as he provides an original for the Stuart dynasty. In Shakespeare's case, this type of character would have had a contemporary symbolic value to the monarch James I and VI, as indeed would the whole debate about primogeniture and the inheritance of thrones and power through proven genealogical background.

Holinshed's Chronicles

It is clear by now that the historical Macbeth was a very different person indeed from the character portrayed by Shakespeare. In essence, it must be concluded that the play *Macbeth* and the man Macbeth were totally separate.

Shakespeare drew mainly from Holinshed's *Chronicles*, published in 1577 and 1587. These early history books provided much of Shakespeare's source material for his historical plays, and we can detect a curious bridge between history and drama if we read the chapters of Holinshed that Shakespeare would have used. In the following extracts, which are all taken from the second edition of Holinshed published in 1587, we can detect the fictioinal elaboration which the author developed from earlier chroniclers such as Wyntoun or Boece, whom he undoubtedly consulted. We may also find certain powerful themes, such as the scene with the Three Witches, that have little basis in history, but which made Shakespeare's drama so distinctive.

In reading these extracts, with their original style and period spelling, it is fascinating to consider that these were the words read by Shakespeare before or even as he created his masterpiece. The extracts are the most direct and

Spears of the time (above and opposite), *with decorated silver inlays.*

obvious, but scholars have frequently commented that Shakespeare drew material from very diffuse sources; the subtitles before each section are for identification only, and are *not* part of the original text. There is no suggestion here that these are the only parts of Holinshed used in *Macbeth*, but they are those that relate closely to some of the most famous scenes in the play – and that relate also to our true historical Macbeth, so altered through the circumstances of both time and literature.

Duncan and Macbeth

'After Malcolme succeeded his nephue Duncane the sonne of his daughter Beatrice: for Malcome had two daughters, the one which was this Beatrice, being giuen in mariage vnto one Abbanath Crinen, a man of great nobilitie, and thane of the Iles and west parts of Scotland, bare of that mariage the foresaid Duncane; the other called Doada, was maried vnto Sinell the thane of Glammis, by whom she had issue one Makbeth a valiant gentleman, and one that if he had not beene somewhat cruell of nature, might haue beene thought most woorthie the gouernement of a realme. On the other part, Duncane was so soft and gentle of nature, that the people wished the inclinations and maners of these two cousins to haue beene so tempered and interchangeablie bestowed betwixt them, that where the one had too much of clemencie, and the other of crueltie, the meane vertue betwixt these two extremities might haue reigned by indifferent partition in them both, so should Duncane haue proued a woorthie king, and Makbeth an excellent capteine. The beginning of Duncans reigne was verie quiet and peaceable, without anie notable trouble; but after it was perceiued how negligent he was in punishing offendors, manie misruled persons tooke occasion thereof to trouble the peace and quiet state of the common-wealth, by seditious commotions which first had their beginnings in this wise.

Banquho the thane of Lochquhaber, of whom the house of the Stewards is descended, the which by order of linage hath now for a long time inioied the crowne of Scotland, euen till these our daies, as he gathered the finances due to the king, and further punished somewhat sharpelie such as were notorious offendors, being assailed by a number of rebels inhabiting in that countrie, and spoiled of the monie and all other things, had much a doo to get awaie with life, after he had receiued sundrie grieuous wounds amongst them. Yet escaping their hands, after hee was somewhat recouered of his hurts, and was able to ride, he repaired to the court, where making his complaint to the king in most earnest wise, he purchased at length that the offendors were sent for by a sergeant at armes, to appeare to make answer vnto such matters as should be laid to their charge: but they augmenting their mischiefous act with a more wicked deed, after they had misued the messenger with sundrie kinds of reproches, they finallie slue him also.

Then doubting not but for such contemptuous demeanor against the kings regall authoritie, they should be inuaded with all the power the king could make. Makdowald one of great estimation among them, making first a

confederacie with his neerest friends and kinsmen, tooke vpon him to be chiefe capteine of all such rebels as would stand against the king, in maintenance of their grieuous offenses latelie committed against him. Manie slanderous words also, and railing tants this Makdowald vttered against his prince, calling him a faint-hearted milkesop, more meet to gouerne a sort of idle moonks in some cloister, than to haue the rule of such valiant and hardie men of warre as the Scots were. He vsed also such subtill persuasions and forged allurements, that in a small time he had gotten togither a mightie power of men: for out of the westerne Iles there came vnto him a great multitude of people, offering themselues to assist him in that rebellious quarell, and out of Ireland in hope of the spoile came no small number of Kernes and Galloglasses, offering gladlie to serue vnder him, whither it should please him to lead them.

Makdowald thus hauing a mightie puissance about him, incountered with such of the kings people as were sent against him into Lochquhaber, and discomfiting them, by mere force tooke their capteine Malcolme, and after the end of the battell smote off his head. This ouerthrow being notified to the king, did put him in woonderfull feare, by reason of his small skill in warlike affaires. Calling therefore his nobles to a councell, he asked of them their best aduise for the subduing of Makdowald and other the rebels. Here, in sundrie heads (as euer it happeneth) were sundrie opinions, which they vttered according to euerie man his skill. At length Makbeth speaking much against the kings softnes, and ouermuch slacknesse in punishing offendors, whereby they had such time to assemble togither, he promised notwithstanding, if the charge were committed vnto him and vnto Banquho, so to order the matter, that the rebels should be shortly vanquished and quite put downe, and that not so much as one of them should be found to make resistance within the countrie.

And euen so it came to passe; for being sent foorth with a new power, at his entring into Lochquhaber, the fame of his comming put the enimies in such feare, that a great number of them stale secretlie awaie from their capteine Makdowald, who neuerthelesse inforced thereto, gaue battell vnto Makbeth, with the residue which remained with him: but being ouercome and fleeing for refuge into a castell (within the which his wife and children were inclosed) at length when he saw how he could neither defend the hold anie longer against his enimies, nor yet vpon surrender be suffered to depart with life saued, hee first slue his wife and children, and lastlie himselfe, least if he had yeelded simplie, he should haue beene executed in most cruell wise for an example to other. Makbeth entring into the castell by the gates, as then set open, found the carcasse of Makdowald lieng dead there amongst the residue of the slaine bodies, which when he beheld, remitting no peece of his cruell nature with that pitifull sight, he caused the head to be cut off, and set vpon a poles end, and so sent it as a present to the king, who as then laie at Bertha. The headlesse trunke he commanded to bee hoong vp vpon an high paire of gallows. . . . Thus was justice and law restored againe to the old accustomed

course, by the diligent means of Makbeth. Immediatlie wherevpon woord came that Sueno king of Norway was arriued in Fife with a puissant armie, to subdue the whole realme of Scotland.'

The Three Witches

'Shortlie after happened a strange and vncouth woonder, which afterward was the cause of much trouble in the realme of Scotland, as ye shall after heare. It fortuned as Makbeth and Banquho iournied towards Fores, where the king then laie, they went sporting by the waie togither without other companie, saue onelie themselues, passing thorough the woods and fields, when suddenlie in the middest of a laund, there met them three women in strange and wild apparell, resembling creatures of elder world, whome when they attentiuelie beheld, woondering much at the sight, the first of them spake and said: 'All haile, Makbeth, thane of Glammis!' (for he had latelie entered into that dignitie and office by the death of his father Sinell). The second of them said: 'Haile, Makbeth, thane of Cawder!' But the third said: 'All haile, Makbeth, that heereafter shalt be king of Scotland!'

Then Banquho: 'What manner of women' (saith he) 'are you, that seeme so little fauourable vnto me, whereas to my fellow heere, besides high offices, ye assigne also the kingdome, appointing foorth nothing for me at all?' 'Yes' (saith the first of them) we promise greater benefits vnto thee, than vnto him, for he shall reigne in deed, but with an vnluckie end: neither shall he leaue

The Three Witches or Weird Sisters, first described in Scottish chronicles several centuries after the reign of Macbeth, and later made famous by William Shakespeare. There is no historical evidence that Macbeth consorted with witches. On the contrary, he was a supporter of the established Church.

Macbeth was finally slain by Malcolm Canmore and his men, after a prolonged war for the Scottish crown. According to the chronicles, he was killed in The Peel Ring at Lumphanan, a prehistoric worship site.

anie issue behind him to succeed in his place, where contrarilie thou in deed shalt not reigne at all, but of thee those shall be borne which shall gouerne the Scotish kingdome by long order of continuall descent.'' Herewith the foresaid women vanished immediatlie out of their sight. This was reputed at the first but some vaine fantasticall illusion by Mackbeth and Banquho, insomuch that Banquho would call Mackbeth in iest, king of Scotland; and Mackbeth againe would call him in sport likewise, the father of manie kings. But afterwards the common opinion was, that these women were either the weird sisters, that is (as ye would say) the goddesses of destinie, or else some nymphs or feiries, indued with knowledge of prophesie by their necromanticall science, bicause euerie thing came to passe as they had spoken. For shortlie after, the thane of Cawder being condemned at Fores of treason against the king committed; his lands, liuings, and offices were giuen of the kings liberalitie to Mackbeth.

The same night after, at supper, Banquho iested with him and said: ''Now Mackbeth thou hast obteined those things which the two former sisters prophesied, there remaineth onelie for thee to purchase that which the third said should come to passe.'' Wherevpon Mackbeth reuoluing the thing in his mind, began euen then to deuise how he might atteine to the kingdome: but yet he thought with himselfe that he must tarie a time, which should aduance him thereto (by the diuine prouidence) as it had come to passe in his former preferment. But shortlie after it chanced that king Duncane, hauing two sonnes by his wife which was the daughter of Siward earle of North-umberland, he made the elder of them, called Malcolme, prince of Cumberland, as it were thereby to appoint him his successor in the king-dome, immediatlie after his deceasse. Mackbeth sore troubled herewith, for that he saw by this means his hope sore hindered (where, by the old lawes of the realme, the ordinance was, that if he that should succeed were not of able age to take the charge vpon himselfe, he that was next of blood vnto him should be admitted) he began to take counsell how he might vsurpe the kingdome by force, hauing a iust quarell so to doo (as he tooke the matter) for that Duncane did what in him lay to defraud him of all maner of title and claime, which he might in time to come, pretend vnto the crowne.

The woords of the three weird sisters also (of whom before ye haue heard) greatlie incouraged him herevnto, but speciallie his wife lay sore vpon him to attempt the thing, as she that was verie ambitious, burning in vnquenchable desire to beare the name of a queene. At length therefore, communicating his purposed intent with his trustie friends, amongst whome Banquho was the chiefest, vpon confidence of their promised aid, he slue the king at Enuerns, or (as some say) at Botgosuane, in the sixt yeare of his reigne. Then hauing a companie about him of such as he had made priuie to his enterprise, he caused himselfe to be proclamed king, and foorthwith went vnto Scone, where (by common consent) he receiued the inuesture of the kingdome according to the accustomed maner. The bodie of Duncane was first conueied vnto Elgine, & there buried in kinglie wise; but afterwards it was remoued and conueied

vnto Colmekill, and there laid in a sepulture amongst his predecessors, in the yeare after the birth of our Sauiour, 1046.'

King of Scotland

'Mackbeth, after the departure thus of Duncanes sonnes, vsed great liberalitie towards the nobles of the realme, thereby to win their fauour, and when he saw that no man went about to trouble him, he set his whole intention to maintein iustice, and to punish all enormities and abuses, which had chanced through the feeble and slouthfull administration of Duncane. . . . Mackbeth shewing himself thus a most diligent punisher of all iniuries and wrongs attempted by anie disordered persons within his realme, was accounted the sure defense and buckler of innocent people; and hereto he also applied his whole indeuor, to cause yoong men to exercise themselues in vertuous maners, and men of the church to attend their diuine seruice according to their vocations.

To be briefe, such were the woorthie dooings and princelie acts of this Mackbeth in the administration of the realme, that if he had atteined there-vnto by rightfull means, and continued in uprightnesse of justice as he began, till the end of his reigne, he might well haue beene numbred amongest the most noble princes that anie where had reigned. He made manie holesome lawes and statutes for the publike weale of his subiects. . . .

These and the like commendable lawes Mackbeth caused to be put as then in vse, gouerning the realme for the space of ten yeares in equall justice.'

179

Macbeth's Cruelty

But this was but a counterfet zeale of equitie shewed by him, partlie against his naturall inclination, to purchase thereby the fauour of the people. Shortlie after, he began to shew what he was, in stead of equitie practising crueltie. For the pricke of conscience (as it chanceth euer in tyrants, and such as atteine to anie estate by vnrighteous means) caused him euer to feare, least he should be serued of the same cup, as he had ministered to his predecessor. The woords also of the three weird sister would not out of his mind, which as they promised him the kingdome, so likewise did they promise it at the same time vnto the posteritie of Banquho. He willed therefore the same Banquho, with his sonne named Fleance, to come to a supper that he had prepared for them; which was in deed, as he had deuised, present death at the hands of certeine murderers, whom he hired to execute that deed; appointing them to meete with the same Banquho and his sonne without the palace, as they returned to their lodgings, and there to slea them, so that he would not have his house slandered but that in time to come he might cleare himselfe, if anie thing were laid to his charge vpon anie suspicion that might arise.

It chanced yet, by the benefit of the darke night, that, though the father were slaine, the sonne yet, by the helpe of almightie God reseruing him to better fortune, escaped that danger; and afterwards hauing some inkeling (by the admonition of some friends which he had in the court) how his life was sought no lesse than his fathers, who was slaine not by chancemedlie (as by the handling of the matter Makbeth wooould haue had it to appeare) but euen vpon a prepensed deuise: wherevpon to auoid further perill he fled into Wales.'

Macbeth and Macduff

'But to returne vnto Makbeth, in continuing the historie, and to begin where I left, ye shall vnderstand that, after the contriued slaughter of Banquho, nothing prospered with the foresaid Makbeth: for in maner euerie man began to doubt his owne life, and durst vnneth appeare in the kings presence; and euen as there were manie that stood in feare of him, so likewise stood he in feare of manie, in such sort that he began to make those awaie by one surmized cauillation or other, whome he thought most able to worke him anie displeasure.

At length he found such sweetnesse by putting his nobles thus to death, that his earnest thirst after bloud in this behalfe might in no wise be satisfied: for ye must consider he wan double profit (as hee thought) hereby: for first they were rid out of the way whome he feared, and then againe his coffers were inriched by their goods which were forfeited to his vse, whereby he might better mainteine a gard of armed men about him to defend his person from iniurie of them whom he had in anie suspicion. Further, to the end he might the more cruellie oppresse his subiects with all tyrantlike wrongs, he builded a strong castell on the top of an hie hill called Dunsinane, situate in Gowrie, ten miles from Perth, on such a proud height, that, standing there aloft, a man might behold well neere all the countries of Angus, Fife, Stermond, and Ernedale, as it were lieng vnderneath him. This castell, then, being founded on the top of that high hill, put the realme to great charges before it was finished, for all the stuffe necessarie to the building could not be brought up without much toile and businesse. But Makbeth, being once determined to haue the worke go forward, caused the thanes of each shire within the realme, to come and helpe towards that building, each man his course about.

At the last, when he turne fell vnto Makduffe, thane of Fife, to build his part, he sent workemen with all needfull prouision, and commanded them to shew such diligence in euerie behalfe, that no occasion might bee giuen for the king to find fault with him, in that he came not himselfe as other had doone, which he refused to doo, for doubt least the king, bearing him (as he partlie vnderstood) no great good will, would laie violent hands vpon him, as he had doone vpon diuerse other. Shortlie after, Makbeth comming to behold how the worke went forward, and bicause he found not Makduffe there, he was sore offended, and said: ''I perceiue this man will neuer obeie my commandements, till he be ridden with a snaffle; but I shall prouide well inough for him.'' . . . Macbeth could not afterwards abide to looke vpon the said Makduffe, either for that he thought his puissance ouer great; either else for that he had learned of certeine wizzards, in whose words he put great confidence, (for that the prophesie had happened so right, which the three faries or weird sisters had declared vnto him), how that he ought to take heed of Makduffe, who in time to come should seeke to destroie him.

And suerlie herevpon had he put Makduffe to death, but that a certeine witch, whome hee had in great trust, had told that he should neuer be slaine with man borne of anie woman, nor vanquished till the wood of Bernane came to the castell of Dunsinane. By this prophesie Makbeth put all feare out of his heart, supposing he might doo what he would, without anie feare to be punished for the same, for by the one prophesie he beleeued it was vnpossible for anie man to vanquish him, and by the other vnpossible to slea him. This vaine hope caused him to doo manie outragious things, to the greeuous oppression of his subiects. At length Makduffe, to auoid perill of life, purposed with himselfe to passe into England, to procure Malcolm Cammore to claime the crowne of Scotland. But this was not so secretlie deuised by Makduffe, but that Makbeth had knowledge giuen him thereof: for kings (as is said) haue sharpe sight like vnto Lynx, and long ears like vnto Midas. For Makbeth had, in euerie noble mans house, one slie fellow or other in fee with him, to reueale all that was said or doone within the same, by which slight he oppressed the most part of the nobles of his realme.'

Macduff flees to England
'Immediatlie then, being aduertised whereabout Makduffe went, he came hastily with a great power into Fife, and foorthwith besieged the castell where Makdaffe dwelled, trusting to haue found him therein. They that kept

Decorated sword hilt from the large Viking settlement at Hedeby, Denmark.

the house, without anie resistance opened the gates, and suffered him to enter, mistrusting none euill. But neuerthelesse Makbeth most cruellie caused the wife and children of Makduffe, with all other whome he found in that castell, to be slaine. Also he confiscated the goods of Makduffe, proclamed him traitor, and confined him out of all the parts of his realme; but Makduffe was alreadie escaped out of danger, and gotten into England vnto Malcolme Cammore, to trie what purchase hee might make by means of his support, to reuenge the slaughter so cruellie executed on his wife, his children, and other friends.'

Malcolm Canmore

'At his comming vnto Malcolme, he declared into what great miserie the estate of Scotland was brought, by the detestable cruelties exercised by the tyrant Makbeth, hauing committed manie horrible slaughters and murders, both as well of the nobles as commons; for the which he was hated right mortallie of all his liege people, desiring nothing more than to be deliuered of that intollerable and most heauie yoke of thraldome, which they susteined at such a caitifes hands.

Malcolme, hearing Makduffes woords, which he vttered in verie lamentable sort, for meere compassion and verie ruth that pearsed his sorrowfull hart, bewailing the miserable state of his countrie, he fetched a deepe sigh; which Makduffe perceiuing, began to fall most earnestlie in hand with him, to enterprise the deliuering of the Scotish people out of the hands of so cruell and bloudie a tyrant, as Makbeth by too manie plaine experiments did shew himselfe to be: which was an easie matter for him to bring to passe, considering not onelie the good title he had, but also the earnest desire of the people to haue some occasion ministred, whereby they might be reuenged of those notable iniuries, which they dailie susteined by the outragious crueltie of Makbeths misgouernance. Though Malcolme was verie sorowfull for the oppression of his countriemen the Scots, in maner as Makduffe had declared; yet doubting whether he were come as one that ment vnfeinedlie as he spake, or else as sent from Makbeth to betraie him, he thought to haue some further triall, and therevpon, dissembling his mind at the first, he answered as followeth:

"I am trulie verie sorie for the miserie chanced to my countrie of Scotland, but though I haue neuer so great affection to relieue the same, yet, by reason of certeine incurable vices, which reigne in me, I am nothing meet thereto. First, such immoderate lust and voluptuous sensualitie (the abhominable founteine of all vices) followeth me, that, if I were made king of Scots, I should seeke to defloure your maids and matrones, in such wise that mine intemperancie should be more importable vnto you, than the bloudie tyrannie of Makbeth now is." Herevnto Makduffe answered: "This suerlie is a verie euill fault, for manie noble princes and kings haue lost both liues and kingdomes for the same; neuerthelesse there are women enow in Scotland, and therefore follow my counsell. Make thy selfe king, and I shall conueie the matter so wiselie, that thou shalt be so satisfied at thy pleasure, in such secret wise that no man shall be aware thereof."

Then said Malcolme, "I am also the most auaritious creature on the earth, so that, if I were king, I should seeke so manie waies to get lands and goods, that I would slea the most part of all the nobles of Scotland by surmized accusations, to the end I might inioy their lands, goods, and possessions; . . . Therefore" saith Malcolme, "suffer me to remaine where I am, least, if I atteine to the regiment of your realme, mine vnquechable auarice may prooue such that ye would thinke the displeasures, which now grieue you, should seeme easie in respect of the vnmeasurable outrage, which might insue through my comming amongst you."

Makduffe to this made answer, how it was a far woorse fault than the other: "for auarice is the root of all mischiefe, and for that crime the most part of our kings haue beene slaine and brought to their finall end. Yet notwithstanding follow my counsell, and take vpon thee the crowne. There is gold and riches inough in Scotland to satisfie thy greedie desire." Then said Malcolme againe, "I am furthermore inclined to dissimulation, telling of leasings, and all other kinds of deceit, so that I naturallie reioise in nothing so much, as to betraie & deceiue such as put anie trust or confidence in my woords. Then sith there is nothing that more becommeth a price than constancie, veritie, truth, and iustice, with the other laudable fellowship of those faire and noble vertues which are comprehended onelie in soothfastnesse, and that lieng vutterlie ouerthroweth the same; you see how vnable I am to gouerne anie prouince or region: and therefore, sith you haue remedies to cloke and hide all the rest of my other vices, I praie you find shift to cloke this vice amongst the residue.''

Then said Makduffe: ''This yet is the woorst of all, and there I leaue thee, and therefore saie: Oh ye vnhappie and miserable Scotishmen, which are thus scourged with so manie and sundrie calamities, ech one aboue other! Ye haue one curssed and wicked tyrant that now reigneth ouer you, without anie right or title, oppressing you with his most bloudie crueltie. This other, that hath the right to the crowne, is so replet with the inconstant behauiour and manifest vices of Englishmen, that he is nothing woorthie to inioy it; for by his owne confession he is not onelie auaritious, and giuen to vnsatiable lust, but so false a traitor withall, that no trust is to be had vnto anie woord he speaketh. 'Adieu, Scotland, for now I account my selfe a banished man for euer, without comfort or consolation:'' and with those woords the brackish teares trickled downe his cheeks verie abundantlie.

At the last, when he was readie to depart, Malcolme tooke him by the sleeue, and said: ''Be of good comfort, Makduffe, for I haue none of these vices before remembred, but haue iested with thee in this manner, onelie to prooue thy mind; for diuerse times heeretofore hath Makbeth sought by this manner of meanes to bring me into hands, but the more slow I haue shewed my selfe to condescend to thy motion and request, the more diligence shall I vse in accomplishing the same.'' Incontinentlie heerevpon they imbraced ech other, and, promising to be faithfull the one to the other, they fell in consultation how they might prouide for all their businesses, to bring the same to good effect.'

Malcolm and Siward

'Soone after Makduffe, repairing to the borders of Scotland, addressed his letters with secret dispatch vnto the nobles of the realme, declaring how Malcolme was confederat with him, to come hastilie into Scotland to claime the crowne, and therefore he required them, sith he was right inheritor thereto, to assist him with their powers to recouer the same out of the hands of the wrongfull vsurper.

In the meane time, Malcolme purchased such fauor at king Edwards hands, that *old Siward* earle of Northumberland was appointed *with ten thousand men* to go with him into Scotland, to support him in this enterprise, for recouerie of his right. After these newes were spread abroad in Scotland, the nobles drew into two seuerall factions, the one taking part with Makbeth, and the other with Malcolme. Heerevpon insued oftentimes sundrie bickerings, & diuerse light skirmishes; for those that were of Malcolmes side would not ieopard to ioine with their enimies in a pight field, till his comming out of England to their support. But after that Makbeth perceiued his enimies power to increase, by such aid as came to them foorth of England with his aduersarie Malcolme, he recoiled backed into Fife, there purposing to abide in campe fortified, at the castell of Dunsinane, and to fight with his enimies, if they ment to pursue him; howbeit some of his friends aduised him, that it should be best for him, either to make some agreement with Malcolme, or else to flee with all speed into the Iles, and to take his treasure with him, to the end he might wage sundrie great princes of the realme to take his part, & reteine strangers, in whome he might better trust than in his owne subiects, which stale dailie from him; but he had such confidence in his prophesies, that he beleeued he should neuer be vanquished, till Birnane wood were brought to Dunsinane; nor yet to be slaine with anie man, that should be or was born of anie woman.

Macduff kills Macbeth

'Malcolme, following hastilie after Makbeth, came the night before the battell vnto Birnane wood; and, when his armie had rested a while there to refresh them, he commanded euerie man to get a bough of some tree or other of that wood in his hand, as big as he might beare, and to march foorth therewith in such wise, that on the next morrow they might come closelie and without sight in this manner within view of his enimies. On the morrow when Makbeth beheld them comming in this sort, he first maruelled what the matter ment, but in the end remembred himselfe that the prophesie which he had heard long before that time, of the comming of Birname wood to Dunsinane castell, was likelie to be now fulfilled. Neuerthelesse, he brought his men in order of battell, and exhorted them to doo valiantlie; howbeit his enimies had scarselie cast from them their boughs, when Makbeth, perceiuing their numbers, betooke him streict to flight; whom Makduffe pursued with great hatred euen till he came vnto Lunfannaine, where Makbeth, perceiuing that Makduffe was hard at his backe, leapt beside his horsse, saieng: "Thou traitor, what meaneth it that thou shouldest thus in vaine follow me that am not appointed to be slaine by anie creature that is borne of a woman? come on therefore, and receiue thy reward which thou has deserued for thy paines!" and therwithall he lifted up his swoord, thinking to haue slaine him.

But Makduffe, quicklie auoiding from his horsse, yer he came at him, answered (with his naked swoord in his hand) saieng: "It is true, Makbeth, and now shall thine insatiable crueltie haue an end, for I am euen he that thy wizzards haue told thee of; who was neuer borne of my mother, but ripped out of her wombe:" therwithall he stept vnto him, and slue him in the place. Then cutting his head from his shoulders, he set it vpon a pole, and brought it vnto Malcolme. This was the end of Makbeth, after he had reigned 17 yeeres ouer the Scotishmen. In the beginning of his reigne he accomplished manie woorthie acts, verie profitable to the common-wealth (as ye haue heard) but afterward, by illusion of the diuell, he defamed the same with most terrible crueltie. He was slaine in the yeere of the incarnation, 1057, and in the 16 yeere of king Edwards reign ouer the Englishmen.'

GENEALOGY OF CHARACTERS

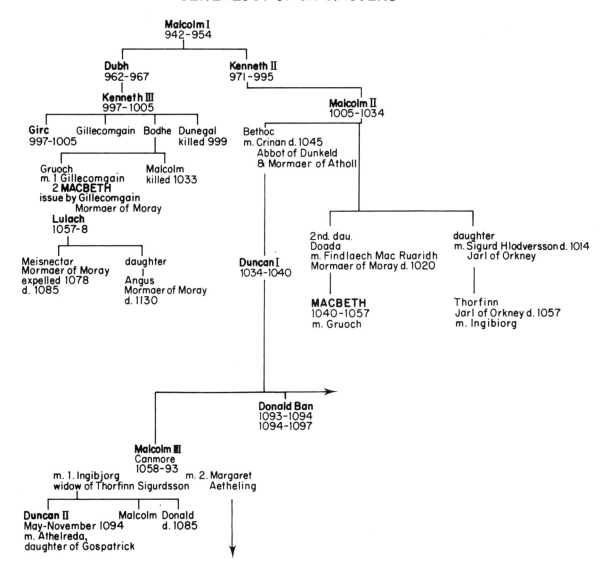

Further Reading

Dorothy Whitelock (ed) *Anglo-Saxon Chronicle* London, 1961

W.M. Hennessy (ed) *Annals of Loch Ce* Dublin 1871

B. MacCarthy (ed) *Annals of Ulster* Dublin 1887–95.

Wilson, D. *Archaeology and Prehistoric Annals of Scotland* Edinburgh, 1851

Rev. John Williams Ab Ithel (ed) *Brut Y Tywysogion* (Rolls Series) London, 1860

A&B Rees, *Celtic Heritage* London, 1961

W.F. Skene, *Celtic Scotland* (3 Vols) Edinburgh 1886

W.F. Skene (ed), *Chronica Gentis Scotorum, De Fordun*, (14th C) Edinburgh 1871

Holinshed, *Chronicles of England, Scotland and Ireland*, London, 1577

B. Thorpe, (ed) *Chronicon ex Chronicis, Florence of Worcester* London, 1848

G. Wutz (ed) *Chronicon, Marianus Scotus*, 1844

R.F. Walker, *Companion to the study of Shakespeare's Macbeth* London, 1947

Dr. A. Ross, *Folklore of the Scottish Highlands* London, 1976

J. Stevenson (ed), *Historia Dunelmensis Ecclesiae* 1855

Hector Boece, *Historia de Scotia*, Paris, 1527

W. Blackwood, *History of the Celtic Place Names of Scotland* Edinburgh, 1926

Lloyd Laing, *Late Celtic Britain and Ireland*, London, 1977

J. MacBeth, *MacBeth, King, Queen and Clan* Edinburgh, 1921

William Shakespeare, *Macbeth* various editions

R. Carruthers, *Macbeth, being an Historical figure* Inverness, 1930

Alexander Burt Taylor (ed), *Orkneyinga Saga* Edinburgh, 1938

Dr. A. Ross, *Pagan Celtic Britain* London, 1974

Bannatyne Club, *Prioratus Sancti Andree in Scotia*, 1841

MS 23/G4, Royal Irish Academy, *Prophecy of St. Berchan* Dublin.

Andrew Wyntoun, D. Ley (ed), *The Orygynale Cronykil of Scotland* Edinburgh, 1879

J. Graham Campbell, *The Viking World* London, 1980

Index

Page numbers in *italics* refer to illustrations.

Illustrations
Colour plates by James Field
All line illustrations by Chesca Potter
Maps and diagrams by Chartwell Illustrators
Photographs courtesy of: British Tourist Authority (page 65); Cardiff City Council (page 71); Chris Lloyd/National Portrait Gallery, Scotland (page 169); Colchester and Essex Museum (pages 62, 78, 81 and 87); HMSO/Department of the Environment, Northern Ireland (page 48); Irish Tourist Board (pages 15, 103, 119, 121 and 137); Museum of Antiquities, University of Newcastle (page 79); National Museet, Copenhagen (page 54); National Museum of Wales (page 59); Northern Irish Tourist Board (page 101); Peter Newark's Historical Pictures (pages 10, 11, 173 and 182); Royal Museum of Scotland (page 57); Scottish Tourist Board (pages 17, 153, 158, 164, 168 and 171); Trinity College Library, Dublin (page 107); Trustees of the British Museum (pages 9 and 60).